T0345641

BILL CLAY

A Political Voice at the Grass Roots

BILL CLAY

MISSOURI HISTORICAL SOCIETY PRESS
ST. LOUIS
DISTRIBUTED BY UNIVERSITY OF MISSOURI PRESS

© 2004 by the Missouri Historical Society Press

08 07 06 05 04   1 2 3 4 5

Library of Congress Cataloging-in-Publication Data

Clay, William L.
    Bill Clay : a political voice at the grass roots / by Bill Clay.
        p.   cm.
    Includes bibliographical references and index.
    ISBN 1-883982-52-9 (hardcover : alk. paper)
    1. Clay, William L. 2. Legislators--United States--Biography. 3. United
States. Congress. House--Biography. 4. African American legislators--
Biography. 5. Saint Louis (Mo.)--Politics and government. 6. Missouri--
Politics and government--1951- I. Title.
    E840.8.C54 A3
    328.73'092--DC22
        2004019508

Distributed by University of Missouri Press

Design: Creativille, Inc.
All photos courtesy of Bill Clay unless otherwise noted.
Printed and Bound by Friesens, Canada

TABLE OF CONTENTS

v   Foreword by Pearlie Evans

vii   Foreword by Dr. Robert Archibald

viii Preface

xi   Introduction

I   CHAPTER 1: Genesis of Black Politics in St. Louis: The Historic Pythian Meeting

11   CHAPTER 2: Early Days of Bill Clay: From Childhood to Manhood

23   CHAPTER 3: Entering the Political Arena

53   CHAPTER 4: Hectic Days Following the 1959 Election

69   CHAPTER 5: 1960: A Year of Decisive Political Results for Negroes

87   CHAPTER 6: Road to Political Respect

107   CHAPTER 7: Jefferson Bank Demonstrations

131   CHAPTER 8: Warren E. Hearnes: My Choice for Governor

143   CHAPTER 9: A. J. Cervantes: Gifted, Innovative Politician

155   CHAPTER 10: Barriers Overcome in Electing a Black U.S. Congressman
       and a Black Citywide Official

173   CHAPTER 11: Influence of Women on My Political Career

189   CHAPTER 12: The Politics of Self-Destruction

209   CHAPTER 13: Bruising 1974 Candidacy for Congress

223   CHAPTER 14: Bait Your Hook with a Snake to Catch a Bass: Bass's
       Campaign Undermined by Blacks

245   CHAPTER 15: Vincent Schoemehl: Hope for Inclusion

269   CHAPTER 16: Payback Time: Revenge or Retribution

283   CHAPTER 17: Bill Clay Sr.: Labor Born and Bred

303   CHAPTER 18: A Summary of the Black Struggle

319   Notes

324   Index

FOREWORD

Without a doubt, this book is a must-read for anyone who seeks to explore the diverse history of combative and racially polarized politics in St. Louis from the 1950s to current times. Mr. Bill Clay, my valued friend, former boss, confidant, and political leader, writes powerfully on the yesteryear struggles of black elected officials. Generally, these struggles were led by him to achieve offices in a city that was a rock-solid bastion of segregation and overt racism.

Bill Clay frames the issues of the black community in a decisive way by pointing out that blacks voted overwhelmingly for whites and that whites rarely, if ever, voted for black candidates. Another overriding issue was that of economics. In essence, black people were not only powerless but also poor. As a leader in the Jefferson Bank challenge, Bill Clay describes in detail the turbulent struggle that confronted the protesters and the entire black community. The real story was about jobs, respect, and equal rights. It was to be heralded as the greatest effort in mobilization that St. Louis had ever seen. Because he confronted the establishment and status quo of politics, he was long the subject of derision and attack from politicians, the press, and even some black leaders. His strong community support base enabled him to keep the faith in institutional change in the economic and political dynamics of black political participation.

Mr. Clay, in this political saga, lets the chips fall where they may. He takes the reader through a journey of rage, humiliation, deceit, triumph, and hope for a better time in St. Louis political arrangements. He challenged blacks to step up to a new way of thinking about their votes and their worthiness to seek and hold office. Another significant aspect of his long career was the uplifting of the status of black women to become political equals. His ability to nudge his male colleagues to accept women in the political arena was key to the success of women holding committeeships and other appointments. This includes my appointment in 1972 as his congressional district assistant, against great odds from some of his male supporters. We are told in no uncertain terms that racism and sexism have no place in the politics of the future and must be totally eradicated.

Clay takes bold and deliberate steps to empower black St. Louisans to gain more offices of influence and power. This is a serious book about the fight for a sea change from the status quo of whites holding real power and blacks holding only small-time appointments and low-level jobs. The book is also a blueprint for politicians, black and white, of today to build upon past achievements. Clay demands that St. Louis political relationships reflect equity among citizens, not relationships of master and slave.

Clay's message is that the politics of deceit and trickery must be confronted head on. On his watch as alderman, committeeman, and congressman he soundly rejected the politics of accommodation and appeasement and embraced the politics of inclusion and coalition when all interests were served. To be tougher, smarter, and uncompromised is the mandate he asks of today's politicians as they move through uncharted political waters. In this hard-hitting autobiography there is much to learn about the challenges of the past; it also details the need to continue the struggle for black leadership and not to surrender to petty promises of greatness. The different kinds of leadership Clay faced are with us still, such as the old guard, young turks, and nihilists. The leaders of today are reminded that to abandon policies and programs beneficial to their people will be to the detriment of others who follow them.

Mr. Clay faced and survived the criticisms of standing alone at times with leaders in his Democratic Party, labor friends, the media, and some black people to win a place at the table of political respect and dignity. It is for the black leaders of today to seek the broader vision of serving their citizens who honor them by electing them.

—Pearlie I. Evans

former district assistant to Congressman Bill Clay

FOREWORD

F undamental change characterizes the immediate past century in our country. Our nation is democratic in ways that our predecessors could not have predicted nor imagined. We have become a country that increasingly takes pride in the many hues and textures of our national culture. Voices previously silenced are raised in a rich and complex chorus; now we both hear and hearken to the voices of racial and cultural minorities, women, gays and lesbians, people with disabilities, and an abundance of other groups who represent a whole spectrum of interests and concerns. Our society has moved from one in which exclusive homogeneous groups wield the power to a society in which power and decision making are more broadly shared than ever before. Bill Clay was one of those voices, disturbing, determined, often raucous, ultimately effective.

For an objective, unbiased, dispassionate discussion of St. Louis's political landscape over the last forty years, do not choose A *Political Voice at the Grass Roots*. Bill Clay's memoir of his four decades in public life could be nothing less than passionate, personal, and courageously, sometimes brazenly, outspoken, for that is his voice, heard and heeded by his own African American community in St. Louis and eventually by the broader population of our region and of the nation.

We, as a community and as a nation, continue to labor under the burden of racism, elitism, and inequality, but we also claim a legacy of hope, compassion, and determination to overcome our iniquities, to expand opportunities, and to make this a better place for all, including the unborn generations who will inherit it. Bill Clay's story is about this determination. It's about building a shared story and a shared future. It's a chronicle for all of us, a story full of foibles and strengths, setbacks and successes that we must incorporate into our community story. We will be richer and stronger for it and the lessons it provides.

—ROBERT R. ARCHIBALD, PH.D.
President, Missouri Historical Society

PREFACE

I wish to thank the thousands of persons who actively campaigned to make my political life a success. Especially, I acknowledge the contribution of my immediate family. I thank my mother and father, my wife Carol, and my two lovely daughters, Vicki and Michele, for always being there when I needed them. I appreciate my son Lacy following in my footsteps and becoming a leader in the political affairs of the nation. These people encouraged my participation in politics, nurtured my career without necessarily agreeing to every phase, and cared for me when I was battered and bruised by the opposition.

I cannot possibly acknowledge all the beautiful people who helped make it possible for me to reach the pinnacle of success. Each performed a critical part in my career development and upward mobility. Without their significant contributions, I would probably still be driving a bus for the St. Louis transit system or collecting a debit for a weekly insurance company. Without their unshakable confidence in my ability to make a difference in the social, economic and political life of St. Louis, I doubt that my career would have been as successful.

In addition, I owe a debt of gratitude to the stalwarts who were there from the beginning, for the bad times as well as the good. Among them are Nat Rivers, Pearlie Evans, John Curtis, Herdy Miller, Gwen Giles, John Bass, Leroy Tyus, Marian Oldham, Margaret Wilson, and others too numerous to name. It is impossible to identify and acknowledge all who canvassed door-to-door in the rain and snow, who conducted registration campaigns, and who drove others to the polls. To them, I also say thanks.

This book attempts to assess the character and contributions of my cohorts, colleagues, and co-conspirators in our drive to make African Americans a relevant factor in St. Louis politics. Disclosing pertinent facts about our relationships in no sense betrays a trust among us. Future generations engaging in politics have a right to know what took place during the turbulent years of my political participation. Past manipulation of the black vote should be discussed. The young must know the truth if they are to prevent future abuses. Our race must realize that American politics was and is polarized along racial lines and divided along economic groupings. Contrary to contemporary political spin doctors, the polarization and division is more the fault of systemic racism than black abrasiveness.

Black politicians must continue to advocate self-expression, self-determination, and self-pride, even if they are branded racist by the media. Those vying to use their political strength to enhance the economic stability of African American communities, as some do, will be targeted for media harassment and grand jury investigations. They will also be assaulted by black leaders who seek to enhance themselves within the white power structure by undermining legitimate efforts to eliminate racist conditions. I exposed those who impeded the fight for freedom. I feel that I must take the risk of alienating blacks and whites, if this writing is to be meaningful. I contend that politics is as much a science and a profession as medicine, law, engineering, and architecture. Those of us dedicated to black political advancement and committed to developing our knowledge, improving our skills, and performing the hard, tedious work required to make politics work for our people now find our progress threatened by a new phenomenon of politics based on racial genocide.

Many encounters with black politicians have not been exceptionally inspiring. In times of critical problems facing our community, some African American leaders abandoned all pretense of commitment to justice and equality for our people. They were more preoccupied with a desire for personal enrichment than with people empowerment. In recent years, a cadre of young black elected officials have attempted to inject race into every political situation. These novices are best characterized, in my opinion, as lacking basic understanding of the dynamics involved in protecting the interests and advancing the cause of our race. Polarization of the races threatens the foundation and the continued existence of our political power.

These ventures could be rationalized in bully terms if certain basic political factors existed in St. Louis: if blacks were the overwhelming majority of the population, registered to the maximum, and voted in numbers proportionate to the white community. Then, seeking complete control of the political process and electing blacks to all the public offices would be possible, though not wise. But the simple truth is that blacks may not even be able to retain the elected positions already achieved.

Turning every election into a black-white encounter is precisely what many white politicians relish. In recent elections, that idiotic notion has been the catalyst for perfecting the concept that only one white candidate at a time can run for each citywide office. White aspirants for office have been so intimidated that many refuse to file against another white for fear of being labeled a "spoiler."

It does not take a great deal of courage for elected officials representing all-white or all-black districts to embark on a racially oriented campaign. Such provocative campaigns do not jeopardize their own political futures, but the adverse ramifications for the electorate are untold.

Coalition building between the predominantly black North Side and the predominantly white South Side is beneficial to both communities and should be encouraged. The real power of black politics is vested in genuine coalition building and productive compromise. It takes fifteen votes to pass legislation in the St. Louis Board of Aldermen, eighty-two votes in the Missouri House of Representatives, eighteen votes in the state senate. Until blacks attain those numbers, if ever, it is insane to polarize the voting public.

The responsibility of leadership is a serious one. Black leaders must analyze the facts, consider the consequences, determine the political interests, then make judgments for endorsing candidates. They must not be intimidated, coerced, or cajoled into supporting candidates simply because they filed first, they accused other bona fide aspirants of attempting to split the vote, or they are black.

—WILLIAM L. CLAY, SR.

Introduction

This book documents my personal involvement spanning forty-two years as an elected official interacting with politics and politicians in the St. Louis community. It is a detailed review, focusing on the rough and tumble highlights of my infighting with Missouri's most famed politicians. It is the revelation of an "insider's" view as a civil rights activist, alderman, ward leader, and member of Congress: a politician who did not sit on the periphery of decision making but was intimately involved in it.

The experiences cited here are by no means uniquely identified with black St. Louisans. In the early 1960s, most large northern cities engaged in the same discriminatory hiring practices and political chicanery as southern metropolises. Insult, injury, and injustice were heaped upon black citizens below and above the Mason-Dixon line. Harassment of civil rights activists, infringement on the right of blacks to vote, and denial of equal access to places of public accommodation were impediments confronting us nationwide. Although racist acts were more overt in the South, the subtle, offensive behavior of whites in the northern and border states like Missouri was just as dehumanizing.

I wrote this book to expose certain hypocritical aspects of Democratic politicians during the last half of the twentieth century, and to reveal how white elected officials related to the concerns of their black constituents. My mission is to educate a black St. Louis community sorely in need of exposure to its history. This writing is not based on some idealistic pipe dream about what politics in black St. Louis should have been, but rather a pragmatic interpretation of what it was for several decades. I discuss the problems, the failures, and the shortcomings of black leaders.

I believe it is important to inform aspirants who seek public service careers through elective office and administrative appointment that they will face trials and tribulations based on their blackness. I document the extreme measures used to restrict black political influence and to deny fair employment to a people who constituted 40 percent of the city's population. I bluntly describe those black politicians who personally waged the battle and endured the consequences of destabilizing our community.

I cover many confrontations with the local media over my refusal to remain silent in matters of racial and social injustice. My outspoken resistance to the undemocratic assaults on the right of free speech, the right of privacy, and, above all, the right to publicly disagree subjected me to unfavorable news coverage. No matter what positions I took, my motivation was always called into question. News articles and editorials critical of my political activities became the expected thing. I describe in unambiguous terms how some elements of the media ignored objectivity, producing unbalanced news articles and biased editorial presentations. I cite examples of the preponderance of derogatory, inflammatory articles deliberately written to diminish my ability to influence city voters. My independence guaranteed that I would be subjected to attacks by those elements who resented strong, black leaders. Yet however strained my relationship with the media became, it never inhibited my faith in the people of Saint Louis.

I do not attempt to project political involvement as a panacea for resolving all of the numerous crises facing our people. But alongside picket lines, economic boycotts, and sit-ins in the 1950s, 1960s, and 1970s, it was a most effective means to confront racism and to ameliorate injustices. I emphasize that the right to vote and the obligation of judiciously exercising it were the paths to tempering the many societal wrongs confronting us.

The Politics of Exploitation

For forty-two years, I was in the thick of battle on every major political campaign in Missouri. If anyone can speak authoritatively about scams, games, and trickery employed to enlist support in black wards, it is I. In the development of a political force capable of advancing the economic and social status of African Americans, our race experienced major successes in some areas, frustration and disillusionment in others. Ironically, our thrust for political equity was often rebuffed by politicians who were the recipients of large black voter support.

From 1959 until 2000, I played a pivotal role in producing a generation of political Horatio Algers. They indeed rose from rags to riches because of support provided by people associated with my organization. Some were pariahs of the first order, devouring anything and anybody in their paths. Others were honest and decent, possessing a sense of fair play and genuine concern for those with whom they made alliances. During a stormy career, I fraternized with Missouri's most influential political movers and shakers: the sincere, the con artists, the reformers, the scavengers. I probably know them better than most because of our closeness.

During this era, I met the most unforgettable—some unforgivable—characters in the political arena. After four decades, I am no longer the wide-eyed optimist expecting politicians to keep all their commitments. Based on my experiences, political rhetoric is meaningless. What you get from the victor is what you can take. Slogans such as "A man's word is his bond" should be excised from the political lexicon. Handshakes, swearing on the graves of dead relatives, pledges to Hannah, Buddha, and Christ have no significance with most politicians I encountered.

I can only speak with firsthand knowledge of Democrats. But from personal observation, I find most Republicans in Missouri more honest in regard to the question of race and politics. Through words and deeds, they make it clear that black voters are not a priority consideration in the campaign and will not be a major factor in governance thereafter. To Missouri Republicans, black voters are an expendable commodity, neither sought nor welcomed in their inner circle.

To most Democrats, black voters are prized treasures, eagerly sought during the campaign and disgracefully discarded afterward. That scenario adequately and oftentimes sums up the conventional relationship between white Democrats and black voters. This Dr. Jekyll/Mr.

Hyde characteristic emerges shortly after the votes are counted. Black leaders who supplied the margin of victory know the romance is over when the winner delivers his election night speech, declaring: "Farewell my deep and Africonic brothers, be brave" (from *Purlie Victorious* by Ossie Davis, 1961). The knights in tainted armor immediately retreat back to groups and individuals in their own communities, attempting to consolidate their newly acquired power in surroundings where they feel more comfortable.

In traditional political headquarters and in exclusive country clubs, white elected officials are embarrassed to acknowledge they wield power that depends on such tenuous grounds as the whims of minority leaders and civil rights activists. To dispel the image, blacks who provided the initial clout for their victories must now become excess baggage. Politicians who tried to prevent their elections now become friends and personal advisers in the nefarious scheme of political reality. The appointments, government contracts, and easy accessibility that were promised must never materialize. Instead, the winners usually appoint key workers from the organizations to insignificant positions, bypassing the endorsement of black leaders who supported them. This is an attempt to establish a campaign committee in the black community that is independent of the influence of black leaders.

Sadly, many white officeholders believe they are rewarding black constituents by appointing blacks who are personally tied to their "navel cords"—like next-door neighbors, chauffeurs, gardeners. They also appoint blacks from the corporate world who in many instances are unknown to leaders in the black community.

Sadly, too many black supporters faithfully hang on to shattered dreams, expecting remarkable accomplishments from their victorious candidate. But all they receive are Christmas cards and invitations to fund-raising events. Unfortunately, that scenario too often describes the conventional relationship between white politicians and their black voters.

In this memoir, actual names of businessmen, civil rights leaders, and politicians are used to avoid the possibility of confusing the roles played by each. I used descriptive adjectives and nouns that were prevalent in depicting our race during specific time periods. The usage of the words *colored*, *Negro*, *black*, *Afro-American*, and *African American* was employed for emphasis and realism. In many instances they are interchangeable. Some designations resulted from insistence of the white race to demean and insult. Others were the creation of blacks intending to extract a measure of respect and recognition. Still other usages were the result of intensive debate within the black community concerning the proper citation to be used.

The term *African American* was not generally acceptable to blacks until the mid-1970s. It came into being around the turn of the twentieth century and continues to be used in the present day. *Black* was a term employed during slavery to denote chattel property and to distinguish between the two races. It is notable that Asians were not referred to as *yellows*, Mexicans as *browns*, or Indians as *reds*. *Colored* was a preferential salutation, at least for blacks, from the seventeenth century until the early 1970s.

I hope this book will serve as a guide to young blacks in St. Louis who have become disillusioned with the present state of affairs in black politics. I also hope that my activities inspire others to follow in my path, and, more important, I hope that I have made a difference in the struggle for decency, justice, and equity.

CHAPTER

1

GENESIS OF BLACK POLITICS IN ST. LOUIS:
THE HISTORIC PYTHIAN MEETING

The modern-day Negro political movement in St. Louis had its genesis in a meeting of the Citizens Liberty League at the Pythian Hall on December 17, 1919. Six young Negro men assembled to express their disgust with local Republican leadership and to devise a plan to expand the role of Negroes in the affairs of government. The group consisted of Crittenden Clark, George L. Vaughn, J. E. Mitchell, Aaron W. Lloyd, Captain Walter Lowe, and Charles Udell Turpin. Each was a source of community influence; they constituted the legitimate core of leadership in the Negro community, commanding respect as leaders and spokespersons for black people. Mitchell was publisher of the *St. Louis Argus* newspaper; Lloyd, the grand chancellor of the Knights of Pythians; Turpin, owner of the Booker T. Washington Theater; Lowe, a ward worker; Vaughn and Clark, prominent attorneys. They were individuals of unquestionable ability and impressive credentials who spoke for members of the Citizens Liberty League.

For 40,000 registered Negro voters, the Citizens Liberty League represented an avenue of hope for achieving political justice. At the conclusion of the meeting, an ultimatum was issued that dramatically redefined and drastically altered relations between the white Republican establishment and the black community. The declaration put the party of Abraham Lincoln on notice that the passive, accommodating behavior of Negroes was a thing of the past. In the clearest language possible, Republicans were told that Negroes were demanding concessions commensurate with their contributions to the party. Party bigwigs were put on notice that black people were not seeking political philanthropy from benevolent white leaders but justice as a right of citizenship.

The Pythian declaration denounced the system of blacks begging for crumbs from the political table and discarded the idea that those who provided the most political muscle to the success of the Republican Party had to suffer the most in personal humiliation. Prior to the meeting, whites had made all the important decisions affecting the lives of Negroes. The boldness and audaciousness of the Citizens Liberty League set in motion a confrontation of radical import. The Republican Party, which had received 90 percent of the black vote since the end of the Civil War, was faced with a "fish or cut bait" situation. Negroes were outraged, and several proposed bolting the party of Abraham Lincoln.

But the leaders, thinking better of that notion, finally approved and published a list of far-reaching proposals to be fulfilled if they were to remain in the Republican Party. The Pythian rebels proclaimed the following thirteen demands:

1. A Negro to be elected from the state of Missouri to serve as a congressman in Washington, D.C.

2. A Negro to be elected as a judge (justice of the peace, similar to the presiding officer in small claims court).

3. A Negro to be elected as constable (the executive officer assisting a justice of the peace).

4. A Negro to be elected as the committeeman of a ward.

5. A Negro woman to be elected as committeewoman, if women obtained the right to vote and hold office in time for the next election, or as soon as possible after women received the right.

6. A Negro to be appointed superintendent of garbage collection.

7. Negroes to serve on grand juries, which consisted of twenty-four persons (generally made up of intellectuals, persons in business, or other professionals).

8. Negroes to be selected to serve on petit juries (misdemeanor and traffic courts).

9. A Negro city undertaker (to bury paupers).

10. Negro uniformed policemen (there were several Negro detectives in plain clothes).

11. A Negro on the board of education.

12. A Negro fire department (really a fire station).

13. A city hospital staffed entirely by Negro doctors, nurses, and orderlies.[1]

The document outlined a list of priorities that consumed the next forty years of community attention. It detonated a chain reaction of events aimed to achieve these goals. Some were attained within months. Others were not accomplished until the early 1950s and late 1960s. Less than a year after the manifesto was issued, Republican Charles Udell Turpin was elected the first Negro constable. His election, however, was not without scandalous opposition from the ruling Republican Party. The press announced the morning after the election that Turpin had been defeated by an overwhelming margin. History is fuzzy as to what happened next. Some contend that blacks seized ballot boxes at gunpoint, and, for six months, the recount was contested in the courts. A second story is more plausible: twelve police officers were assigned to protect the ballots around the clock. Six months later, the court finally declared Turpin the winner by a margin of two to one. "And so a black man," stated Nathan B. Young, "who was born in Georgia, lived in Mississippi, and was a gold prospector and one-time jewelry salesman in Mexico became the first black man to be elected to public office in the city of St. Louis and the state of Missouri."[2]

The next year (1920) another Republican, Walthal M. Moore, was elected the first Negro to the Missouri House of Representatives. He represented the Third District until his defeat in 1922. In 1925, he returned to the statehouse from the Sixth District for three more terms (1925–1930).

Richard "Dick" Kent, a taxicab owner, was elected the first Negro committeeman of the Sixth Ward in 1920. After passage of the Nineteenth Amendment to the U.S. Constitution ratifying suffrage for women in 1920, a Negro woman, Rosa Madison, became committee-woman of the Sixth Ward. Within three years of the Pythian meeting, Negroes had been trained to serve as uniformed policemen, to operate two fire stations (on Jefferson Avenue near Market Street and the 3900 block of Enright), to bury unclaimed Negro paupers for the city, to serve on petit juries and grand juries, and to supervise garbage collection.

What began as a list of overly optimistic requests—perceived by whites as another publicity stunt—materialized into a fait accompli. The attitude and determination of the black community were destined to continue, to grow, and to flourish for the next several generations. They were destined to alter the way in which white officials dealt with the minority community. The initial success of the Liberty League was so inspiring to the community that it was impossible to relax until the other five conditions were met: A Negro in Congress, a justice of the peace, a member of the board of education, a member of the board of aldermen, and a city hospital staffed by Negroes. These goals became causes célèbres to Negroes for the next five decades.

A major effort was made by both John W. Hayes in 1929 and Julia Child Curtis in 1931 to be the first Negro elected to the Board of Education. Both ran a far distance behind the winners. Others followed their efforts and lost each time during the ensuing thirty-five years.

Yet, after the success of the Pythian declaration and increased agitation from Negroes, the Republican Party continued its resistance to sharing power with blacks. The local administration refused to deliver jobs or services in proportion to the contributions of black voters. In 1933 George Vaughn, David Grant, Frank Bledsoe, and Jordan W. Chambers convinced a sizable number of blacks to vote for the Democratic ticket. Prominent blacks ran for the Board of Education in 1939, 1945, 1951, 1952, 1955, and 1957.[3]

It was many years before the entire list of demands developed by the Citizens Liberty League was achieved, but the flame of hope sparked by the effectiveness of the Pythian group never dimmed. Ten years later, in 1928, the community almost elected the first Negro to the U.S. Congress in the twentieth century; since 1901, no person of color had served in Congress. Blacks in St. Louis launched a major thrust to elect one of their own to the U.S. House of Representatives. Joseph L. McLemore ran as a candidate on the Democrat ticket. In this race, the

Democratic Party officially endorsed a black congressional candidate for the first time. In the general election, McLemore was pitted against the white Republican incumbent, Congressman L. C. Dyer, who had represented the heavily populated black district since 1910 and had never been seriously challenged during his nine terms in office.

Most blacks were aligned with the Republicans and saw nothing admirable or worthwhile in supporting a Democrat—even a black Democrat. McLemore, however, waged a vigorous campaign, losing by only 7,000 votes. (Dyer received 24,701 to McLemore's 17,609.) Voter support for Dyer in black wards made the difference for the white incumbent. Despite his spirited, issue-oriented campaign, McLemore was not able to overcome the Lincoln mystique: he had freed the slaves, and that was sufficient reason for blacks' everlasting loyalty to the Republican party.

Black St. Louis Republicans, like blacks in other cities, were to a great extent persuaded by party propaganda accusing McLemore and other black Democrats of running merely to garner electoral votes for Al Smith, the Democratic candidate for president. At the time, the black vote played a key role in determining which candidates would win the states of Ohio, Kentucky, Maryland, and Missouri. Black Republicans feared that a Democratic victory would be the rebirth of the policies of Woodrow Wilson, who as president had re-established segregation of the races in government hiring, dining rooms, and toilet facilities. Wilson appointed bigoted southern white Democrats to key government positions. Since a majority of blacks were Republican and Baptist, Al Smith, a Catholic Democrat running for Congress in the Twelfth District, had two strikes against him from the start. Political loyalty and religious bigotry prevailed as both McLemore and Smith were defeated.

McLemore's chances would have been better if Congressman Dyer had not been so popular a national figure among black voters. His exalted image was established when James Weldon Johnson, the secretary of the National Association for the Advancement of Colored People (NAACP), persuaded him in 1921 to introduce an anti-lynching bill which would "assure to persons within the jurisdiction of every state the equal protection of the laws, and to punish the crime of lynching."[4]

Lynching was a very emotional issue in black communities, and Dyer's introduction of a bill to make it a federal crime was a meaningful political gesture for blacks. Between 1889 and 1922, 3,436 blacks had been officially designated as lynched victims. Between 1918 and 1921, twenty-eight black people were publicly burned in the streets by white mobs. Thousands more died at the hands of racist terrorists but were not recorded as lynched (the circumstances did not meet the legal definition of lynching as an act of mob violence resulting in the death or maiming of a person who was taken from the custody of a law enforcement official).

Dyer's bill, similar to the first anti-lynching bill introduced on January 20, 1900, by the last black congressman of the Reconstruction era, George H. White, was debated in the House and stringently opposed by southern congressmen who openly advocated mob rule as the only remedy for maintaining civilized conditions. Despite the acrimonious ranting of the congressmen, the anti-lynching bill passed the House by a vote of 230 to 119, and Representative Dyer earned the respect and loyalty of many Negro citizens. However, the bill was stalled in the Senate by a filibuster led by Democratic senators from Mississippi and Alabama.[5]

As for the other demands, in St. Louis the election of a black justice of the peace had to wait until the late 1930s. In 1937 Homer G. Phillips Hospital (HGP), staffed and administered by blacks, opened. On April 20, 1943, Reverend Jasper C. Caston, age forty-four, fulfilled another milestone, becoming the first black elected to the St. Louis Board of Aldermen. The pastor of Memorial Baptist Church won the seat with 1,674 votes to his opponent's 422 votes. The minority community was, however, denied an elected representative on the Board of Education until 1960.

The amazing accomplishments of those who met at Pythian Hall were followed with remarkable success in the 1950s and 1960s. But, in recent years, the commitment and the vision of black leaders have diminished appreciably.

Unrealistic Black Expectations

If I were mandated to cite the most crippling deficiency in the present struggle to reach political parity, it would be black voters' high expectations of white politicians. Most of our unsolvable problems emanate from this sad perversity, which allows white politicians to tell black leaders that our community is not in sync with demands for racial justice.

It is the mentality of blacks to ask nothing of substance from white elected officials whom they support but to expect the impossible from black leaders. The list of expectations is as long as it is preposterous: personally returning all telephone calls, regardless of the simplicity of the alleged problem; attending all PTA and block unit meetings; securing jobs; cosigning personal loans; fixing traffic tickets; providing free legal service; acting as a marriage counselor, child psychologist, and medical adviser. None of these is required, expected, or indeed requested of white officials. Blacks who vote in the same proportion or contribute the same finances, if not more, as whites expect little return on their investments. They are satisfied with being placed on a long mailing list, being invited to fund-raising cocktail parties with nondescript functionaries, and being asked to serve on re-election committees.

More detrimental to their cause than these misconceptions is the lack of understanding of real power and how execution of that power affects their lives. When ghettoized neighborhoods experience high rates of unemployment, poor street lighting, inadequate sewers, bumpy roads, and unconscionable health facilities, the blame is normally transferred to black leaders. Since no blacks serve as U.S. senators or governors, every black in the country lives in the middle of a district represented by whites. Failure to shower equal blame and reluctance to expect resolution of these conditions poignantly highlight a cancerous affliction eating away at the black body politic.

Our politics cannot be fair, sensible, productive, and meaningful unless all who represent us are held to the same standard. Blacks have made significant gains in St. Louis politics. Although our achievements have been notable, failure to reach more of our goals can be placed at the door of timid black leaders who have surrendered to reactionary forces. What our politicians need today is the same type of courage and integrity displayed in 1919 by the group of pioneering Negroes from St. Louis who met to challenge their Republican Party leaders at Pythian Hall.

Mau-Mau Mentality

More disturbing than the distant relationship between white officials and their black constituents are the uncivilized attacks by blacks on one another, which make it impossible to direct an effective, preemptive assault against our enemies.

This psychopathic diversion is similar to the Mau-Mau syndrome. Mau-Maus were a fanatical group of Kenyans led by Jomo Kenyatta, who forged independence for their African colony from the British Empire. They massacred other Africans who performed menial tasks for white colonialists. Seeking to overthrow European rulers, the Mau-Maus murdered maids, chauffeurs, gardeners, and cooks. Kenyatta's freedom fighters operated under the misguided assumption that those aiding and abetting whites were the real enemy. Kenyatta and his followers won their rightful struggle for freedom, but as a result of identifying other blacks as the enemy, black people began to perceive whites as friends. Consequently, Brits still run the commerce of this independent African nation. Not much has changed for the vast lower class of black inhabitants. They still own little land, operate few businesses, enjoy hardly any material pleasures, and are treated by black leaders just as ruthlessly as they were by the former white colonists.

Too many in the African American community here at midcentury adopted a similar attitude. They possessed a mentality that was anathema to the new militant mood engulfing Negroes. On questions of racial advancement, they were passive almost to the extent of timidity. Their positions were ambivalent, constantly in flux, and mostly in confusion. Unless this trend is reversed, the years of struggle by Homer G. Phillips, Sidney Redmond, DeVerne Calloway, and hundreds of others will have been for naught. Black people must never take their eyes off the prize.

Chapter

2

Early Days of Bill Clay:
From Childhood to Manhood

I was born on the banks of the Mississippi River and grew up in a neighborhood of dilapidated three-story, rat-infested tenement houses with no hot running water or indoor toilet facilities. Regrettably, these sordid conditions were not hidden behind the railroad tracks, out of the sight of the city's fathers. Thirty-three thousand city residents lived in cold-water flats without indoor toilets or central heating. Food was cooked on an open stove fueled by kindling wood and coal. Water was heated for baths taken in a number-ten washtub, and a curtain was draped for privacy. This took place just blocks from the downtown business district, adjacent to city hall, and in plain sight of three daily newspapers: the *Star-Times*, the *Post-Dispatch*, and the *Globe-Democrat*.

I was delivering newspapers by the age of eight. By age eleven the Second World War had begun, and I was selling scrap metal, paper, and rags. By age twelve I was working at a clothing store in downtown St. Louis. Our neighborhood was racially mixed but also rigidly segregated. Irish, Polish, Italians, and blacks lived in the same blocks but in different worlds. Tenement houses were rented according to race or nationality. Five schools were in walking distance: two blocks south was a Catholic school for Italians, three blocks north a Catholic school for Irish, two blocks away a public school for whites, three blocks away a public school for Negroes, and ten blocks away a Catholic school for Negroes.

Whites frequented restaurants, movies, and hotels open to whites only. Even the public playground in our community was racially "separate but inherently unequal." One side was reserved for whites, the other for us. There were two ball diamonds, two swimming pools, two sets of swings, and two volleyball courts. The white swimming pool was deep enough for diving (5 feet). Ours was a wading pool (2 feet deep).

There was one white recreation staff and one Negro staff. The quarters for changing clothes and securing athletic equipment were on different sides of the playground. The different races did play together on vacant lots and at the public playground after closing hours, on weekends, and during the winter months.

Within a six-block radius of my living quarters were persons of various ethnic, religious, and cultural backgrounds. I had personal associations with Salvatore Polizzi, now a monsignor in the Roman Catholic Church; Sonny Liston and Virgil Akins, former world boxing champions; Robert Williams, now known as Robert Guillaume, of the television show *Benson*; and an assortment of other fascinating characters.

I lived in this area for twenty-one years with my mother, father, two brothers, and four sisters. I was the fourth child born—all on the kitchen table—to Irving and Luella Clay. We grew up in the heart of a major city and, like others in the same predicament, were unaware that most people did not suffer a lack of such basic facilities.

The happiest times of my youth were the seven days each year I spent at Boy Scout camp. There were trees and grass. The air was clean. I loved playing softball in the city's recreation league for Negro youth. I grew up like others in the neighborhood, very happy-go-lucky. Astonishingly, from my present vantage point, I now realize life was more happy than lucky. And, amazingly, I remained in that state of suspended animation about my well-being until the roof literally caved in on my world of naïveté.

My First Encounter with the Political System

When I was eighteen, a single incident convinced me of the power and importance of political connections. Its impression was so indelible that I still occasionally relive the grim details. Oblivious to the world around me and its intricate workings, I journeyed off into life innocently adjusting to the transition from adolescence to maturity. Still working after school in the downtown clothing store, attending Saint Louis University

(SLU), and frequenting a nearby pool hall every available moment assured that my teen years would be normal as well as carefree. The lifestyle I lived in the late 1940s was typical of that experienced by other blacks across the breadth of America. We idolized the feats of Joe Louis and Jesse Owens. We cheered for Jackie Robinson, even when he struck out or bobbled a ball. Success in sports was a source of pride and inspiration for a race of people sorely in need of heroes. In fact, success in sports was the greatest hope we tenaciously clung to in our effort to overcome the terrifying effects of racial discrimination and segregation. Athletic accomplishment provided a sense of group importance, opposed to the bombastic haranguing from a society that constantly told us of our worthlessness.

In 1949 a brutal crime was committed at a neighborhood grocery. Two blacks were sought by the police for murdering a white couple who owned the delicatessen. The usual fear and panic swept our area whenever crimes with racial overtones were committed. The media always dramatized the incidents in savage detail, emphasizing the racial aspects. Hundreds of black men would be indiscriminately arrested, charged under suspicion of homicide, and held for days without bail. This case was no different.

At about 5:15 p.m.—three days after the slaying—a white policeman, Eddie Burke, walked into the store where I had worked for five years. He handcuffed me and placed me under arrest, punched me several times, and refused to tell my employer why I was being arrested. I was taken in a police car to the Fourth District police station, four blocks from where I worked and one block from where I lived. My employer immediately called to inform my mother, who was waiting at the station with her sister, my Aunt Teddy, when we arrived. Burke, who had a reputation for brutalizing blacks, used profanity to instruct my mother that my "ass was his" and that there was no need to explain anything to "two black b———s." Once inside, he took me into a small room for interrogation. Interrogation in 1949 was a euphemism for beating the hell out of a "nigger." I was the "nigger" in question—and a scared, confused, and horrified one at that.

In that dirty little back room, sitting on a backless stool, I was informed that the manager of the poolroom had fingered me as driving the killers to the bus depot. Standing before me was a pathological misfit with a rubber hose in his hand, clothed in the authority of law, about to dispense his special form of justice. He had earned his reputation the hard way by physically and publicly brutalizing Negro people.

Before he could force a confession, the door opened, and two plainclothes detectives appeared. They were dispatched from police headquarters bearing orders to take charge of the investigation. Burke screamed that I was guilty and that he would get the credit for solving the case. The officers calmly explained their orders from the chief and transported me to headquarters, where I was given a lie-detector test, judged to be uninvolved, and released.

Why was I so fortunate when many others would have suffered the physical abuse and a forced confession? The answer is quite simple: political influence. My Aunt Teddy telephoned the man whose house she cleaned and whose children she sometimes cared for. As a member of the Board of Police Commissioners, he had influence and instantly decided how the case of Bill Clay would be resolved. All the Eddie Burkes in town had no recourse to countermand his decision.

The experience convinced me that survival and political influence are inseparable in American society.

1952: My Baptism by Fire

My first real encounter with partisan political activity was as a college student in my first year at SLU. My professor of political science suggested that it was worth getting involved in many of the interesting races in the 1952 Democratic primary. Along with Herman Thompson, a fellow student, I followed this advice and decided to hook up with the Nineteenth Ward Regular Democratic Organization, which was led by the renowned Jordan W. Chambers. He was often and deservingly characterized as the most powerful black in St. Louis's political history. Chambers had dictated the course of politics in black St. Louis since the late 1930s.

We went to several ward meetings before it became apparent that those surrounding Chambers were not going to allow intruders to penetrate the inner circle. At one meeting, I did go up to the front of the hall to introduce myself. Forty-eight years later, having been the target of such overtures by well-meaning interlopers, I now understand how futile it was for us to try to gain recognition in such a close-knit group.

Unable to breach the protective wall around Chambers, we ventured to the corner of Sarah Street and Easton Avenue in the Eighteenth Ward. There, Al Wallace had opened a headquarters. He was a ward heeler for John "Jack" Dwyer, the city treasurer and chairman of the Democratic City Central Committee, and he was running for the state senate. The incumbent of many years, Edward "Jellyroll" Hogan, was a notorious Depression-era gangster. After several days we were convinced that Wallace did not possess the leadership qualities with which we wanted to be associated. With only limited political knowledge, we were aware that his operation lacked organization and public involvement.

My girlfriend and future wife, Carol Ann Johnson, informed me that Olivia Calloway was running for committeewoman in the Eighteenth Ward. She lived two doors down from Janet Price, who had been Carol's friend since kindergarten. Later we attended an outdoor rally sponsored by Frederick N. Weathers and Calloway, candidates for Eighteenth Ward committee posts. Weathers, streetwise and dedicated to improving the lot of his people, was a protégé of Chambers. Wayman Smith II roused a crowd of some three hundred persons with dazzling oratory and hard-hitting rhetoric. In an impassioned speech, he introduced Weathers as the person qualified to lead our people out of the wilderness of "political and economic isolation." Thompson and I worked that summer distributing handbills and canvassing door to door. Weathers and Calloway defeated incumbents Charles "Turtles" Reardon and Hortense Curry for the Democratic committee posts. (Curry had died several weeks before election day, but her name had remained on the ballot.)

Activities at Fort McClellan

In 1953 I was drafted into the army. A year later I was stationed at Fort McClellan in Alabama, assigned to the Army Chemical Corps. In direct contravention of President Harry S. Truman's 1948 Executive Order 9981 banning racial segregation on military facilities, the post was thoroughly and officially segregated by race. Despite sincere efforts by President Dwight Eisenhower to wipe away the last vestiges of racial separation in the military, in 1954 Fort McClellan still resisted with all the insobriety of the last Confederate general and the insolence of the last Confederate infantryman. I was forced to soldier at a facility that prohibited blacks from getting a haircut except on Saturdays, when a black barber was brought in from a nearby town; that closed the noncommissioned officers' club to blacks on Thursdays, when white girls were imported from Anniston, Alabama, for dances; that had a "whites only" PX restaurant; and that kept blacks out of the swimming pool by claiming it was reserved for national guardsmen in training.

Under the circumstances, I became incensed and organized a campaign among the black soldiers to protest these illegal activities. We boycotted the barbershop for several months (many refusing to get haircuts), and I, along with my wife and several kids from the housing project where we lived off-post, swept past the guard at the swimming pool one day and integrated it.

At that point, the commanding officer of the post threatened to court-martial me. I immediately appealed to army headquarters and the Negro press to investigate the situation and also to inquire into the allegations of racial discrimination at the newly constructed Women's Army Corps unit on the campgrounds. Several black newspapers carried the story. Within weeks I was transferred to an army base in Missouri. Later Congressman Charles Diggs of Michigan initiated a full-scale investigation.

Organizing the NAACP Youth Council

Returning to St. Louis after my discharge from the army in 1955, I called together ten or twelve friends to discuss plans for combating racial discrimination. I was twenty-four years old and married with one child, working full-time at the federal government's mapping agency and selling insurance part-time. While most others in our age group were involved in social clubs, arranging picnics and river cruises, my wife and I were more serious about our future. We were a little different, and some thought us a little odd. It was our impression that black people should be interested in more important issues.

So we organized the NAACP Youth Council, feeling that our lives would be more productive and more fulfilling by fighting racism. My co-workers at the Aeronautical and Information Chart Center of the United States Government formed the core of the group. After several meetings, it was decided that we would form the Council. Youths we were not—our ages ranged from twenty-two to thirty. But compared to those in charge of the adult branch of the NAACP, we were infants. The group elected me president, and we secured a chapter through the national office of the NAACP in New York City. Theoretically, the local adult membership had little control over our activities.

Within days our group launched a series of picket lines at eating establishments that refused to serve blacks. Within months our membership had grown to over five hundred, and our picket lines were attracting hundreds of youths and older people. Newspapers gave us extensive coverage, and politicians showed great interest in this new development.

Our group captured the attention and imagination of many blacks looking for a mechanism to fight racial bigotry. In less than six months we had opened eating facilities for blacks at the White Castle drive-in chain restaurants, the Parkmoor Diner, and the Orange-Front FootLong Drive-in. In less than a year, we had broken the color line against hiring black truck drivers at bread companies and dairies. We then moved on to force chain supermarkets (Kroger, A&P, and National) to hire black butchers, cashiers, and warehousemen.

Training Ground for My First Election

In 1957 revision of the St. Louis city charter was the major initiative of the two daily newspapers, businessmen, and constituents in silk-stocking wards. Previous attempts to restructure the composition of the Board of Aldermen had been rejected by the voters. No matter how tactfully the proposal was couched, two variables were constant: a desire to neutralize the political influence of labor unions and a desire to stymie the political potential of a rapidly increasing black population.

The size of political units basically determines what special interest groups will control government. The larger the district, the less likely grassroots organizations or unorganized citizens will wield a meaningful voice. The smaller the geographical boundaries, the more probable that block units, small merchants, PTAs, and minorities will influence who represents them. Editorial writers, large financial contributors, and societal elites usually have greater leverage in excessively large districts.

The city charter proposal called for reducing the size of the Board of Aldermen from twenty-eight representatives of wards and a president elected citywide to fifteen members (seven at large, seven from wards, and a president citywide). Enlarging ward boundaries and electing over 50 percent of the Board of Aldermen citywide endangered the possible election of more Negroes. At the time no black had ever been elected citywide, but, according to demographics, it would be possible to elect several in the foreseeable future.

I learned a valuable lesson in the campaign to revise the city charter, which enabled me to succeed in later encounters. As president of the NAACP Youth Council, I was assigned the task of rallying my members to work against the charter in the Fourth Ward.

Jack Dwyer, chairman of the Democratic City Central Committee and committeeman of the Fourth Ward, favored passage of the charter amendment. Ernest Calloway, president of the NAACP and research director for Joint Council Thirteen Central States Teamsters, served as adviser and confidant to members of the NAACP Youth Council in developing our tactics. He was an astute politician with an analytical mind. His guidance and strategies were helpful. We developed most of our campaign ploys by bouncing them off of him and evaluating his reactions. Our appeal to voters was broad-based in refuting the drab, nebulous ranting for "good government" and reform.

Our appeal dealt with the hope that twelve blacks would someday sit on the Board of Aldermen and help to determine the future of St. Louis. We contended that the new charter calling for the 7–7–1 election of aldermen was designed to restrict the increase of Negro representation. We charged that it had no logical purpose other than to create a permanent political ghetto for the 240,000 black citizens who were underrepresented.

Despite support of the charter revision by some black leaders aligned with the white power structure, mathematics was on the side of those of us who opposed the plan. The probability of electing twelve blacks out of twenty-nine made the possibility of electing two blacks out of fifteen ring hollow.

In our door-to-door canvassing, we pointed out that the new city charter offered Negroes little enticement to support it. There were no provisions in the charter that would prohibit discrimination in restaurants, hotels, theaters, movie houses, or rental apartments. There was no mention of a law banning employment discrimination.

We met the challenge and measured up to the task. Dwyer and his veteran precinct workers were trounced. Citywide, the charter proposal went down in a resounding defeat, losing in twenty-two of the twenty-eight wards. Our troops earned their wings the hard way, going door-to-door with a message of hope. We learned in this campaign the two most difficult lessons in politics: how to get voters excited and how to get them to the polls. The campaign served as a testing ground for the fight that was to come eighteen months later in the Twenty-sixth Ward. I envisioned an episode similar to the Spanish Civil War, where allied and axis powers tested their raw, untrained troops and new battle equipment in readiness for the Second World War that everyone knew was coming.

Transferring that knowledge, experience, and enthusiasm was simply a matter of time and occasion. The chosen time was 1959, and the occasion was my running for alderman of the Twenty-sixth Ward.

A Twenty-Five-Year Feud with the *Globe-Democrat*

Little did I realize that as my political career blossomed, detractors in the media and leaders of the business sector would oppose my efforts in such vehement fashion. But as my respect among constituents and colleagues increased, so too did the hostility toward the positions I advocated.

For a period of more than twenty years, the publishers of the *St. Louis Globe-Democrat* conducted a campaign to curtail my influence and to derail my upward mobility. My refusal to compromise on matters of racial justice or to cower from pressures to temper my stance for equal rights prompted most of the opposition. The power of the mass media to twist truth to fit its cynical purposes is astounding. The *St. Louis Globe-Democrat* was a great transmitter of half truths, pseudo values, and irresponsible, false interpretations of life in the black community. The paper always called into question my motivation whenever I took positions on public policy. Critical news articles and demeaning editorials were expected from those who resented strong, black leadership. Consequently, I found myself in a struggle for political survival with the *Globe-Democrat*, which often portrayed me as corrupt and incorrigible. The newspaper and its two publishers were the primary architects of the serious animosity among the races that existed throughout the city during my career. Their distorted news coverage and racially inflammatory editorials were directed toward persons or groups that fought to eliminate discrimination and segregation.

Politically, the powerful downtown financial cartel tacitly agreed with the muckraking tactics taken by the *Globe-Democrat* and, in every election, supported my opponent. Our disagreement was based mostly on a difference of ideology of what constitutes fair treatment for the minority community—specifically, my belief that blacks were entitled to all of the rights of citizenship as others. My consideration of those rights as non-negotiable put me at odds with the power structure.

Any discussion with them was futile because my political philosophy left no room for compromise on certain tenets they possessed: that the black community was for sale, that Martin Luther King Boulevard was viewed as the "Cimmaron Trail and North Side voters could be herded to the polls like cattle," and that the white establishment should have carte blanche in designating black leaders.

Amazingly, their desire to influence decisions in the black areas has never waned. They still attempt to appoint African American spokespeople and confer on them the mantle of legitimate, respectable leadership. They are motivated by a fear of dealing with the real leadership because negotiations might be difficult. This position defies reality. No other group is held in such scorn. The business leaders do not presume a right to pick the leadership of B'Nai B'rith, the American Federation of Labor–Congress of Industrial Organizations (AFL-CIO), the American Civil Liberties Union (ACLU), or other similar organizations.

CHAPTER

3

ENTERING THE POLITICAL ARENA

When I filed as a candidate for the Board of Aldermen in 1958, St. Louis was as "separate and unequal" as any place south of the Mason-Dixon line. The political system had failed miserably in delivering justice to its citizens of color. The history of racism was consistent with the temperament of racial intolerance endemic throughout the nation. Based on custom and tradition, the city denied Negroes basic rights of citizenship. Although signs such as For Whites Only and For Colored Only were not displayed, the policy of separation was evident, effective, and enforced. St. Louis was a city that spent time and money to convince America that it had eliminated most of its racial problems without social upheaval and that it was committed to providing fair and equal opportunity to all its inhabitants. But closer analysis of the advertised racial haven revealed the existence of a politically suppressed and economically exploited Negro community.

Employment for Negroes in the public and private sectors was almost nonexistent in management and white-collar positions. Only 3.6 percent of Negro workers were working as professionals or technicians. Although the city had a 40 percent black population, of the city's 2,221 policemen only 326 (15 percent) were black. The fire department was worse. Only 5 percent of the firemen were black, and they worked in two firehouses staffed entirely by blacks.

Negroes were grossly underrepresented in public office. The four members of the Board of Police Commissioners, appointed by the governor, were white males. Only four Negroes served on the twenty-nine-member Board of Aldermen: T. H. Mayberry (Fourth Ward), Archie Blaine (Sixth Ward), Wayman Smith II (Eighteenth Ward), and Dewitte Lawson (Nineteenth Ward). Only three blacks—John Green, James P. Troupe, and Leroy Tyus—were members of the state legislature. Eleven citywide-elected county offices that controlled more than one thousand patronage jobs were held by whites. A Negro had never been elected to the twelve-member school board. The fifty-six-member Democratic City Central Committee controlling the political machinery of the city had only four blacks as members. In the eight wards where Negro voters were in the majority, only two were represented by blacks. Of the six state senators, none were black. There were no Negroes serving in the mayor's cabinet and none appointed under the civil service system as commissioners of any agency. State government did not have a black in any position of administrative authority.

Because black citizens did not have the power to impact decisions that critically affected their lives, immediate and drastic measures were required to address the crisis. The record was clear: In a rigidly segregated community, the lack of human services almost bordered on criminality. Existing conditions caused Negroes like myself to determine that race did play a major role in the social, political, and economic affairs of St. Louis. The bleak prospect of improving the situation prompted a sizable group of determined individuals to plan to reverse this obscene denial of opportunity.

We were no longer content to accept the pleasant platitudes and paternalistic phrases traditionally used to appease the concerns of blacks victimized by harsh policies of discrimination. Our hostility was not directed exclusively at white officials. We also indicted a cadre of Negro civil rights leaders who viewed themselves as a buffer between the white establishment and abrasive black activists. The forward advancement of the Negro race was stymied during the first half of the twentieth century because some blacks considered it a privilege to serve the interests of the white community, and they eagerly opposed the enhancement of black rights.

A growing segment of the black population was becoming increasingly disgusted with the lack of progress. Young activists, neighborhood leaders, and disgruntled, jobless adults aggressively sought tangible advancement through nonviolent protest. They insisted on playing a pivotal role in the formulation of policies and positions for addressing the situation. The chant for more jobs, more black elected officials, and better city services surfaced across the width and breadth of the inner city. Some elderly black leaders failed to recognize this sea change in Negro attitudes.

Negroes had stopped playing around the fringes of the political game and had plunged into the heart and soul of it. The "have-nots" and the deprived began to recognize common concerns, interests, and enemies. But, more significantly, there was a general awareness that we had latent power that, if developed, was sufficient to overthrow the white political bosses. This awareness and unity represented a milestone in establishing effective political forces in St. Louis. Our race was yearning to be represented in legislative bodies by officials who prioritized civil rights and conspicuously promoted human needs. We expected those representing us to initiate debate about racial matters. We were determined that passive responses to our conditions would not be tolerated.

Race for Twenty-sixth Ward Alderman

My first election to public office in 1959 did not occur because I possessed any amazing skills, charismatic charms, or unusual powers. It was not because my opponents in the contest lacked talent, dedication, or commitment. The campaign for alderman in the Twenty-sixth Ward offered voters a choice between five well-qualified and educationally prepared candidates. The incumbent alderman was white. The four challengers, including myself, were Negroes. One challenger was a prominent attorney. Another was the pastor of a large African Methodist Episcopal (AME) congregation located in the ward, and the other was a seasoned political veteran.

The incumbent had served honorably for twelve years, but his status was in jeopardy because the tide of racial pride had arrived and nothing or no one could hold back its rising waters. It was the beginning of the great civil rights movement.

I was successful because I was the challenger whom most identified with the struggle for racial equality and the one possessing a reputation for not tolerating racial injustices. I had been in the forefront of the civil rights movement, leading picket lines for jobs, sitting in at restaurants for equal access to public accommodations, and challenging police brutality.

As often happens, the smallest incidents can determine the greatest outcomes. Sheriff Martin L. Tozer and the considerable power vested in his patronage-laden political machine were toppled because of an arrogant, rude remark uttered in the wrong place at the wrong time. A friend approached me about helping him to get an appointment as special assistant to the state attorney. The position was a part-time patronage plum coveted by most young, struggling lawyers. It paid only $2,400 a year, but the hours required to work were minimal and provided attorneys with a base for paying overhead expenses in their private practices.

I persuaded twenty of my cohorts to attend the monthly meeting of the Twenty-sixth Ward Regular Democratic Organization. My friend Daniel Tillman,[6] who was vying for the position, also had about twenty of his friends on hand. There were approximately 120 persons in attendance. My curiosity was aroused by the four people sitting at the front of the hall at a long table. One had a ledger; she gave receipts to those who deposited cash on the table. Tillman informed me that those were dues-paying members of the organization who held patronage jobs at city hall. He stated that a small percentage of their annual salaries was paid to cover the normal expenses of the ward organization. My curiosity was aroused because only eight of the fifty or sixty dues-payers were black, although at least half of the residents of the ward were black.

The chairman, Tozer, rose and declared that there were no problems worthy of discussion and recognized Tillman for remarks. Afterward, Tozer asked if there was any new business and then announced that free beer and hot dogs were available in the rear of the room.

Tillman and I entered the back room to seek Tozer's endorsement of Tillman for appointment as an assistant state's attorney. But Tozer was not polished, educated, or diplomatic. In a very rude manner, he informed us that $2,400 a year was too much to give to a Negro lawyer.

Instead he announced that he would hire two Negroes and give each $1,200 annually. We were appalled. His contemptuous attitude left us somewhat perplexed. At that very moment, it crossed my mind to file against him and rid our ward of this insensitive person.

The next day I went to the Board of Election Commissioners to file for office. Much to my surprise and embarrassment, I learned the next election was for the alderman, not the committeeman. Unshaken by this lack of basic political knowledge, I spent many hours evaluating the pluses and minuses of throwing my hat into the race for alderman. Initially, my interest in elective office was sustained by a desire to teach the committeeman a lesson.

I discussed the matter with some of those involved with me in the civil rights movement. At a meeting we expressed our anger at Tozer's intolerance and concluded that blacks needed a strong voice in elective office. The solution became obvious: The Board of Aldermen could eliminate most of our frustrations by passing legislation to open all places of public accommodation and a bill to prohibit employment discrimination.

After determining that the pluses outweighed the minuses, it was decided that I should file for alderman. Something I remembered reading in *Janet's Repentance*, by George Eliot, gave me encouragement to enter the race. As she wrote in 1857, "Any coward can fight a battle when he's sure of winning; but give me the man who has pluck to fight when he's sure of losing."

This adequately describes the dilemma I faced in 1958 when deciding to file for alderman of the Twenty-sixth Ward. The odds were all stacked against me. None of the political insiders gave me an outside chance of winning. I had no money, no political organization, and no media support. To compound the problem, I had virtually no possibility of attaining money or media support. Being neither coward nor hero, but somewhat conceited, I decided victory was mine for the taking.

I did have some positive, sellable assets. I had a sizable amount of name recognition. I knew many of the people who lived in the Twenty-sixth Ward and believed I could eventually transform those relationships into votes. A major stumbling block would be my ability to convince them that, despite my youth, I was old enough to make a difference in improving the quality of life for them and their children. I was the assistant manager of Supreme Liberty Life Insurance. But, before my promotion, I had worked as a debit agent collecting weekly premiums from policyholders. I went in and out of hundreds of households in the ward. For many I served as lawyer, notary public, social worker, or even marriage counselor. I knew their family members by their first names, and they knew me by my first name. What more qualification did a person need to get elected?

I opened my headquarters twenty feet from the White Castle eating establishment where I had conducted my first picket line to secure service for black people. I had negotiated with the Brod-Dugan paint store to hire its first black salesman. The store was only seventy-five feet from my headquarters. The die was cast. I would win or lose on familiar home ground. The task, however, was more difficult, more tedious, and more revealing than I had imagined. My first eye-opening experience was when I asked for the support of a young black woman who was one of ten students in my high school graduating class. We had started school in elementary grades and continued in the same building throughout high school. We were friends for over twenty years. She refused to assist me because the committeeman employed her as a watcher in the polling place on election day.

I knew then that the battle would be hard and long. My next step was to pay a personal visit to each person on my insurance debit to talk politics. This venture proved more profitable. Many were sympathetic with my mission and were encouraged by my youthful ambition. I met several who later became active in the campaign. One was an agent for another black weekly insurance company.

Next I lined up the support of numerous relatives and gave them specific assignments. Some did not live in the ward. My family, as others in the ghetto, was legendary. They enjoyed the good times together and agonized over the bad ones. My father had eight brothers and sisters. My mother had seven. They had scores of children and grandchildren. I had been to family reunions with more than six hundred people. Scores of Clays on my father's side and Rhodeses, Diggses, Hyatts, and Wilsons on my mother's side—all born in Missouri and all living in St. Louis—eventually became the nucleus of my campaign organization. Cousins, nephews, uncles, and aunts came from all over town as crusaders to make sure that the first Clay seeking public office would be victorious. My relatives knew somebody on every block and persuaded their friends to join the movement. No stone was left unturned. Hundreds of Clay feet trampled throughout the ward, upholding the honor of the family name.

I spent countless hours in the houses of people who were perfect strangers to me but had close association with members of my immediate family. They would tell stories from my childhood, of how they had watched me grow and mature. It was a good feeling to know that my parents had so many friends. This all gave me the confidence to continue with what was perceived, initially, as an impossible dream: the toppling of an entrenched white political machine.

During the campaign it was necessary to expose those Negroes who supported white officeholders merely because they had jobs at city hall or received protection from the police for their illegal activities. Early in the campaign, I was confronted by one of Tozer's patronage workers who attempted to berate me because I had graduated from SLU. Most people are impressed by the scholastic achievements of others. The more education people attain, the more they are respected by those without it. This is especially true in the black community; blacks have had to overcome formidable obstacles to achieve educational success.

I had gone to a cocktail lounge in the center of the ward to visit a longtime family friend, Nathaniel Rivers. He and my father had been close associates since childhood. He had also been influential in East St. Louis, Illinois, politics for many years. Now he was living in St. Louis and was part owner of Juanita's Cocktail Lounge.

The bar was crowded. Although Rivers and I discussed the matter in rather subdued tones, others did hear the conversation. Tozer's black supporter approached us in a defiant, almost threatening manner. He was flashily dressed, sporting a large diamond stickpin in his tie and wearing a ring of at least one carat on his pinkie finger. Interrupting our conversation in a rather rude and loud voice, he began to demean me as a person and to berate my credentials for public office.

Rivers immediately came to my defense, pointing out that I had a degree from SLU while the incumbent had only finished the tenth grade. Tozer's "man Friday" then stated that it was stupid to believe I could defeat a man as powerful as the sheriff merely because I had a college degree. Rivers, in his matter-of-fact, smooth manner, softly stated that he would bet one hundred dollars that my chance of becoming sheriff was far greater than the sheriff's chance of graduating from SLU. His ghetto-like rebuttal ended the discussion. The crowded lounge became filled with laughter. By nightfall everybody in the neighborhood was privy to the humiliation of Tozer's booster. Shortly thereafter, Rivers agreed to play a leading role in the campaign.

The Three Musketeers

In the development of my organization to conduct the campaign, I established a chart clearly identifying key persons and assigned responsibilities. As a part of my campaign organization, I devised numerous ways for individuals to play important roles. I believed it was essential to designate appropriate titles for workers to signify their authority.

But, more important, I understood that politics was a profession, not a hobby, and I realized that the ward headquarters did not have the same connotation as a fraternity or social club. Drinking, dancing, and socializing were important to political clubs only in the sense that these activities facilitated organization for the next election and helped build a support group to assure massive get-out-the-vote drives. The ability to balance the two imperatives—seeking the greater community good and simultaneously amassing personal power to achieve that goal—became the hallmark of my career.

After setting out certain disciplines for myself, I was fortunate to meet three unforgettable characters. When they crossed my path, my confidence was rekindled. I met each at different times and under different circumstances.

The first was John Curtis. One rainy day early in the campaign, while I was sitting in my headquarters alone, the door opened and in walked Curtis. He was about five foot five, weighing no more than 125 pounds. He said that he wanted to be a policeman, and, if I promised to get him on the police force, he would work for my election.

I knew that John did not and would not ever meet the physical qualifications for the force. A candidate had to be a high school graduate, stand five foot eight, and weigh 165 pounds to be considered. But my enthusiasm for workers allowed me to dismiss such incidental, arbitrary rules as trivial. Curtis was assured that my first objective as an elected official would be to zealously attempt to put him on the police force. Deep in my heart, I knew it did not matter how much power I attained—Curtis would never go on the force. Emphasizing the word "attempt" turned a big lie into a little fib. I felt Curtis also knew that he would never qualify for the force. But, being a wise and perceptive individual, he must have known the truth. I think he was swayed by my sincerity to challenge the establishment and his own opportunity to pursue a worthwhile mission. He, too, had been victimized by racism and was determined to contribute to its eradication.

Curtis had powers of persuasion equal to successful refrigerator salesmen at the North Pole. When other precinct captains had trouble convincing voters to support our efforts, Curtis was dispatched to the scene. Time after time, they became supporters. He rallied the largest meetings, placed more signs inside windows, and enlisted more volunteer canvassers than any other precinct captain. He worked incessantly and brought one of his relatives into the camp who was the personal dining-car waiter for the president of a large railroad. This relative introduced me to the next most influential member of our organization, the wife of a dining-car waiter. He also persuaded two of my neighbors, James and Addie Rice, to become active in politics. Addie and Curtis became the most productive precinct captains in my operation. Addie, gracious and refined, added a touch of class to the free-spirited group surrounding me. She organized her precinct into a smooth-working machine, although living next door to Mary McDermott, the ward's elected committeewoman, caused her some personal discomfort. She outsmarted, outworked, and outmaneuvered the opposition at every turn. Her husband, James, quiet but respected, enlisted the assistance of five other railroad workers. Their contributions were invaluable. Trained for all sorts of protest activity under the tutelage of A. Philip Randolph of the Brotherhood of Sleeping Car Porters, they readily jumped into the political trenches of the Twenty-sixth Ward. Their presence gave maturity and direction to our cadre of energetic but inexperienced adolescents.

The third most unforgettable character I came in contact with was Magnolia Dease. She had been affiliated with Chambers's organization. She smoked a pipe and drank 100-proof bourbon without a water chaser. Her political instincts were perfect; her ability to sway voters was unmatched by ordinary political workers. She was the life of the organization, enlisting the support of people from many diverse backgrounds who worshiped her down-to-earth style. Maggie, as most of us called her, knew the political game inside out and upside down. Years of active duty with the Chambers folk tended to produce this kind of streetwise fighter committed to victory at any cost. Defeat was not in her vocabulary.

Maggie used her wealth of experience to train others and to neutralize many blacks who were tied in some way to the incumbent organization. Her major effort was one-on-one contact with those appointed as election clerks and judges by Committeeman Tozer. Elections during this period were won or lost (and many simply stolen) inside polling places. Tozer appointed all officials, including the Republican judges and clerks. This was possible because his machine also handpicked and elected the Republican committeepeople. Hanky-panky after the polls closed was expected in all the so-called delivery wards. Policemen were assigned to prevent disturbances at the polling places, not to assure honest counts. The police were also selected by the ward bosses.

Dease convinced a substantial number of Tozer's polling clerks to give us a fair count. Her appeal to racial pride was enhanced by the fact that none of the clerks was able to secure a full-time patronage job through the committeeman. Earning $15 one day a year was really not a job worth protecting, and Dease leaned heavily on that fact.

These three precinct leaders influenced others with a similar ability to cultivate and educate the voters. Curtis, Rice, and Dease made the campaign run smoothly.

A Learning Process

The old adage "politics makes strange bedfellows" took on a new meaning for me. I anticipated that a number of forces would oppose my candidacy. Others were quite revealing and, in fact, educational. Behind each supporter, there was a real or imagined motive. My principal occupation was attempting to discern the reason some people supported me and others did not.

Knowing the reasons why people joined political organizations allowed me to develop plans to keep supporters and also to neutralize opposition. Several people hated my opponent without loving me. That was understandable: At some time or another, incumbents make lasting enemies. The longer they hold office, the more enemies they accumulate. Others were hopeful of city employment when I won. A large number were active in politics because, for the first time, someone had asked them to get involved.

Well-organized political machines are similar to high-wage-rate labor unions that hold down membership to an absolute minimum for the purpose of ensuring full employment of all active participants. Tozer's group was no different. Therefore, many disgruntled, unsuccessful job seekers volunteered to work for me as a way of settling a score with the ward leader. Substantial support for me came from young blacks discontented with their inability to find employment. Older blacks supported me with the hope that their children would not suffer the same indignities they had. Both groups viewed political involvement as the most viable means of throwing off the yoke of discrimination and oppression.

Others refused to endorse me because they contended that four black candidates nullified the chances of any one of us winning. Frank Mitchell Sr., publisher of the oldest black business in the state, the *St. Louis Argus* newspaper, was not one of these people. He encouraged me to stay in the race. He also agreed to print my literature for actual cost. That was a big concession. I became able to buy one thousand handbills for seventeen dollars.

The price was affordable; the deal was very profitable. A ploy was developed to make other candidates spend large sums of money to refute our accusations. The one thousand handbills printed each week were carefully distributed to the doors of each candidate, to their neighbors on each side, and across the street. This strategy created the impression that distribution was ward-wide. My opponents resorted to rebutting the charges with ward-wide distribution of literature denying the charges. Our goal was accomplished: Those voters we could not reach because of lack of money were informed by our opponents of the major issues in the campaign.

Later we improved on the system by making electronic plates and reproducing the handbills in large numbers. That was possible because T. H. Mayberry, a real-estate broker and member of the Board of Aldermen, allowed us to use his mimeograph machine and ink without cost. The reams of paper were donated to us by supporters.

Amen, Reverend, Amen

In the fall of 1958, after almost a year of campaigning, my chief opponent, incumbent Bill Brady, viewed me as a serious candidate. My group began earning endorsements from community leaders and organizations.

One of the most influential groups in any black community is the organization of churches. I addressed the Baptist Ministers Association. Arriving at the scheduled time, I sat through two hours of routine organizational business before I was called upon to speak. I painstakingly explained my background and qualifications for office, outlined my platform for legislative action if elected, documented the failure of the incumbent to address our problems, and stressed the failure of the present political ward organization to represent the interests of an area becoming predominantly black. I spoke of the incumbent's lack of aggressive leadership on issues such as public accommodations, discrimination in employment, and fair housing.

My remarks were interrupted many times by applause. One minister made the motion that the organization go on record as endorsing my candidacy. Six or seven others spoke in glowing terms supporting the motion. The vote to endorse was unanimous.

As I was about to leave the room, one minister who had been silent said, "Mr. Clay, I see in your brochure that you graduated from Saint Louis University. That's a Catholic institution. Does that mean you are a Catholic?" The answer was yes. Then several of the ministers who had so eloquently praised me recanted. Despite the gallant effort of Reverend Curtis Faulkner and several others to counter this blatant religious bigotry, the endorsement was rescinded. Apparently, the majority felt that an elected official, in order to give voice to the drive for racial equality, must be not only black but also Protestant. It was not relevant that the incumbent alderman I sought to replace was also Catholic. Reverend Faulkner came to my rescue, but his brethren would not be influenced by reason or Christian charity.

Bleeding, but not mortally wounded, our camp redoubled its efforts within the churches of those voting to rescind the endorsement. We were remarkably successful in finding deacons and women auxiliary leaders to openly defy their pastors on this score. The failure of the ministerial group to lend support had only a minimal impact on the outcome of the election.

Not all of my experiences during the 1958 campaign were as disappointing or disconcerting as the one with the Baptist preachers. Many were light, comical, and refreshing. They helped to relieve the tension, strain, and anxiety of exhausted campaign workers.

The Missing Precinct Captains

The pastor of a large black church in the ward, Reverend Samuel Pointer of Wayman Temple AME Church, also threw his hat into the ring. That decision caused some consternation within my camp because of his more than one thousand parishioners, most of whom lived in the ward. In fact, several of our precinct captains were leaders in the church and members of the deacon board. We did not know how Pointer's candidacy would affect their status in our organization. A strategy meeting was called to devise a plan against what we anticipated would be a tough opponent and an even tougher campaign. It was agreed that an effort would be made to infiltrate Pointer's organization. Five persons, not publicly identified with our group, were designated to become double agents. Their initial assignment was to attend Pointer's first public meeting at his newly opened headquarters, make notes of those in attendance, volunteer for key positions, and report back to the strategy committee all details and discussions.

About forty people came to the opening of the headquarters. The candidate made brief remarks, outlined his reasons for seeking office, and proceeded to introduce his campaign manager. None of our precinct captains who were members of his church was in attendance. During the session, the campaign manager mentioned that to win it was necessary to find people who would serve as precinct captains in each of the twenty-four precincts. Reverend Pointer interrupted to make an inquiry. He asked why they could not use the precinct captains who were already in the ward. The room broke out in laughter, with our spies leading the way. Needless to say, from that day forward, our campaign committee did not take Pointer's candidacy seriously. We knew his limited knowledge of political workings would not enable him to split the black vote, and the election results showed that we had not only the first laugh but the last as well.

Divided Community

My election was complicated, to say the least. The residential area was in a stage of racial change. An all-white, lower-middle-class community of blue-collar workers was now being replaced by blacks who formerly lived in the Mill Creek redevelopment area, an older inner-city section of town. Demolition of the area under the guise of urban renewal displaced thousands of blacks and dispersed them into wards such as the twenty-sixth. By 1959 the ward had gone from mostly white to approximately 65 percent black. Many black residents were well-educated, professional employees. Most, however, were factory and assembly-line employees striving to buy homes and educate their children.

All of the elected officials of the ward were white and con-nected to the Catholic Church. Their job security was dependent on the Catholic vote. Two homes that housed almost eighty Catholic nuns were located in the ward; they represented the base of voter power in the regular Democratic club. For years, membership and active partici-pation in the affairs of St. Mark's Catholic Church were necessities for election to any post in the ward.

Tozer's decision to support a black, Sterling Cooper, for alder-man increased the odds of defeating the incumbent. He needed total support in the white area of the ward and a portion of the black vote in order to win. But when a very popular black attorney, James Bell, filed to run, the pendulum swung back in favor of the white incumbent. Four blacks—in a district only 65 percent black—seeking election against one white incumbent presented a serious problem for each seeking to replace the incumbent. Mathematically, the numbers were just not there for a black to win.

But again, our group was determined that we could get 50.1 per-cent of the vote, and the other candidates could split the remainder. We continued to wage a vigorous campaign. We produced over one hun-dred large canvas signs that were displayed from second-story porches at major intersections in the ward. The canvas for the signs was donated by a variety store in the ward. The wood backing was given by a cam-paign worker who demolished his old garage. Art students provided the lettering work. The weather-resistant paint was the kind used on the nose of airplanes. (We never asked the employees of McDonnell Douglas where they got the red and blue paint.)

Organizing the Unorganized through Home Meetings

The eighteen-month campaign was the most grueling physical exercise I had ever encountered. It was common to work twelve to fourteen hours daily, including weekends. Scores of people donated thousands of man-hours in putting all the pieces together. Many of them worked long hours each day, creating the climate for the victory that followed.

One of the most time-consuming tasks was the home meetings. A conservative estimate of the number of house gatherings during the campaign is about six hundred; that included houses where meetings were held more than once. The purpose of the meetings was twofold: to build support at the block level and to introduce the candidate.

Home meetings became the most crucial element in the campaign. We determined that victory or defeat rested on the success or failure of them. The strategy behind the meetings was elaborate, well planned, and programmed to achieve two purposes: to educate those in attendance on the issues and to develop a network of volunteers for canvassing, telephoning, and election day balloting.

It was decided that the initial home meetings would take place in what we termed "center of influence" houses. The job then became to accurately identify the havens of activity in every block and concentrate on befriending the decision-maker in each. By "activity haven," we meant a place where others in the neighborhood felt comfortable taking their problems to a person in whom they had confidence. Our small cadre of supporters worked hard at searching out those centers of influence before we even attempted the first meeting.

We found that the kind of person who wielded the most influence differed from block to block, and, in some blocks, more than one existed. In one area it was an insurance man or barber. In others it was the man running an illegal gambling establishment or the owner of the confectionery. But all were leaders in their own right and held sway over many others. Our first objective was to personally make contact and convince them that the future of the ward was tied to my election. Sometimes it took three or four trips by three or four different people. But the time and effort were well spent once they were convinced to hold a meeting.

The second objective was then to plan in minute detail what the meeting should accomplish. That required imagination, artistic skills, and creative writing. Brochures outlining a platform and program of action were developed. Handbills with brief, to-the-point messages were produced. Forms for compiling information about those in attendance were prepared. A committee was established to make follow-up phone calls to all who attended the meetings. They were enlisted to do volunteer work in the area and to have similar home meetings. The key to this strategy was that many of those friendly with the center of influence had friends and relatives who lived in other parts of the ward. The meetings had a ripple or domino effect. One generated another, and so forth.

Two workers from our inner circle were assigned to start and finish each meeting. Their responsibility was to see that refreshments— usually coffee, tea, and pastries—were served. They also opened the sessions by following a script placed on huge placards sitting on an easel. The first card displayed a picture of the candidate and his family. They talked about this family man, his education, and his background in community affairs. The second outlined the problems of the ward and the need for strong, black leadership. The third spoke to the platform and program for action. The remaining cards addressed the need for change and the ways each individual could get involved in a meaningful way.

These meetings were well attended. Often as many as forty or fifty people gathered. Each night two or three meetings took place in different parts of the ward. I attended each of them. When I arrived, because of the tight time schedule, the meeting was temporarily interrupted, and I was introduced. I made brief remarks, opened the session for questions, thanked those in attendance, and apologized for having to leave for another meeting. The meeting was then continued. We found that my appearance, after having already been discussed, created the impression that everybody now knew me personally.

After six or seven months of this educational program, the campaign took on a sort of crusade atmosphere. Our thought-provoking sessions began to pay dividends. People who had been connected with and felt obligated to the old Tozer political machine because of some trivial favor started to question their reason for remaining loyal. Fixing a traffic ticket, getting an alley cleaned, and paving a hole in the street suddenly appeared insignificant compared to what my election victory promised black citizens: new hope, more respect, due process, and equal opportunity in jobs, housing, and education. We succeeded in smoking out and crippling the most effective weapon of any entrenched political machine: its relevancy. Open discussions evaluating the machine's performance and contributions exposed its blatant failures and injustices, virtually guaranteeing its defeat at the polls.

Meeting with the Undisputed Black Political Leader

Near the end of the campaign, my troops were exhausted, but I could see victory in the making. Oliver Thornton, a friend of my wife, was one of Jordan Chambers's close allies, and he suggested that I meet with Chambers. He arranged a meeting between us that took place at 1 a.m. at Club Riviera. Chambers was an imposing figure with an impeccable reputation for frankness. He not only enjoyed the role he played, but he savored every minute of it. He was important, sincere, and bigger than life. However short in stature, he towered head and shoulders above most men and, certainly, above anyone I had encountered in my brief career. He was a black man oozing self-confidence and beaming in self-respect. It was an exhilarating experience for a young upstart like me just to be in his presence.

The conversation, however, was not to my liking. Chambers opened by chastising me for being a disruptive force in North St. Louis politics. He detested the activities of the sit-ins, picket lines, and boycotts in which I had been involved. He admonished me for destabilizing political race relationships that he had so carefully nurtured for the past twenty-five years. He accused me of pitting black against white and young against old. He rained on the parade of a young aspiring politician, yet he expressed a great deal of respect for the poise, grit, and mission of the "young turks."

I was flabbergasted but still filled with awe in the presence of this incomparable individual. The bottom line, as I saw it, was not to lose my cool. Advice, assistance, or at least neutrality on the part of the old master was needed if I were to win the election. There was a rumor that Chambers and Weathers were planning to send their patronage

Clay addressing a group celebrating the opening of a park named for Jordan W. Chambers.

workers to work for Tozer. I knew that Chambers could field an army of precinct workers to work against my candidacy. I also knew he had reason to do exactly that because Tozer had fifteen of Chambers's supporters on his payroll.

The news media highlighted for months Chambers's basic disagreements with the civil rights movement. It was no secret that he disapproved of aggressive confrontation with the power structure; neither did he cater to picket lines and sit-ins. It had nothing to do with his lack of militancy. He was fearful that such direct challenges would be detrimental to plans to increase the political power base of Negroes. He also had a deep-rooted resentment toward old-line civil rights leaders who had endeared themselves to certain repressive forces in the business community. We shared that perception. The NAACP was loaded with middle-class blacks who openly opposed Chambers in most elections, and he viewed them as "dangling dolls" on the strings of white puppeteers. In his opinion, I did not fall into that category. He viewed me as restless, impatient, and, most of all, dangerously uncontrollable.

The encounter was vintage Jordan Chambers. He opened the session by displaying that he was master of the situation and commander in chief of a vast army awaiting his signal to help or to frustrate any other designs for election. His initial remark was, "Little n——, who do you think you are? Why in hell do you believe I will help you to defeat a man whose plate I eat from?" Then he poured himself an eight-ounce water glass of 100-proof bourbon and continued to berate both Thornton and me. He chastised Thornton for bringing such a character to his club. At this very moment, both Thornton and I knew that Chambers liked something about the little nincompoop who was rising, phoenixlike, from the ashes of poverty to an exalted position worthy of his berating.

The rest of the conversation was a matter of protocol. I paid the proper respect to the most dynamic personality I had ever met by praising his unmatched record of accomplishments. Carefully, I discussed the importance of taking charge of Twenty-sixth Ward politics, elaborating on the theory that advancement of the people should dictate the course of action. Chambers understood that victory in the ward would signal the downfall of several other white kingpins in North St. Louis who constantly worked to neutralize his influence. Ultimately, he knew my win would mean that never again would he have to go hat in hand, begging for legitimate concessions from white politicians. It meant he could deal with one of his own who respected him and recognized his political genius.

My request was simple and straightforward. I wanted a commitment from him to stay out of the Twenty-sixth Ward. I knew better than to ask for his outright endorsement. My only desire was to place the old pro in a position of impartiality. I also wanted assurance that he would persuade other blacks obligated to him not to support the incumbent. Finally, I boldly asked him for financial support.

That was a mistake that paid handsome dividends. He looked at me for almost a minute. Then he looked in the direction of Thornton and asked, "Where did you find this fool?" Thornton smiled. I smiled. Jordan grunted. Much to everyone's surprise, he stated, "I will not give you any money, but I will keep the wolves from your door. I will speak to a few of your key workers if you can arrange a private and secret meeting." He concluded by saying that anybody with guts should be inside the political system, not outside criticizing it.

The meeting went better than expected. He agreed to provide assistance to me through his friend and future state representative Joseph Ames. Ames, a white labor leader, funneled money for canvassers, signs, and election day workers into the campaign. In addition, he supplied a cadre of union members for telephoning and getting out the vote. Chambers himself arranged a secret meeting with my most trusted supporters. It was held at midnight in the basement of my home.

It was long after Chambers's death that I learned the truth about my first meeting with him. Once again he had outsmarted a young whippersnapper. A trusted friend of mine recalled in detail how Chambers had suggested to Thornton that a meeting would be advantageous. The old fox had read the mood of the community and was taking no unnecessary chances of allowing a new political force to develop without his support. I bit hook, line, and sinker in accepting Thornton's invitation.

I remember Chambers with awe and respect.

Victory: How Sweet It Is!

Finally, the long campaign reached its closing days. After a year and half of backbreaking, bruising campaigning, an act of God almost caused my defeat. For several weeks our supporters had joked about Tozer's people counting the ballots and that it would take an act of God for me to win. Ten days before the election, there *was* an act of God, and we were convinced it was intended to help my opponent.

A tornado ripped across St. Louis, killing several people in its wake. Homes in the ward were destroyed, and families were forced to move out of the area. Many of our main supporters were scattered throughout the city—thank God they returned on election day and cast their votes. Early in the morning after the tornado struck, Alderman Wayman Smith II called and invited me to tour his ravished, torn ward. We rode for several hours, assessing damage and offering assistance.

Despite the tornado, the weekend before the election our organization was clicking on all fronts. Our well-oiled machine was purring like a kitten; we felt confident of victory. Hundreds of volunteers prepared for election day. Calling and re-calling voters who had attended our home meetings dominated the agenda. Plans for getting out the vote were meticulously laid and included assigning workers to shifts and designating areas of responsibility.

As Jackie Gleason used to say, "How sweet it is!" On March 10, 1959, the long election campaign finally came to an end. The polls closed at 7 p.m., and the few paid workers, joined by hundreds of volunteers, gathered at our headquarters. Several hours passed in what seemed like an eternity, waiting, hoping, and praying, but there was still no knowledge of the winner available. My group had campaigned for eighteen months, two weeks, three days, and fourteen hours. All past preparations, strategies, efforts, and even designs for the future had now boiled down to results that would be announced shortly.

Tozer held most of the aces in this loaded deck. Under Missouri law, the Republican and Democratic committeepeople hired the polling judges, clerks, and watchers. In North St. Louis, where the Republican Party was inoperative, the Democrats also hired the Republican polling officials. Stealing elections in 1959 was a common practice. The federal government seldom, if ever, got involved, especially in local races, and local prosecutors were all elected Democrats. Those pseudo-Republicans inside the polls, supposedly there to assure honest counts of the ballots, were like the proverbial monkey who saw no evil, spoke no evil, and heard no evil. The longer it took for the count, the more suspicious our workers became that ballot tampering was taking place inside the polls.

However, there was nothing that could be done about it except to wait and speculate. We were all gathered in the headquarters listening to the radio for any partial report on the returns. But nothing came. It was now nine o'clock, and most of the winners from other wards had been declared.

Finally, the door to the headquarters opened. The incumbent of twelve years, Bill Brady, slowly walked down the aisle. Before he reached the front of the room where I was sitting, it dawned on our horde of workers that his mission was to congratulate me. There was pandemonium. Brady was lifted to the shoulders of several of my jubilant workers and paraded through the crowd. Some shouted, while others cried. The celebration was so wild that, when sheets listing registered voters were pulled from the walls, the wallpaper came with them.

Other black leaders started to enter the room shortly thereafter. I remember State Representative James Troupe and former representative Walter Lay being the first to arrive. Then there was Hubert Brown, former president of the NAACP, Alderman Wayman Smith II, and others. I was elated to see such celebrities.

The final results showed that the black vote was not sufficiently split to deny my election. Bell received 452; Cooper, 519; Pointer, 113; and Brady, 1,064. I was the winner, with 1,530 votes. Paper ballots and adept vote counters inside the polls meant they probably voided one thousand of my votes. We later found out what had delayed the tallying of votes. Dease had succeeded in infiltrating the Tozer forces. In many of the precincts, arguments developed between white and black poll workers about efforts to destroy ballots for me. It was reported that in some places police officers had to break up skirmishes.

The festivities at my headquarters lasted until about 4 a.m. It was only a Democratic primary victory, but, in St. Louis, that's tantamount to election. The general election to be held one month later was only a formality. I was befuddled and bewildered. I knew I had won, but, like Robert Redford in the movie *The Candidate*, I had no idea of what it was that I had won: "only time [would] tell."

A Fraudulent Election

For thirty years the black community had engaged in a continuous effort to place a person on the school board without success. John W. Hayes in 1929 and Julia Child Curtis in 1931 attempted to become the first Negro elected to the Board of Education. Both lost by large margins. Others who followed in their footsteps over the next thirty-five years but lost included Zenobia Shoulders Johnson, Charles Gates, Robert Witherspoon, Sidney Redmond, Dr. Edward Grant, Father Joseph Nicholson, and Dr. Walter Younge.

In 1939 Attorney Witherspoon received 23,751 votes; in 1945 Attorney Redmond received 31,898 votes; in 1951 Dr. Grant received 33,340 votes; and, in 1952, Father Nicholson received 53,898 votes. At the same time, victorious white candidates were garnering in excess of 70,000 votes each.

Grant was the first Negro to serve on the school board, when he was appointed in 1950. He was defeated in 1951. In 1955 and again in 1957, Dr. Walter Younge ran fifth to the winners in elections where four candidates were elected. He polled 53,683 and 48,005 votes, respectively. Younge served from 1956 to 1957, appointed by Mayor Joseph Darst. Grant and Younge were both appointed by mayors to fill unexpired terms, and both were defeated in their bids to remain on the school board.

But in the April 7, 1959, general election, one month after my primary victory, another attempt was made. In those days the public education system provided a vast array of patronage jobs for Democratic politicians. Certified employees (teachers, principals, and counselors) were free from political interference. Non-certified employees (custodians, cafeteria workers, maintenance men, electricians, carpenters, pipe-fitters, and truck drivers) were dues-paying members of political organizations who got jobs by recommendations from committeemen. Ward leaders cherished the hundreds of patronage jobs and worked hard to elect their friends to the school board.

Democratic leaders formed their usual coalition to back a slate of candidates to fill the four school board positions up for election in 1959. The presence of a black minister of the African Methodist Church, Reverend John J. Hicks, added tension and doubt to traditional slate-makers. Usually, white candidates received overwhelming support in the black community if endorsed by black leaders.

The results in prior elections were unusually close, as black candidates ran fifth in races to fill only four positions. In every election since 1929, Negroes had made serious efforts to win election to the school board, but the same pattern had emerged. The entire black political strength was pledged to support three white candidates. In return, white politicians supporting the same three whites endorsed the one black. By far, they got the better end of the deal.

What happened in each election was the same: Whites always got the most votes to fill the four slots, and the black candidate always ran fifth because his support in white wards was superficial and minimal. While the three whites were receiving overwhelming numbers of votes in our community, the black candidate was getting only token support in the white wards.

Hicks, however, presented a difficult problem for those whites who really did not want a black on the board. He was the thirteenth black to seek the school board in thirty years of effort. He was supported by a phalanx of supporters, which included the AFL-CIO Committee on Political Education (COPE), the *Post-Dispatch*, the twelve Negro ward leaders, numerous community and religious groups, and the independent "good government" that endorsed three other non-politically associated white persons. In addition, the regular politicians of the Democratic machine representing the twenty-eight ward organizations had their slate of four candidates, which also included Hicks.

But it was obvious, at least to me, that this paper support in the past had been insufficient to produce victory. I advocated defeat with honor. In my opinion, if we were to lose, it should not be the result of our continued stupidity. My position was that if and when white politicians needing our votes responded to our candidates in kind with equal numbers of votes, then and only then should we endorse their favorites. Hicks's candidacy presented for us the first real opportunity to openly attack the insidious practices engaged in by a coalition of whites and blacks. Others in the community were fearful that publicly encouraging blacks to vote only for the black candidate would produce counterreactions in the white communities. I contended that those racist conditions already existed. My advice was to cast "bullet" votes—only for the black candidate. My efforts were not confined to the Twenty-sixth Ward but expanded and were accepted throughout the entire community.

Calloway served as campaign manager and did a yeoman's job in organizing the black community for a massive turnout of voters on election day. Hicks was victorious. He ran second in an eleven-man race for four vacancies. His total of 46,608 votes was surpassed only by Daniel L. Schlafly's 50,939 votes. Hicks ran 4,280 votes ahead of the third place finisher, 11,786 ahead of fourth place, and 11,756 ahead of the fifth place entrant. In the six black wards, he ran between 16,369 and 11,686 votes ahead of the three whites in the coalition.

In six of the white wards endorsing him as part of the package, Hicks averaged 9,000 fewer votes than the three whites without them publicly advocating bullet voting. That was par for the course and the primary reason blacks had never been elected to the school board. I think I played an important part in redefining the rules that enabled us to accomplish a goal first expressed forty years prior at the Pythian meeting in 1918.

The election, however, was not without casualties. Georgia Buckowitz, one of the white coalition candidates allied with the ward leaders, ran fourth. She defeated Robert Rainey, the fifth place runner-up, by twenty-eight votes. Rainey, a white doctor with a large practice catering to the wealthy, was a staunch Republican with fairly liberal views.

Mrs. Buckowitz was the wife of Louis Buckowitz, the Democratic committeeman of the Tenth Ward delivery organization. He was also one of the most outspoken advocates of strict racial segregation who made no bones about his feelings about white superiority and missed no opportunity to publicly characterize blacks as unfit for public office. His reputation for race-baiting and his scurrilous attacks on minorities were well documented.

In the Ninth Precinct of the Twenty-sixth Ward, Georgia Buckowitz received 83 votes to Rev. Hicks's 122. She received fewer than 35 votes in each of the other precincts. That fact prompted my supporters to secure 130 notarized statements from the electorate in the Ninth Precinct, swearing they had voted only for Hicks as the organization had recommended. This number was sufficient when subtracting from the total cast in order for Mrs. Buckowitz to prove she could not have received 83 votes in the precinct. The affidavits were delivered to Rainey, who lost by only 28 votes. He filed a lawsuit contesting the outcome.

The court ordered the ballot box opened and the votes recounted. Buckowitz, instead of receiving 83 votes, was credited with only 12 votes. Rainey was declared the winner by 53 votes and seated on the Board of Education. The attempted vote theft in the Twenty-sixth Ward was not an isolated case. Investigations by the Board of Elections found major irregularities in fifteen precincts throughout the city and asked ninety election clerks and judges to resign their commissions.

Republican Harold I. Elbert Supported by Democrats

During the 1959 general election, the white Democratic candidate in the Twenty-eighth Ward, Charlie Hunt, declared that if he were elected he would oppose the public accommodations bill and fight "to preserve property values in the ward." This proved to be his Waterloo. The "neighborhood preservation" utterance was a code word for opposing Negroes who were moving into the ward. Although a Republican had represented the ward for years, the white population was evenly divided between Republicans and Democrats. Blacks recently moving into the area constituted about 15 percent of the ward, and their lopsided Democratic Party vote shifted the odds for Democrats being elected.

The Republican challenger, Attorney Harold I. Elbert, was running for the first time. He was a graduate of the University of Oklahoma College of Law and held a master of laws degree and a doctorate of law from the University of Michigan. He taught part-time at Saint Louis University. Elbert publicly campaigned in favor of opening all public accommodations to all people. The Congress of Racial Equality (CORE) endorsed him. Since I had very little opposition in the general election, my entire organization was able to campaign on Elbert's behalf. We were effective in campaigning and successful in convincing a sufficient number of blacks to switch parties and vote Republican for Elbert, who won by a slim margin. His vote for public accommodations was secure and provided a hope of victory for enactment of the law.

CHAPTER

4

HECTIC DAYS FOLLOWING THE 1959 ELECTION

T he days immediately following the 1959 election were not all "peaches and cream" or "boxes of Cracker Jacks," as former Cleveland mayor Carl Stokes once described politics. The laughs, tears, and jubilation of victory-night euphoria quickly vanished as daily political life recaptured its previous state of reality. Many supporters expected overnight change in their intolerable living conditions and their lack of job opportunities. Precinct workers expected instant employment at city hall or with state agencies, but aldermen did not possess the power to appoint political jobs. That function was the prerogative of the ward committeepeople. My burden, therefore, was twofold: to keep the political organization intact until the 1960 and 1962 elections were held for committee posts, constable, magistrate, and state representatives, and to cause a fundamental change in the way constituents evaluated their elected officials.

Ward Activities

Keeping the campaign organization intact was relatively easy. It meant establishing programs of interest and importance to the precinct workers. The ward club accomplished that goal by continuing registration drives and assisting residents in resolving problems with the government. It also became an outpost for various activities, with emphasis on the community and civil rights.

The ward organization set up a typing class at the ward headquarters; a public-school typing teacher taught the classes twice a week to sixteen students. The course lasted ten weeks, and the ward furnished typewriters, paper, and other supplies. There were weekly parties at the headquarters, annual picnics, and Christmas dances to keep the members in touch with one another. A small college scholarship program was set up for children of active precinct workers. Joining with CORE, the club was able to collect tons of clothing and food for Negroes in Fayette County, Tennessee, who were victims of a devastating economic boycott conducted by whites because Negroes sought to register and vote. Tuesday night was the ward meeting. Hundreds attended and were treated to the most current analysis of city politics. Thursday night the headquarters were open for use by community groups, free of charge. On weekends the ward held fund-raising activities.

Norman R. Seay, chairman of the ward club, continued his activities as president of the Federation of Urban League Block Units. He also headed up an investigation of the state penitentiary at Jefferson City, issuing a blistering attack on the policy of neglecting Negro inmates. He charged that quarters for Negroes were unheated, old, and dilapidated. Seay was appointed by the NAACP as chairman of a special committee on police affairs to act as a liaison with the Metropolitan Board of Police Commissioners. He doggedly campaigned for more Negro officers and the creation of an aggressive policy of upgrading and promoting blacks on the force. Seay charged that there were fifty Negroes on the force with some college education, and ten of them held degrees. Only one was above the rank of patrolman. Of the eighteen hundred white officers, seven had college degrees and six held ranks of sergeant or better.

The necessity of re-educating constituents about the proper relationship between the elected and the electors was of paramount importance in preserving the vitality of the organization. Altering the misconception of what constituted effective political leadership was more difficult and more sensitive. Fixing parking tickets, getting people out of jail, providing baskets of food at Christmas, and protecting illegal activities had to be replaced by a system that offered more substance and less vaudeville. It was my belief that government largesse and basic subsistence should be entitlements of citizenship and not favors doled out by committeemen, aldermen, and other elected officials.

To offset the emphasis placed on these misguided values, I embarked on an issue-oriented course of action as the criteria for justifying the right to hold public office. I had to maintain high visibility as a

1960 rally to re-elect Senator Edward Long. From left: Clay, Magistrate Frank Bledsoe, state senate candidate T. D. McNeal, 26th Ward committeeman candidate Norman Seay, Representative Hugh White, and Committeeman Leroy Tyus.

legislator in the Board of Aldermen. Without maximum exposure, properly publicized, we would never succeed in wresting control of the ward committee posts and the jobs accompanying them from the old regime.

On the first day of my first session, I introduced a resolution proposing the establishment of a committee to investigate discrimination against black workers on a city-financed, privately owned construction project. Attorneys Margaret Bush Wilson, Charles Oldham, and I developed a strategy for pursuing the issue. The resolution called for an investigation of "patterns and practices" of discrimination in hiring at the Plaza apartment buildings. The resolution read in part: "It appears that . . . numerous workmen have been hired on said Plaza project, but to date not a single skilled worker from the Negro community in the city of St. Louis or the state of Missouri has been hired or employed on said project, and only two skilled workers who are Negroes now have such jobs, both of whom are nonresidents."

There were no federal, state, or city laws prohibiting discrimination in employment against minorities. Historically, skilled Negro mechanics had been barred from joining labor unions and denied employment by construction contractors, both union and nonunion. The resolution challenged a contract that the city had awarded to the Fruin-Colnon Construction Company. The project covered four square blocks in close proximity to the city hall complex. The construction site for the six thirteen-story buildings containing 1,090 luxury apartments was taken by the city under the power of "eminent domain" and transferred to the developer, granting favorable treatment through abatement of taxes for twenty-five years. A bond issue of $1.5 million was passed to cover one third of the cost of clearing the blighted area. The federal government paid the other two thirds.

The twenty-five Democratic aldermen hurriedly called a caucus to discuss my resolution. The four Republican members were excluded. The discussion, however, did not center around the merits or demerits of the proposal but around whether the body had the legal authority to obstruct a project already in progress. The parliamentarian expressed doubt and refused to rule. David Grant, a black lawyer and legislative director of the board, expressed no such apprehension. He cited the verse and chapter of law supporting the proposal. Alphonse J. Cervantes, who, with my support, had been elected president of the board two weeks prior in the same election as myself, supported the resolution.

The measure was referred to the resolutions committee, where other black members succeeded in broadening its scope to include all projects receiving tax money. The next week it was reported back to the full body and passed by a vote of seventeen to six. The resolution provided the power of subpoena and the ability to arrest anyone not responding to it. This provision gave the committee its best potential for exposing the racial practices of labor unions and construction companies.

Cervantes, in a courageous decision, appointed me chairman of the committee. Veteran members of the board criticized him, contending that a senior member should have been named chairman. He countered that similar affronts to black citizens had existed in the past, and none with seniority had shown any interest. Also named to the committee were Elbert (R-28th Ward), Mayberry (D-4th Ward), Joseph Noel (D-27th Ward), and Joseph P. Roddy (D-17th Ward).

The president of the electricians' union, H. Lee Bruns, also an elected member of the Board of Education, appeared before the committee, angrily protesting his subpoena. He alleged that it was pushed under the door of his office and discovered there the next morning. I graciously acknowledged his indignation for the record and expressed my sincere gratitude to him for not compelling the committee to force his appearance.

Mayberry, inquiring about the absence of Negroes in the apprenticeship program conducted jointly between his union and the public school system, asked Bruns, "If the nine hundred people enrolled as apprentices all had blonde hair and Scandinavian names, wouldn't you concede there had been some sort of selective process?" Bruns angrily snapped, "No, I would not!"

The committee held three public hearings, receiving testimony from eighteen witnesses during the summer months. Portions of the hearings were televised. It was documented that three labor unions had 16,000 members but only 26 Negroes. The committee also established that only 2 Negroes were working on the site, discovered evidence of discrimination in construction unions, and learned that no blacks were enrolled among the 1,735 apprenticeship students in various programs underwritten by federal, state and, city money.

While the proceedings were taking place, I announced my intention to introduce a bill to cancel the contract between the city and the developer. It was not known if ample votes existed for passage, but it stirred much controversy. The mayor, the contractor, and labor leaders did not know either and did not want to chance a vote. Before the conclusion of the investigation, blacks had been hired at the project as bricklayers, carpenters, electricians, plumbers, and cement masons. For the first time, the cycle of discrimination against skilled black mechanics in hiring on public projects was broken.

Public Accommodations Bill

The next major legislative battle was that of enacting a public accommodations law. For many years, the four black members on the board had waged a strenuous fight to open all public facilities on a nondiscriminatory basis. Restaurants, cocktail lounges, hotels, recreational parks, movie houses, barbershops, and beauty parlors denied accommodation to Negroes. Civil rights groups had conducted a protracted campaign to end these practices. CORE, in addition to sit-ins and picket lines, had turned its attention to active partisan ward politics in order to defeat aldermen who voted against the measure.

The legislation had been losing by a small margin as some white aldermen switched their votes back and forth. In 1953 it died in committee. In 1954 it received token support; in 1955 it again died in committee. In 1956 it was defeated on the floor by a vote of 16–10. In 1957 and 1958, it was defeated by votes of 14–12 and 15–13, respectively.

The 1959 election provided what we anticipated would be a sufficient margin for passage if white aldermen elected from wards with substantial black voters continued their support of it. In the Twentieth Ward, Lawrence "Jaybird" Woodson, a black businessman, was elected the same day as I was. He defeated Alderman Edgar J. Feely, the most senior member of the board—a twenty-year veteran. Black leaders accused Feely of being in the hospital every time a civil rights bill was voted on. The hope of speedy passage was dashed when several white aldermen again changed their votes to no. That was the history of this piece of legislation.

On Sunday, August 9, 1960, at a regular weekly meeting of CORE, the group voted to renew negotiations with the Howard Johnson restaurant, insisting that it change its policy of refusing service to Negroes. Three members of the committee—Raymond Howard, a law student at Saint Louis University; Robert Schwerdtman, a legal reporter; and I, a member of the Board of Aldermen—were selected to test the restaurant policy before requesting a meeting. We entered the premises and asked to be served. When the waitress refused and the manager affirmed that the policy had not changed, we continued to sit. A uniformed police officer eating at a counter was summoned and ordered us to leave the premises. Refusing to obey his illegal order, the three of us were arrested on charges of disturbing the peace. Despite the fact that there were no loud voices and no pushing or shoving at any time, the arrest took place.

Robert Schwerdtman, Alderman Bill Clay, Herman Thompson, and Raymond Howard just before the trial of those arrested for seeking service at a Howard Johnson restaurant.

The arrests sparked demonstrations at the restaurant. Under the supervision of Norman Seay, CORE picketers marched day and night, seven days a week, for more than six months. Students from Vashon and Sumner High Schools participated in the demonstrations and were arrested for sitting in at the restaurant. Two seniors from Vashon High School, Arthur Shaw and Cecil Wright, who had organized students and demonstrated at a number of restaurants, joined the pickets at Howard Johnson.

Three black members of the Board of Aldermen—Mayberry, Woodson, and I—wrote to Governor James T. Blair, informing him that more than fifty young students had been arrested while peacefully sitting in the restaurant awaiting service and that the "action of the police in these circumstances protect[ed] the private acts of discrimination practiced by licensed owners of such restaurants."

In 1961, after nine years of struggle, the Public Accommodations Bill finally became law by a vote of 20–4. Three white Democrats with large black constituencies continued to play the game of hide-and-seek. Barney Mueller of the Twenty-first Ward was present but did not vote. James Noonan of the Third Ward and Raymond Leisure of the Seventh Ward left the chamber just prior to the tally. Each represented wards with approximately 40 percent black voters. James Geiger of the Tenth Ward and Albert "Red" Villa of the Eleventh Ward voted in favor of the legislation. They represented two deep–South Side wards with more than 95 percent white voters. Two of the three Republicans on the board (Fred Haag and Elbert) voted for the bill. George Grellner, the other Republican, was absent. Elbert spoke eloquently in favor of passage.

The vote was not close because the 1961 elections saw several aldermen who opposed the measure defeated by its supporters. A vociferous opponent of the bill, Republican Joseph P. McDonald of the Twenty-fifth Ward, was replaced by a Democrat who voted to pass it. McDonald had been the most obnoxious foe of public accommodations. In the 1960 debate, he declared:

> I have full sympathy with the Negro who suffers embarrassment of being
> deprived of certain accommodations, and I certainly do not take the part of

proprietors who deny him these privileges. But there is a difference between right and privilege. A right is something you have. A privilege is something you merit. The Negro probably has been held back by the white man. The Negro should improve himself and advance his economic advantages and then both he and his dollars will be sought.

The restaurant association that had opposed the bill for years reversed its stand and convinced several aldermen to change their vote.

Fair Employment Bill

Alderman Elbert was a person of impressive credentials and impeccable integrity. He had the ability to speedily read volumes of print and remember not only what was written but also the pages on which it appeared. Continuing to educate a black community about the benefits of aggressive, affirmative leadership, Oldham and I approached Elbert

Mayor Raymond Tucker signs the Equal Employment Opportunities bill in 1960. From left: Clay, Tucker, Harold Elbert, and the Human Rights Commission chairman.

about drafting legislation for a fair employment ordinance. He readily agreed. In a matter of days, he put together the basic framework of the bill with references to many legal arguments and court cases pertaining to the subject. His insight into the issue and his depth of knowledge about the subject were superb. We gave the proposal to David Grant for review, who made minor changes and approved it. Elbert and I thus cosponsored the Equal Employment Opportunities bill. It was one of the most comprehensive bills of its kind. After lengthy debate but no major changes, the bill was enacted.

Purging Arrest Records

My legislative prowess was reaping huge dividends, but controversy still followed my career. Another bill that I introduced would prohibit the police department from releasing records of persons arrested but not convicted. The preface of the bill questioned the "reasonableness and advisability" of disclosing to anyone other than investigative police officers and prosecuting authorities the arrest records "upon which no convictions were obtained." Publicly releasing this information had a devastating impact on the ability of Negroes to attain employment. Employers who wished to evade the equal employment law often cited the fraudulent arrest record.

Charging individuals as suspects was a common scheme in black neighborhoods. The arrest records carried such notations as suspicion of robbery, suspicion of assault to kill, suspicion of gambling, and suspicion of selling alcohol without a license. Seventy percent of those apprehended under this legal but questionable procedure were released within a matter of hours because no reasonable cause existed for the arrest. But once the arrest was entered on the police blotter, it remained there permanently.

The incident that brought the matter to the forefront was the alleged rape of a white woman who described in graphic detail how three Negro males, in a convertible automobile with leopard-skin seat covers, had kidnapped and raped her repeatedly over a two-day period. Racial tensions were at a dangerously high level.

Exacerbating the situation was the inflammatory coverage of the *St. Louis Globe-Democrat*. For years, the newspaper and its publishers were the primary architects in developing a wall of resistance to racial progress for Negroes. Their shortsighted policies of support for reactionary, anti-black causes gave encouragement to every bigot in the paper's reader area. Their sensational news coverage and inflammatory editorials may have sold newspapers, but it lost them respect in the circles of fair-minded people. On important issues, it was impossible for the newspaper to influence or shape opinion in the black community. Many blacks viewed the newspaper as a race-baiting, race-hating scandal sheet.

In this instance, the newspaper racially exploited the incident to its fullest. For five consecutive days, it published front-page stories arousing the worst emotions in people. Editorializing on the sanctity of white womanhood and the need to punish the Negroes responsible for the reprehensible crime, it wrote one editorial titled "As Bad as the Congo!" To fully understand the demonic significance of this characterization, it is necessary to note that St. Louis is a predominately Catholic city, and at the time, the Congolese people were engaged in a war to overthrow white colonial rule. They were vigorously murdering whites, including Catholic priests and nuns. The *Globe-Democrat* editorial stated:

> Last Sunday at three o'clock in the afternoon, a young woman was standing on the corner of Broadway and Lafayette, waiting for a bus. Three men, reeking of alcohol, grabbed her, threw her into an auto and drove to a cornfield, possibly in Illinois, where she was raped time after time.

> She was held captive all day and assaulted again that night. On Sunday she was driven to an empty garage, apparently in St. Louis, and attacked again. Revolting as this story is, we think it needs telling and emphasized.

> After holding the girl captive for more than twenty-four hours, her attackers discarded her near Carondelet Park. She is in serious condition in City Hospital. The attackers, she said, are Negroes. She is white.

> This bold and brutal crime is as bad as any committed during the recent riot-
> ing in the Congo. St. Louisans should be especially alarmed since the girl was
> grabbed up in broad daylight off a busy city street corner.
>
> If the culprits are caught, the facts corroborated, this savage crime should be pun-
> ished by the maximum penalty Missouri statute sets for forcible rape. The men
> should be put to death in the gas chamber.[7]

The editorial and news coverage had the city teetering on the verge of a riot. In its haste to spread hysteria and racial hatred, the newspaper hit all of the high points for arousing a lynch mob. Nowhere in the editorial were the words "allegedly" or "supposedly" used. It was starkly implied that a virtuous white lady had been assaulted and ravished numerous times by brutal Negroes. It was meticulously pointed out that she was taken across the state line to Illinois and then transported back to Missouri, which also made it a federal crime. The accused were compared with savages in Africa, and the struggle for freedom in the Congo was described as "rioting." Without confirmation of medical professionals, the article stated that she was raped repeatedly and was hospitalized in serious condition. Finally, the death penalty was the only punishment the editors determined to be fit for the degenerates.

More than 300 blacks were taken into custody—104 booked and suspected of rape. The majority had no prior record of entanglement with the law. Many were stopped while on their way to work, taken to jail, interrogated, and released without arrest or notation of detention. Others were arrested at shopping centers in downtown St. Louis. A few black professionals and businessmen were apprehended. Once the notation of "arrested on suspicion of rape" was put on the record, it stayed forever.

After several weeks, the *Post-Dispatch* decided that the story merited further investigation. As a result of the paper's diligent inquiry, the truth was uncovered. A lovely, young married white lady—the personification of womanhood—had willingly spent the weekend with a white sailor on leave from his ship in Baltimore, Maryland. Afraid of personal consequences, she fabricated the sordid story that caused others such personal suffering. But what about the arrests of 104 black men accused of rape? Too bad, said city fathers—the law was the law, and its application was applied equally to whites and blacks.

The *Globe-Democrat* refused to admit that its reporting was excessive and sensational or even that the hoax was a miscarriage of justice. The newspaper proceeded to defend its original position and to demand that the police clear the city of the likes of those who could have "grabbed" a woman off a street corner "in broad daylight."

I intended to expunge all records where arrests did not result in convictions. The purpose was to protect innocent citizens from damage, loss of reputation, and loss of employment. At the press conference after my introduction, I stated, "Too often in the past, citizens have been denied jobs and opportunity for employment because of arrests when no conviction has been obtained and the person released with no formal charges brought." It was a common practice for prospective employers to procure transcripts of arrest records. The equal employment ordinance, however, declared that such action violated the right of a person to "fair and equal opportunities for consideration for gainful employment."

Initially, white members of the board and the media considered the bill as a means of giving special relief to blacks involved in criminal activities. The aldermen were predisposed to vote to defeat the measure and publicly stated their intention. But on the "road to Damascus," there was a strange conversion. Lightning must have struck some aldermen when their white constituents, who had suffered the same injustices, lobbied them to support the legislation. Whites in low-income neighborhoods who had also been denied employment opportunities based on capricious and arbitrary arrest records pressured their representatives to support the bill. David Grant said, "It's a practice that injures many innocent people of both races—particularly Negroes, who are on the fringe of employment potential and are easily knocked off for any frivolous reason."[8]

The biggest problem facing me was keeping white aldermen from taking charge of the debate. They spoke for the measure in such laudatory terms that it was difficult to determine who had sponsored the bill. The vote was 27–0 on final passage.

Mayor Tucker vetoed the bill. Override of the veto was as overwhelming as the vote for passage. However, it did not become law immediately because Associate City Counselor Eugene P. Freeman, an appointee of the mayor, ruled that the Board of Aldermen did not have legal authority to legislate against the police department (a state agency). Several years later, police officials admitted to the unfairness of the procedure, and the state legislature rectified the injustice by enacting a bill to expunge the records of all arrests not resulting in subsequent prosecution and conviction.

The Absentee Aldermen

My bold legislative initiatives were put on hold by my decision to abide by custom instead of by respect for law. When I was elected to the board in 1959, very few aldermen lived in the wards they were elected to represent. Despite a city charter provision that mandated expulsion for not residing in the ward of election, a fourth of the members ignored the law. I was no exception. I resided in the ward when elected, but that was only a convenience that enabled me to contribute money to my poorly underfinanced campaign.

After filing for office, I leased my house in the Twentieth Ward, moved into my mother's home in the Twenty-sixth Ward, and used the monthly lease payments to cover campaign expenditures. Shortly after election, my family and I moved back into the home we owned. Three aldermen were now residing in the Twentieth Ward: Smith of the Eighteenth Ward, Woodson of the Twentieth Ward, and myself. But the Twenty-sixth Ward, without my presence, was still well represented because DeWitte Lawson of the Nineteenth Ward and Archie Blaine of the Sixth Ward resided there. Mayberry and Woodson were the only black aldermen who lived in the wards that had elected them.

Five white members of the board, to my knowledge, did not live in their wards. These aldermen were John T. Curry of the Fifth Ward,

Thomas J. Finan of the Sixteenth Ward, Alfred Harris of the Twenty-second Ward, Barney Mueller of the Twenty-first Ward, and Raymond Leisure of the Seventh Ward.

In 1960, a front-page *Globe-Democrat* story revealed that Harris had moved to Ladue, an affluent suburb of the city. The photograph depicting his new home signaled a clear warning to those who did not reside in their wards. Immediately, I realized that voter indignation, media agitation, and legal suits to force compliance with the law would take on a much greater meaning.

Within days, my family and I moved into rented quarters in the Twenty-sixth Ward. In 1965, after a long legal battle, the court ruled that Harris, Smith, and Mueller had forfeited their right to office because they resided outside their wards.

Bill Clay and family in campaign photo for 1963 re-election to the Board of Aldermen.

CHAPTER

5

1960: A YEAR OF DECISIVE POLITICAL RESULTS

FOR NEGROES

The 1960 election for sheriff was a classic demonstration of the hostilities the Irish clan harbored against Committeeman Tozer, the man who had broken their total dominance of citywide offices four years earlier. They were willing to give the position to a non-Irish South Side politician in order to re-establish control. Louis "Midge" Berra, a colorful character of Italian descent, was endorsed by most of the Irish clan allied with the pipefitters' union. But the sheriff controlled over two hundred patronage jobs in his office that many ward organizations possessed. The job factor meant that the Irish ward leaders who usually allied with the union would not unanimously support the union's effort.

There was a split in the ranks. Dwyer endorsed Tozer. Jordan Chambers, who had been very close to union leaders Larry Callanan and John "Doc" Lawler, also supported Tozer. So did Weathers and most other black leaders. I was the lone exception. Initially, I knew Berra could not carry our ward because his alderman had been an outspoken foe of blacks in their efforts to attain public accommodation. So I filed for sheriff, giving our organization a candidate to support. The black community viewed that action with mixed emotions. Chambers and Weathers saw it as an effort to aid the pipefitters and the candidacy of Berra for sheriff. Blacks aligned with Chambers and Weathers said I would take votes away from Tozer and cause Berra to be elected. Those in my camp expressed the opposite opinion, citing Tozer's committee-ship and his racist behavior. Our people were challenging Tozer for ward leader, and it made no sense for us to endorse our opposition. Brady, the former alderman, was persuaded to join forces with the Seay-White camp. He also filed for sheriff to assure that voters had an option.

It is quite possible that had I stayed in the race, Berra would have been elected sheriff. But black wards, with the exception of the twenty-sixth, delivered massive majorities for Tozer, and he won the election by less than two thousand votes. The final count was Tozer with 39,080, Berra with 36,786, and Brady with 8,195.

Battle to Control the Twenty-sixth Ward

Before the start of the 1960 campaign for the committee posts in the Twenty-sixth Ward, Benjamin L. Goins and I met at his request. Goins, an impeccable dresser, entered the Supreme Liberty Life Insurance Company office to discuss "our" future in politics. I was district manager of the weekly insurance company, the largest black-owned business in the North. The company proudly boasted that its assets totaled more than $27 million.

Rumor had it that Goins had agreed to serve as campaign manager for Austin Wright, a candidate for committeeman. Unknown to Wright, however, was the fact that Goins desired the committee position for himself. His purpose for meeting with me was to solicit my support for his endeavor. As he explained, if I gave my endorsement he would convince Wright not to seek the office. He said the two of us could influence the majority of voters in the ward and become a dominant force in politics. After winning the aldermanic seat the previous year, I was determined that our organization would select candidates for the committee posts. My victory would have been hollow had we surrendered the real power to those who had not helped to wrest it from the political machine. The session ended as Goins announced his support for Wright and Ida L. Harris, and I reaffirmed my endorsement of Seay and Anna White. Following that encounter, an intense battle ensued for control of the Twenty-sixth Ward.

Two highly organized black groups challenged Committeeman Tozer. Tozer, as sheriff, controlled more patronage jobs than any other city officeholder. Initially, he had the edge in terms of organization, experience, and manpower. There were approximately eighty-five patronage workers paying dues to his club, another two hundred on his payroll as sheriff, and hundreds more indebted to him because of personal favors. In addition, he appointed all of the Democratic judges, clerks, and watchers at the polling places.

The campaign was long, bitterly fought, and costly. A reasonable estimate of expenditures shows the Tozer forces spending $20,000, the Wright forces $15,000, and the Seay group $12,000, a sizable amount for 1960. The $47,000 spent by the three candidates in today's dollars equates to approximately $150,000. No candidate today would or could afford to spend that much money to win a ward. But the stakes were high. If Tozer won, politics as usual would be the order of the day. The winner of the Wright-Seay rivalry would certainly determine a new force in black politics for the next decade.

Seay and Wright were girded for battle and convinced that Tozer would be a minor factor in the race. Each of the three factions devised a different strategy for reaching the voters. Tozer depended on the old method of politicking. He continued to give out baskets of food, pay rent for some, hire canvassers, and pressure his patronage employees to work harder. Recognizing the new demographics of the ward, he appointed seven blacks to patronage jobs at city hall.

Under normal circumstances it would have seemed that the odds of defeating Tozer were insurmountable. But there were inherent flaws in the system that rendered elected officials vulnerable. First, Tozer was white in a district of a recently black majority, and the mood of the black community had changed considerably. Most were determined to take control of the political machinery in their areas. Second, he stood six feet tall, weighed 225 pounds, and always had a cigar dangling from his mouth. He wore a ten-gallon Texas-style cowboy hat, adding greatly to his caricature image as a plantation boss. Third, most of his white jobholders no longer lived in the ward. Fourth, our precinct workers explained that the favors extended to constituents, such as fixing traffic tickets, pruning trees, and cleaning alleys, were those due to them as taxpayers.

Tozer, under pressure from his few black jobholders, endorsed another black patronage worker for committeewoman instead of his longtime friend and incumbent, Mary McDermott. That caused further erosion in his ability to deliver votes.

Unemployment was excessively high for blacks in all parts of the city. Political jobs were extremely attractive to those who were not working or were waiting tables, cleaning offices, or doing domestic work. Most blacks performing these menial tasks were educationally qualified for better positions. Prospects of white-collar employment at city hall were a very glamorous lure that brought many workers into the fold of the black candidates.

The Wright camp resorted to a one-on-one strategy. Wright and his co-workers preferred to meet individually with the electorate, spending countless hours in taverns, pool halls, and barbershops. They also worked hard to garner the endorsements of ministers and block unit chairmen. They produced large amounts of literature written by Ernest Calloway, a prolific writer who served as a behind-the-scenes strategist.

Wright, an entertainer since childhood, was a personable and popular local singer, dancer, and master of ceremonies. He had been involved with many civic and community organizations. His choice for running mate was Harris, who was active in church work. She had been the first black to challenge the Tozer machine when she ran unsuccessfully for the committee post in 1956. Harris brought with her many years of experience in campaigning for other candidates. She had been involved in the Eighteenth Ward with Committeeman Charles "Turtles" Reardon and was on the team that supported Bernard Dickmann when he ran for mayor in 1933. She was one of the first blacks to move into the Twenty-sixth Ward, and she helped organize block units in her neighborhood.

The Wright-Harris team had selected Goins as their campaign manager. He was a workaholic, seemingly always in perpetual motion. What he lacked in political know-how was compensated for by his energetic activity. The group went about the business of reassembling old campaign workers from Harris's prior effort. One of their most effective recruits was Willie Mack, known as "Whisper." Mack owned a barbershop and had dozens of friends who idolized him.

The Seay-White campaign was very exciting for me and for the organization that we had built in the Twenty-sixth Ward. The election was not held until the first Tuesday in August, but the campaign between Seay and Wright started the preceding November. By January window signs and bumper stickers were displayed at numerous locations; handbills and brochures were being circulated. Each of the two teams of Negro candidates was busily preparing for victory.

There was, of course, some serious rupture in the Seay-White campaign group. We had lost some key operatives to the Wright-Harris team. DeVerne Calloway—the wife of Ernest Calloway of the Teamsters union and an important cog in my victory the previous year—departed our company and joined forces with the Goins-Wright-Harris camp. She took with her two of our able precinct captains.

I was the campaign manager for Seay and White. Seay was a schoolteacher by profession. He had been active in the civil rights movement for eleven years even though he was only twenty-eight. He was a neat dresser and a dynamic orator. His running mate, White, had been active in politics for a quarter of a century. Formerly associated with Senator Mike Kinney of the Sixth Ward, she now found herself living in the Twenty-sixth Ward because of Mayor Tucker's program to rehabilitate the Mill Creek area. She was savvy, cunning, and smart. She had put together a group called Community Sisters, consisting of about fifty women who actively campaigned wherever she deemed important.

The nucleus of Seay followers was young professionals, mostly schoolteachers, civil rights workers, and sleeping-car porters. About one third of our precinct captains were either professionals or wives of doctors, lawyers, or teachers, which gave a certain stability and maturity to the campaign. This group was brought in chiefly by Marian Oldham, a schoolteacher and the wife of Attorney Charles Oldham. Both Oldhams were very active in CORE. They were dedicated volunteers who spent a great deal of time canvassing, telephoning, and addressing envelopes. We also had the support of many young college graduates whom I knew from my bartending days at the Musician's Club while in college.

The Seay-White-Clay group was more balanced and more representative of the community than the other two groups. Most of our workers were between twenty-two and thirty years of age because both Seay and I were in that age group. Anna White's followers were older and more seasoned in political affairs.

The Seay camp placed its priority on home meetings with groups of people ranging from five to fifty persons. During the winter months, meetings were held every night—on many occasions, four or five per night. They were duplicates of the meetings I successfully held when campaigning for alderman. In the spring, the rallies were moved outdoors. Streets were blocked off, platforms were erected, and music and soft drinks were provided. Hundreds of people attended and listened to the speeches and live music. The gatherings were similar to old-time church revivals.

One strategy used by machine politicians was to keep voter registration low so that the deliverable votes gave their candidates the advantage. Canvassers for the election board, named by Tozer, were adept in striking from the rolls those they sensed were in opposition to the ward organization, leaving others who had recently moved out of the ward but maintained a connection with the committeeman.

Seay and Wright knew that in order to win it would be necessary to register blacks who had recently moved into the ward. In many cases, it was a simple matter of providing a change of address from their last legally registered address. But in other instances, it required transporting them approximately five miles to the Board of Election Commissioners. The two camps spent months taking eligible voters to be registered. The Seay group rented two buses each Saturday and transported an average of one hundred people weekly. They were accompanied on the trip by articulate precinct workers who informed them of why they should vote the Seay-White ticket. They were also encouraged to join the crusade to elect black representation.

Eight weeks before the August primary, it became apparent that Goins was not equipped to match political wits with the more seasoned Seay forces. The Teamsters union, which had secretly contributed to the Wright campaign, decided to come out of the closet. Ernest Calloway took charge of Wright's campaign operations. Earlier, he and I had engaged in several confrontations; one had caused me to leave the NAACP and join CORE.

NAACP Youth Council Destroyed

The list of NAACP Youth Council accomplishments was a source of embarrassment for the St. Louis senior NAACP branch. They had primarily functioned by filing lawsuits and issuing press releases. Direct confrontation through sit-ins and picket lines was not on their radar scope. The more success we had, the more embarrassed they became. Finally, the disagreement became public knowledge.

The adult branch reacted in typical NAACP fashion. At first it tended to ignore us. Eventually, it attempted to co-opt our agenda and corral our energies. The group was unsuccessful in both efforts, and we became the enemy of its leadership. In 1958 Ernest Calloway gained control of the adult branch of the NAACP from Hubert Brown. His first action as president was an attempt to rein in the NAACP Youth Council, which he considered a loose cannon. We naïvely played into his hands.

We made a fatal mistake several months after he took over the branch by meeting with a group of people working with the Young Women's Hebrew Association (YWHA) and planning a fund-raising project. All proceeds would go to the Youth Council. They recommended and we approved Pete Seeger as the entertainer who could draw a crowd at a concert. Unbeknownst to us, Pete Seeger, a Jewish folk singer, was also regarded as one of the leading communists in the country.

Calloway exploited the incident to its fullest. He charged that communists had infiltrated our group and were now directing policy from Moscow. The national organization in New York, under the leadership of Executive Director Roy Wilkins, was terrified. At the time, FBI director J. Edgar Hoover was attempting to make a case that the civil rights organization was a "Red Front" for the communist party.

I received an airmail special delivery from Herbert L. Wright, the Youth Council secretary, stating, "Do not accept the Pete Seeger concert offer. Mr. Seeger has, in the past, been connected with many left-wing political organizations, and his present political interests are quite dubious, to say the least." Calloway persuaded the New York leadership to rescind our Youth Council charter.

In this encounter, I learned valuable lessons from Calloway: first, what Joseph Stalin had meant by not making a revolution with "silk gloves"; second, that an "iron fist in a silk glove" was the most effective way of persuasion. Both theories enabled me to develop a lethal attitude when encountering my political enemies.

After competing in several political, union, and civil rights skirmishes, it was no exaggeration to say that we knew each other's strengths and weaknesses. When handbills were distributed informing us of the fact that Calloway was new campaign manager for Wright, we were rightfully concerned. In his first act as the new manager, Calloway called for an outdoor rally. Knowledgeable of his great organizational ability and powerful oratorical skills, we approached the situation very cautiously. We contemplated and eventually discarded several plans. One called for a counter-rally at the same time within a few blocks of the Wright rally. That, too, was nixed. Finally, we decided to add some levity and rattle the opposition.

Will the Real Wife Stand Up?

To break the campaign monotony, there was occasionally room for laughter and political tricks. I had studied Calloway so intensively in the years of the Youth Council incident that I could almost predict what he would say and do at any given time. I could also predict the choreography he would use in pumping the crowd for his initial appearance.

My assessment was correct. About four hundred people were in attendance at the parking lot of an abandoned movie house. On the platform were the principals: Wright, Harris, Goins, Calloway, and two ministers. As I predicted, one of the principals was missing: Wright's wife. The meeting began with a prayer that placed God squarely on the side of Wright and Harris. Then Goins introduced Calloway as the new campaign manager.

After reciting his impressive credentials, Calloway announced that it was his honor and privilege to introduce the man of the hour, the next committeeman of the ward. But before exercising such a prerogative, he said it was necessary to introduce the great lady behind this great man—

the one who made it all possible. Of course, it was the wife of Wright. My prediction had panned out. I knew Calloway like a book. I had read him over and over. He never strayed. He never altered his game plan.

I viewed the event from a tree in a dark alley about half a block away. For dramatic and maximum crowd appeal, Mrs. Wright was somewhere in the audience. Calloway taught me that tactic in 1956. He surveyed the crowd and asked that the charming, vivacious little lady please stand. Five charming, vivacious young ladies, all members of the Seay camp, each strategically placed in the audience, rose simultaneously and began to take bows. It was a hilarious event, one that was talked about for several days. Calloway was furious, Goins was confused, Wright was indignant. I was elated.

Battle of the Signs

The Seay and Wright people campaigned vigorously for almost a year. Each had beautifully decorated window signs and displayed them in many homes. Tozer, relying on traditional tactics, ignored this unorthodox method. The battle of the signs became a crucial tactic only for us neophytes. Wright would place a sign in a window, Seay would attempt to talk the home owner into taking it down, and vice versa. This maneuver went on for several months. The competition for signs was intense. Each side had about three hundred signs in the windows of avid supporters that the other camp could not replace. When the Seay people held house meetings in the winter months, we secured forms from those in attendance. In addition to questions such as "Will you work on election day?" "Will you call your neighbors?" and "Will you volunteer your car to get out the vote?" there was another which asked, "Will you place a sign in your window?" However, those signs were not placed.

Two weeks before election day, the Seay group, under the direction of our headquarters manager, Lee Daniel "Pete" Lloyd, carefully went through the cards and separated those who had indicated a willingness to place a sign in their windows. For three days, these people were telephoned and reminded of their pledges. They were told that the following Friday or Saturday a worker would bring a sign and place it in the window. That ploy may well have been the turning point in the election. Starting on Friday afternoon, about fifty workers were given signs and addresses. By 9 that night over one thousand colorful blue and red signs were placed in windows. When the opposition awoke the next morning they were stunned to see such an awesome array of support—to the extent that it took them until Monday to devise a counterattack. By that time, the election was over, for all practical purposes. Their main supporters were so demoralized that for almost forty-eight hours they stopped campaigning altogether.

In assessing the 1960 campaign, Calloway later acknowledged the effects of the signs. But he credited another ploy as being the most significant. He said that the precise moment he knew his team had lost was at 6:30 p.m. on the Sunday before the primary. He admitted to being totally surprised by the last event capping the Seay-White campaign. That admission was uttered fifteen years later in the classroom at Saint Louis University where he was professor of urban affairs and teaching a course in political science.

The Seay group organized a motorcade for the Sunday preceding the election. The plans were developed in secrecy, and arrangements were made in such a way as to catch the opposition off guard. A rumor floated around that many people were abandoning the Seay-White group, which explained the signs disappearing from their windows. However, we had run out of money for materials, so it was agreed that signs already up in the windows would be retrieved on the Saturday evening before election day and used in the parade. It was further agreed that the signs would then be used in front of polling places the following Tuesday.

Each captain asked participants to have their automobiles in the parking lot of the Sears Roebuck department store and two others, which were closed on Sundays. The cars came and came, decorated with signs, crepe paper, and other paraphernalia. The route of the parade was designed so that it would pass the Wright-Harris headquarters between 6:30 and 7:00 p.m. It would be cool by then, and the headquarters would be buzzing with workers preparing for last-minute election day activities. Precisely at 6:30, the lead car of the motorcade arrived in front of the headquarters. Horns were blowing, the band on the flatbed truck was blaring, and workers inside the building rushed to the street.

Calloway was flabbergasted to see 250 cars in a parade that took approximately thirty minutes to pass his headquarters. He remarked later in the classroom that he had known then that the ballgame was over. Tozer received 1,297 votes, Wright received 1,797, and Seay received 2,331. White beat her closest rival, Ida Harris, by less than 100 votes.

As the election returns bear out, "Whisper" Mack knew how to work a precinct. Wright-Harris won only two precincts. Mack delivered his precinct from Wright by a margin of 2–1. Much credit goes to his wife, Jackie, for this achievement. They made the perfect political combination. He influenced the street people, and she was loved by home owners in the neighborhood. The next day I persuaded both Macks to join our organization.

Campaign against Dwyer and the State Senator
In 1960 Edward "Jellyroll" Hogan, the notorious Irish gangster during the era of Prohibition and head of the Egan Rats, an Irish group allegedly responsible for more than one hundred gangland murders, was the state senate incumbent. He had built an effective political machine in past years and accumulated untold political IOUs, even among black politicians and voters. But the mood in the black community was changing; blacks were demanding black representation wherever blacks were in the majority.

Two black elected officials of the Fourth Ward, Alderman Mayberry and Magistrate Judge William Diuguid, decided that the time was ripe to oppose not only Hogan but also Jack Dwyer, committeeman of the all-black ward. Dwyer's influence as chairman of the central committee was key to many white officeholders in black wards maintaining their positions. His ability to raise money for them and to share patronage jobs with them was invaluable.

The plan to challenge Dwyer called for Diuguid to file for committeeman and to file another black against Hogan for the state senate. Among Dwyer's black supporters, that strategy was not looked upon with favor. Dwyer had been one of a few white politicians to dispense patronage to blacks on any kind of equitable basis. About half of his many jobs in the ward were manned by blacks. He was the person primarily responsible for the elections of Mayberry and Diuguid. He also had many black friends in the business community, and the publishers of the two major Negro weekly newspapers were his supporters. Hogan, on the other hand, was instrumental in a number of black policemen being placed on the force and being promoted; he protected blacks engaged in illegal gambling, prostitution, and an after-hours speakeasy.

Diuguid and Mayberry convinced Rev. Frank Madison Reid to run for the Senate. Reid, pastor of St. James AME Church, was the son of a prominent bishop of the AME Church. He was active in the civil rights movement and respected in the community.

At the time, a battle was being fought between the young turks and the old-guard black politicians for control of North Side wards. The youths thought that the older Negro politicians would be forced to support a white candidate for state senator. The Mayberry group solicited and got the support of activist attorney Hugh White, businessman Arthur Kennedy, civil rights leader Margaret Wilson, and myself. Reid was not going to get the faction of the old guard led by Weathers, Calloway, and Theodore D. McNeal. They viewed Reid's candidacy as a threat to their leadership roles. If he won, they lost face, influence, and power. But Reid's candidacy precipitated a change in thinking among the Dwyer and the Weathers people.

It soon became apparent that Hogan was in serious danger of being defeated by Reid. That's when Weathers proved his mastery by sidetracking our efforts without destroying the ultimate goal of electing a black to the senate. The situation was complicated and complex. First, Chambers was not inclined to support anybody other than his friend of many years, Hogan. But Chambers had only a few precincts in the district, and his influence in the others was minimal. Second, Dwyer was neutral at the time but leaning toward the incumbent. Third, Chambers's protégé Leroy Tyus was running for committeeman in the Twentieth Ward, a key part of the district. This appeared to give Chambers an edge in soliciting support for Hogan. Fourth, in the Twenty-sixth Ward, I was in support of Reid. Fifth, it would not have been politically feasible to attack or embarrass Reid.

The Election of the First Black Senator

The district represented by Senator Hogan was in midtown St. Louis, mostly located in the black area commonly called the Ville. Black people had been inhabitants of this area since before the turn of the twentieth century. Most middle-class Negroes lived there; it was also the site of many historic Negro structures: Sumner High School, the Poro Building, Tandy Community Center, Homer G. Phillips Hospital, and Annie Malone Orphan Home. Negro candidates Nathaniel Sweet, publisher of the *St. Louis American*; Joseph W. P. Clark, civil rights activist; and Al Wallace, political ward heeler, had sought office in this black-majority district. They were unsuccessful because white politicians held all but one of the elected ward committee posts and thus the power to deliver—or in many cases manipulate—election returns in the district.

If there was any lingering doubt about Weathers's arrival as an effective leader, the 1960 race for state senate dismissed it. He organized and spearheaded the campaign of T. D. McNeal. Initially, the black press ran a series of articles resurrecting McNeal as the golden boy of the civil rights movement. He was the international vice president of the Sleeping Car Porters' union under the leadership of A. Phillip Randolph and had been a prominent leader in the civil rights struggle of the 1930s and 1940s. He organized the St. Louis component of the March on Washington during the days of World War II.

In early 1941, Randolph announced that 10,000 blacks would parade down Pennsylvania Avenue on July 1 to show their displeasure with the discrimination and segregation sanctioned by the federal government.

He was criticized by some for his position. But as a determined activist, he upped the ante, announcing that 100,000 would march on Washington. Bolstering his optimism, more than 20,000 blacks attended a meeting at Madison Square Garden that was called before the scheduled march.

On June 25, six days before the march, President Franklin Delano Roosevelt—after Randolph refused to call off the march—issued Executive Order 8802, declaring discrimination in hiring to be contrary to the policy of the United States. But the order was ignored by the defense industry, and FDR refused to enforce it. Subsequently, the original massive march announced by Randolph became a series of local protest demonstrations against the U.S. government's refusal to employ blacks in defense plants.

McNeal, the chief organizer and spokesman for the St. Louis chapter of Randolph's March on Washington, was responsible for many blacks being employed in the war effort. He led marches on the largest plants in St. Louis for equal employment rights. He convened a rally of 10,500 Negroes in Kiel Auditorium. More than 7,000 Negroes then obtained jobs at the U.S. Cartridge Company's small arms plant, the Carter Carburetor Company, Laclede Gas, McDonnell Douglas Aircraft, General Cable, and Union Electric. The group also picketed the Southwestern Bell telephone company and won a partial victory when the firm opened an office in the Negro community and staffed it with black employees.

Weathers formed a committee of distinguished, non-political citizens to draft McNeal for the senate race. Simultaneously, Dwyer was convinced by Weathers that a black would win the senatorial seat, and that it would be a person influenced by Mayberry and Diuguid unless McNeal got political support. McNeal, suave and savvy, took a statesmanlike position. While not asking Reid to withdraw, he refused to file unless he, McNeal, were the unanimous choice of the black community.

While the promotion of McNeal was taking place, the bishop of the AME district, encouraged by Weathers, asked Reid to withdraw from the race, and Reid acceded to his bishop's wishes. Diuguid, Mayberry, and the rest of us had only one consolation: a black of stature and commitment would make a serious effort for the seat.

In announcing his withdrawal, the reverend agreed to become chairman of McNeal's Citizens' Committee. He stated that he had filed only to assure that representation of black people would be enhanced in the next general assembly. He believed that McNeal would accomplish that end.

A. Phillip Randolph came to town to boost McNeal's candidacy. With a unified community, including the support of the young turks, McNeal won in a landslide, receiving the largest majority of votes against a senatorial incumbent in modern Missouri history.

The 1960 election was the turning point for blacks in their struggle to attain influence in St. Louis politics. Negro candidates captured a state senate seat (T. D. McNeal), two ward committeemen (Norman R. Seay and Leroy Tyus) and two ward committeewomen (Anna White and Geneva Wright), and three state representatives (Hugh J. White, Henry Winfield Wheeler, and William Wright).

Black Community Network

During the 1950s, an unstructured but positive system of communicating existed among black leaders. The informal arrangement of sharing information centered around two eating establishments and a popular nightclub. Black businessmen, politicians, and professionals met daily in one or two of the places, discussed issues, and exchanged ideas for combating enemies of the Negro race: breakfast at the Tate Sisters' restaurant, followed by lunch at Jesse Johnson's Deluxe Restaurant, and late-night excursions at Jordan Chambers's Club Riviera.

Businessmen Bill Hart, Al Ford, Henry McKell, Arthur Kennedy, and numerous others ate at Tate Sisters' in the west end of the Negro community every morning. Doctors and administrators from Homer G. Phillips Hospital were also there daily. They were joined by a few elected officials, such as Weathers and Tyus, who frequented the establishment and were the carriers of news from the breakfast group to the luncheon conference of leaders.

At noon the rendezvous point was the Deluxe Restaurant, which was located in midtown across from the People's Finance Building and around the corner from the *St. Louis Argus* building. The People's building at the corner of Jefferson and Market Streets was the hub of the black business community. It opened in 1926 and, through the years, housed the most important organizations in the city. It was the home of the NAACP, the *St. Louis American* newspaper, the Brotherhood of Sleeping Car Porters, the Moving Picture Operators' Union, the J. Roy Terry School of Music, and the National Baptist Association. It also provided offices for lawyers, doctors, a pharmacist, and other professionals.

Each day the most involved activists in the Negro community met for soul food and conversation. Five days a week, the restaurant was host to Alderman Wayman Smith; attorneys Frankie Freeman, Al Lynch, James Bell, and David Grant; media personalities N. A. Sweets of the *American*, Howard Woods of the *Argus*, columnist Buddy Lonesome, and Irving Williamson; civil rights leaders Joe Clark and Hugh White; and Committeeman Fred Weathers. Occasionally, T. H. Mayberry and Margaret Bush Wilson joined us for lunch.

It was at these sessions that the affairs of government as related to Negroes were thoroughly discussed, examined, and debated. There was not always agreement as to the resolution of the problems, but everyone there heard and understood the opinions of a cross section of the black community. The camaraderie served to lessen the questioning of motives of those who held opposing opinions.

Some who participated in the luncheon meetings also went to the Club Riviera late at night to converse with Jordan Chambers, who owned the club. He was usually briefed on most developments in the community before the luncheon gatherings. Weathers, on his way to his office in the City Hall complex each morning, stopped at Chambers's home. They discussed and strategized on a daily basis.

The operation and fellowship disappeared when the Mill Creek redevelopment project destroyed the People's Finance Building and the sites of the Deluxe Restaurant and the *St. Louis Argus*. The passage of the Public Accommodation Bill opened other eateries that blacks began to frequent.

CHAPTER

6

ROAD TO POLITICAL RESPECT

After my victorious 1959 campaign for alderman, seasoned political analysts doubted that one election would have a long-term impact on the course of black politics. But when I successfully managed Seay's campaign for committeeman the next year, my respect among my peers increased, and politicians began to seek my support. Endorsement by our organization was equivalent to three thousand votes in the ward and generated between four thousand and seven thousand additional voters who were influenced by "rump" groups we had developed in other parts of the city. Others acknowledged that I had taken the first step on the road to becoming a factor in Missouri politics.

The Struggle for Political Freedom

I benefited from the mood of militant resistance to conditions in our city. It came about as a direct result of fifty years of sustained, ever-increasing defiance on the part of thousands of black St. Louisans who were determined to map their own destinies and chart their own course of life. The pounding of a constant drumbeat for equality and justice, in a system absent of both, rose in acoustic, crescendoed decibels. Each refusal to willingly accept racial indignities, no matter how minuscule, contributed to a mind-set that reached defiant fruition around the time I ran for office in the late 1950s. Through decades of struggle and determination, the black community finalized a simple formula and devised a realistic blueprint for political empowerment. I just happened to be in the right place at the right time and was prepared to accept the mantle of leadership under the right circumstances.

But my rise to the top of the political heap in St. Louis during the 1960s, 1970s, and the rest of the century was not by accident or luck. It was because of grit, skill, ingenuity, hard work, and an ability to organize the unorganized. Our group was able to develop a political apparatus capable of delivering lopsided vote margins and electing endorsed candidates because we surrounded ourselves with people of wisdom, vision, integrity, and commitment to racial equality. We associated with men and women of principle such as state senator John Bass, community activist Pearlie Evans, state senator Gwen Giles, Charles and Marian Oldham, David Grant, Frank Bledsoe, Ivory Perry, Bob Curtis, state senator Franklin Payne, state representative Nathaniel Rivers, Leroy Tyus, Frederick N. Weathers, and others who were more interested in people empowerment than in personal financial enhancement. Together, we overcame community apathy and repelled the insolence of some black leaders. Our organizational skills and understanding of the electoral process, along with our alliances with ministers, civil rights advocates, and key labor leaders, played a major role in our unchallenged dictation of election outcomes.

Because I was the spokesman of the "political family," I was perceived as the mastermind of the victorious political slates. It was because of my association with dynamic precinct captains such as John Curtis, Willie Mack, Herdy Miller, Blondell Cook, Magnolia Dease, and Addie Rice that my ascendancy to the pinnacle of political power was possible. I attribute my staying power to one and only one fact—that I never strayed from or equivocated on the question of entitlement of black people to all rights and opportunities guaranteed by condition of citizenship. As a result, I never lost my base in the black community and earned much respect and many supporters in the white community.

When Irish Eyes Were Smiling

At the time I sought my first public office, ethnic groups (Italians, Lebanese, Negroes) were a negligible factor in the political decision-making of the city. Irish Catholics controlled the political machinery with an ironclad fist. Their domination spanned unchallenged and uninterrupted for approximately twenty years, yet to describe their prowess as a single, cohesive unit similar to New York's Tammany Hall would be misleading. Their pre-eminence was not dependent on one, two, or three strong individuals but on a collection of high-strung, egotistic people who constantly held center stage.

Often, there were personal squabbles among four or five Irish factions in primary elections. But pride of common heritage, an intense desire to counter bigotry against their race, and the wish to dispense patronage to their own kind prevailed in the general elections over their petty differences and personal agendas. Despite division in their ranks, the Irish held a stranglehold on the election of the twelve citywide county offices: sheriff, recorder of deeds, license collector, collector of revenue, clerk of the court of criminal corrections, clerk of the court of criminal causes, clerk of the circuit court, city treasurer, public administrator, circuit attorney, coroner, and prosecuting attorney. These offices were the source of patronage jobs that provided the political muscle for Democratic ward organizations. Theoretically, each ward was designated a number of public employees who were endorsed by the ward committeepeople. In turn, the jobholders became the foundation for viable ward organizations, paying a percentage of their annual salaries in dues, canvassing precincts, and getting out the vote on election day for the Democratic ticket.

At one time, these jobs numbered in the thousands. Hundreds of civil service jobs in trash collection, street cleaning, and parks were considered patronage because politicians endorsed them and influenced the continued employment of the recipient. It was common for some wards to have as many as two hundred patronage workers. In 1950 thirteen of the city's twenty-eight wards, all on the North Side, were represented by Irish elected officials or affiliated with Irish-controlled labor unions. Only one ward, the nineteenth, under the leadership of Jordan Chambers, was represented by blacks.

For more than two decades, the Irish controlled who was elected to the county offices. At various times during this period, they held from seven to ten of the offices. Martin L. Tozer, of Dutch extraction, won an upset victory in the 1956 election by defeating Thomas Callanan, the incumbent Irish sheriff and brother of Larry Callanan. Nine of the other patronage offices were held by the Irish.

Although the Irish composed less than 30 percent of the population, other ethnic groups were unsuccessful in winning elective office. The
Irish domination, however, did not extend to the three most sensitive and
most important citywide offices that controlled the budget and expenditure
of tax money: mayor, comptroller, and president of the Board of Aldermen.

Webbe, Morrell, and Weathers

In 1962 two ethnic groups made an effort to become major players in
the political ball game. A Lebanese, Sorkis Webbe Sr., and a Negro, Fred
Weathers, filed for public administrator and clerk of the criminal court,
respectively. Webbe was supported by most South Side leaders and a few
labor leaders. Weathers, with the promise of support from several white
politicians, was the first Negro to mount a serious campaign for a citywide patronage office. Reverend John J. Hicks and James Hurt had been
elected to the school board within the past two years. Attorney David
Grant and educator C. B. Broussard had been elected to the Board of
Freeholders to draft a new city charter. The four were elected in non-
partisan, multicandidate races, dispensing no patronage or setting any
fiscal policy for the city.

Weathers, a man of extensive background and experience, possessed credentials far superior to his opponent, Patrick Lavin. The incumbent Lavin, a high school dropout, was a typical hand-shaking,
backslapping ward heeler who attended daily mass and evening beer busts.
He was invisible in the general affairs of the community. By contrast,
Weathers was active in community and civic organizations and served
on the boards of the NAACP and the Urban League. He was a member
of the mayor's committees of social services and public housing and a
member of the advisory board of the juvenile court. In addition, he held
a bachelor of arts degree from Atlanta University and a master's degree
from the University of Pennsylvania. Most Irish officials supported Lavin.

Weathers's backers formed a coalition with Jack Dwyer and several others who were supporting committeeman of the Twenty-first Ward
and Assistant Deputy License Collector Leo Morrell. The basis for the

North Side committeemen Leroy Tyus, Franklin Payne, Fred Weathers, Clay, Samuel Goldston, and John Conley in 1968. Photograph by Irving Williamson, 1968. MHS Photographs and Prints Collection.

alliance was the endorsement of three white committeemen for Weathers in exchange for three black ward leaders' support for Morrell. Similar pacts had been formed in the past to no avail. These agreements seldom succeeded because few whites ever voted for black candidates.

The quid pro quo arrangement ignored the resolve of young civil rights activists. The major stumbling block to the arrangement came from CORE, the most effective center of protest activism for young militants, and the Twenty-sixth Ward organization, which was the base of its civil rights and political activity. The ward clubhouse became a forum for discussion and development of critical community issues. CORE and the Twenty-sixth Ward saw no plausible way to support

Morrell and maintain our integrity. As a matter of principle, we felt compelled to oppose him and refused to compromise an inch on his candidacy. Morrell was the wrong candidate to palm off on the black community. He was an unrepentant racist who opposed legislation to provide equal employment opportunity, open housing, and public accommodation. He refused to give patronage jobs to his Negro constituents. If those promoting Weathers's candidacy had only consulted Oldham, Seay, and me, they would have known our attitude before agreeing to the ill-fated alliance.

I'd once resided in Morrell's Twenty-first Ward and experienced the tactics used to exclude blacks from participating in ward activity. Whenever we showed up for monthly ward meetings, he would abruptly rise, rap the gavel, and adjourn. No public announcements were ever made of the ward's next gathering.

Morrell had a long history of racist behavior. In June 1947, Archbishop Joseph E. Ritter declared that all Catholic elementary and high schools would open in September without regard to the race of students. Immediately, Morrell announced opposition to the plan. With his and others' signatures, thousands of letters were mailed, calling for a rally on the Sunday before the opening of school. Ironically, the protest was to be held on the steps of a public school, Beaumont High. Less than one hundred people showed up for the protest rally. What caused the low attendance was a matter of speculation. The archbishop's authority, respect among parishioners, and steadfast insistence on integration certainly played a role. But rumor had it that the mail sack with the invitations was accidentally diverted to Hawaii by a postal clerk. The desegregation of the parochial schools took place in September without incident, less than seven years before the Supreme Court's decision in *Brown v. Board of Education*.

But Morrell and his allies, including state senator Jack Barrett, were also steadfast in their anti-integration beliefs. They formed the Catholic Laymen's Organization and appealed to the apostolic delegate to overturn the order. When their petition was denied, they threatened to take their case to the Vatican but instead decided to take legal action. The archbishop was not easily intimidated. He issued a pastoral letter that was read in all churches in the diocese, warning that those attempting to thwart the integration of the schools or participating in filing legal action "would be subject to immediate excommunication." The protest fizzled.

As the prospect of a viable coalition with Morrell began to deteriorate, a meeting was convened at the home of Weathers, specifically for the benefit of Seay and me. Every black committeeman, state legislator, alderman, constable, and magistrate was present. Seay and I were the only people in the room not supporting Morrell. Attorney Grant, the only nonelected person invited, chaired the session. Surprisingly, the guest of honor was candidate Morrell. The other officials encouraged our cooperation.

They were sincere but not convincing. While I was enumerating my reasons for opposing him and explaining why he was going to be denied the Negro vote, Morrell jumped to his feet and said, "All of these fine Negro leaders have endorsed me. You are nobody. I don't need your support." At that point, Chambers, in his roaring voice, said, "Sit down and shut up, you shit bum. The man is telling the truth. It will be difficult to carry our wards for you with or without his support."

Our decision did not dampen our enthusiasm for Weathers's campaign. There was no evidence that he was damaged by our refusal to join the coalition. He was endorsed by three white committeemen representing wards with substantial black populations, several leaders in South Saint Louis, four black committeemen, and six black aldermen. The Twenty-sixth Ward organization also endorsed Webbe. We conducted an intensive registration and get-out-the-vote drive for him and Weathers. Barbecues, fish fries, and street rallies were held. But the coalition ticket of Weathers and Morrell fell short of the goal. They both lost by close margins.

A huge outpouring of voters in the black wards, combined with limited support from the South Side, almost elected Weathers to be the first black in a citywide position. Lavin received 34,053 votes (52.3 percent) to Weathers's 30,948 votes (47.7 percent). Weathers lost the Twenty-first Ward (Committeeman Morrell endorsed him) with 1,153 votes to Lavin's 1,384 votes. He lost badly in every white precinct in the ward without any visible sign of a viable campaign for Lavin. It meant that in a ward 40 percent black, the agreement of exchanging ward endorsements had little effect on white voters.

The election of Webbe as public administrator began the down-hill slide of the Irish monopoly on citywide offices. In rapid succession came the appointment of Louis "Midge" Berra, an Italian, as collector of revenue; the election of Francis Slay, a Lebanese, as recorder of deeds; the appointment of Benjamin Goins, a black, as license collector; the election of Georgi Solomon, a Lebanese, as clerk of the court of criminal corrections; the election of Freeman Bosley Jr., a black, as clerk of the circuit court; and the appointment of Larry Williams, a black, as city treasurer.

Webbe's election was also the beginning of a new analysis of the dichotomy of sectional political debates. For years, white North Side leaders and their black supporters had framed the issues for Negro voters as a contest between liberal whites in the northern part of the city against those biased South Side politicians. However, the argument defied reality. To define the division of bigoted politicians in such a manner was an insult to intelligent blacks. Outspoken opponents of public accommodations, fair employment, and school desegregation resided on both sides of town. Aldermen James Noonan, Edgar J. Feely, Barney Mueller, and Milt Svetanics of the North Side never voted for civil rights measures. Aldermen James Geisler, Joseph Roddy, and Albert Villa of the South Side provided key votes to pass the public accommodations bill. Fred Haag, a Republican from the South Side, voted for public accommodations. Edward Roach and Leo Morrell of the North Side never supported black candidates for citywide offices, while South Side committeemen James McAteer did support blacks.

Chambers: Leader with Awesome Influence

Jordan Chambers dictated politics in black St. Louis from the mid-1940s. Glorified while alive, canonized since, and now deified by young politicians, Chambers was the undisputed black political leader.

Describing him in such lofty terms may not be a truism in every sense, but debating his positive impact on far-reaching decisions affecting minority conditions is a moot point. The fact remains that Chambers exerted an awesome influence on the times in which he lived and under the impediments he was forced to overcome. His leadership role must be judged by factors and events existing during his era. Then, blacks were victimized by a system of political exploitation, social exclusion, and economic impoverishment. He rose from obscurity to be the undisputed voice of his constituency.

Chambers died several months after Weathers's loss, leaving a void in Negro leadership. The vacuum was filled by Weathers, who was the most influential politician in our community. He was no ordinary, everyday Negro politician. He excelled during a period when other minorities despaired. His Marcella Cab Company was the largest cab company in the city or county. He was the largest employer of blacks in the private sector: He hired more than four hundred drivers, telephone operators, clerks, mechanics, dispatchers, and supervisors. The company grossed more than two million dollars annually.

Weathers displayed unique political acumen in promoting the victorious campaigns that led to the elections of the first black school board member, the first black state senator, and the first black woman in the state legislature. His power was not absolute, but his seniority, knowledge, and independence from the other factions earned him the respect of most politicians.

Goins Elected Twenty-first Ward Committeeman

The determination of CORE and the young activists in the Twenty-sixth Ward to rid our community of Morrell continued after his defeat by Webbe. When Webbe ran for public administrator in 1962, I had established a rump group in opposition to Morrell's Twenty-first Ward regular organization. After the election, I kept the Twenty-first Ward Democratic Improvement Association functioning. Arthur "Chink" Washington, Clarence Holly, and I paid the rent, utilities, and telephone bills. The chairman was Holly. Other key members were Willie Williams and June Dugas.

It was common knowledge—and sometimes aired publicly in the press—that Seay and I were destined to part political ways as our organization experienced an internal struggle for ward leadership. It was a traumatic period for precinct workers who liked and admired both Seay and me. Seay's endorsement of Mayor Tucker for re-election riled Committeewoman Anna White, who despised Tucker. She had been a property owner in the Mill Creek redevelopment area when Tucker and community do-gooders literally stole the homes of black people. I resented Seay's chummy relationship with Dwyer and the downtown elite. Seay accused me of usurping the committeeman's authority.

Goins, aware of the tense situation, approached me in February 1963 to ask my endorsement for the committee post. I had not had a serious conversation with him since our first encounter in the insurance office. He assured me that with his faithful assistance and everlasting allegiance I could in fact become the most powerful official in the city. Allegedly, all he desired was to be my obedient disciple. His plea was embarrassing. My negative impression of him had not changed: I knew he would never speak out on any major issue, especially the highly controversial one of racial equality. I was courteous but candid in explaining that he had no future in Twenty-sixth Ward politics if it depended on my support. It was at this moment that I decided on a ploy to get him out of the ward.

The rump group in the Twenty-first Ward was gearing up for the next campaign when Goins approached me. Holly, a prime mover in the organization, had opted to run for state representative. We were successful in finding a suitable candidate, June Dugas, to oppose the incumbent committeewoman, but she withdrew before the election and was replaced by Jackie Butler. Washington and Williams had no desire to seek the committee post. Everything was in place to challenge Morrell except a candidate for committeeman.

I told Goins that if he wanted to run for the committee post, we had a ready-made organization. He agreed, and I introduced him to the group. I had initially analyzed the ward as a potentially fertile ground for future expansion of black representation. I believed that in two or three years, with proper agitation and a larger influx of black residents, it would be ripe for wrestling control. But under Goins's leadership, thousands of black voters were registered, and it became apparent that the ward committee posts could be won.

Goins and Butler were elected. Holly was defeated.

The Battle Between Good and Evil: "White Hats" v. "Black Hats"

I never found it difficult to separate good politicians from bad ones. Those favoring the elite and catering to the rich and famous are usually showered with praise by establishment forces and represented as wearing "white hats." Supposedly, they are in search of basic reform of conventional standards. Those accused of wearing "black hats" are depicted as defying the rules of social order. They are vilified in scurrilous editorials and ridiculed in degrading cartoons. Subsequently, they become targets of criminal investigations and grand jury inquiries.

I have met many people described as white knights in shining armor. Amazingly, most possessed no knightly qualities and, in many instances, wore tainted armor. The idea that those wearing the "white hats" were the good guys was a farce. The politicians with whom I had the best relations and who treated black leaders as political equals were the ones smeared, hounded, libeled, and slandered by the media. Their motives were impugned even when performing worthwhile civic and community activities. Constant, persistent, and negative reporting over a sustained period earned them reputations as bad guys in "black hats." But during my years of public service, it was the black hats who advanced the cause of black politics.

The so-called bad guys usually delivered on the promises they made before election. If our race had relied on the white hats, we would still be wandering in a political wasteland. Progress for blacks came about because effective coalitions with black hats enabled us to share power. Those hailed as reformers were opposed or absent as blacks were elected

for the first time as state senator, license collector, comptroller, city treasurer, clerk of the courts, mayor, and member of Congress. However, the
white hats were present in a standing-room-only crowd to defeat a black
mayor, a black comptroller, and a black clerk of the court for reelection.

Coalescing with the Webbes, Callanans, and John Lawler made
much of our progress possible. They respected us as individuals. They
treated their black enemies the same as their white enemies and their
black friends the same as their white friends. In the early 1960s, Sorkis
Webbe Sr., another politician destined to be victimized by the media,
entered my life when he ran for public administrator. He and two other

Public administrator Sorkis Webbe Sr., undated.

black hats, Larry Callanan and Lawler, solidified a political deal-making bond with Tyus and me that altered the relationship between white and black politics. Webbe possessed a rare talent for putting together the right people at the right time for the right purpose and achieving a favorable outcome. He could package a deal better than anyone I had ever met. His mind-set rested on the premise that all things were probable and most were possible.

There was symmetry of purpose and of behavior among Webbe, Lawler, and Callanan. They were determined to advance their personal interests, but, unlike many others, they respected their cohorts and repaid their political obligations. The biggest, boldest, and most prominent of the black hat crowd was Larry Callanan, director of the voluntary political fund for Pipefitters' Local 562. Without a doubt, he was a Jesse James to the white hats who considered all black hats to be political outlaws. He was a tough competitor and ran the union in a tough manner. His union exploits were as legendary as his political ones. Among his union members, he was known as "the bully." But the rank and file membership of less than one thousand liked him. This small number does not begin to explain the awesome power that Callanan wielded. During the early 1960s, when other construction union workers were paid $7 to $10 per hour, Pipefitters were making twice that amount.

Most voluntarily contributed $1 a day to the union's political fund. Special card-carrying members from Missouri and Illinois paid no union dues but contributed $2 a day. It is estimated that between $200,000 and $300,000 a year went into the till. It allowed Callanan to be a major player in local, state, and national election campaigns.

There were constant accusations involving Callanan's ties to criminal elements and allegations that he misused the welfare and pension funds. He was once convicted of labor racketeering. The business community and the press were extremely critical of the union's policies and labor demands. Callanan was on the Chamber of Commerce's most hated list. They charged that his practices amounted to extortion and discouraged outsiders from investing in the city. They feared Callanan more than other labor leaders because he had more influence, more money, more nerve, and more political savvy than the rest of his opponents. Unlike others, he was the intimidator and not the intimidated. He did not seek their blessing nor beg their forgiveness.

My relationship with Callanan began in the early 1960s when we met to discuss candidates for local and state offices. I endorsed several candidates in whom he was interested. A year or so later, Tyus and I formed an alliance with Callanan and the Pipefitters, which proved advantageous to the union and beneficial to the black community.

Negro politicians, with the exception of Chambers, refused to make political deals with Callanan. In the black community, the all-white, Irish-controlled union was considered a racist organization. Like all building trade unions, nationally and locally, the local one prescribed to a rigid policy of racial discrimination. In 1962 the union withdrew its training manual from use in the apprentice program at O'Fallon Technical High School rather than allow Negro students to use it.

But Negro politicians continued to work with other white union leaders who enforced the same policy of excluding Negroes. Negro organizations and elected officials dealt with the cement finishers, electricians, bricklayers, operating engineers, and ironworkers. All refused to admit Negroes to their membership. I rejected the illogical arrangement that one discriminating union was worse than other discriminating unions. I believed that if blacks were to change these restrictions, it was necessary to negotiate with them from a position of strength. That became the basis for Tyus and me to form an alliance with Callanan.

In exchange for the political clout we delivered, concessions were made for the advancement of blacks in the union and in elective politics. The combination of shrinking white delivery wards (white union workers moving to suburbia), an expanding black population (migration from the south), and the union's ready cash to finance campaigns constituted a formula for success. The coalition between Callanan, Tyus, and myself was primarily responsible for Goins's appointment as the first black citywide official, the election of John Bass as comptroller, and my election as congressman.

Larry Callanan with attorney Morris Shenker in 1953. Photograph by Buel White, MHS Photographs and Prints Collection. © 1953, *St. Louis Post-Dispatch*.

Pipefitters Integrate: Clay Hired to Coordinate Program

Callanan's number one assistant was another black hat, John "Doc" Lawler. If Callanan was the bully, disliked and feared by many, Doc was the mild-mannered gentleman—one of the few who could talk common sense into Larry. The well-respected Lawler served as a mediator between Larry and those he threatened. Larry would take the low road, demanding the impossible; Lawler would breach the gap by reaching an agreement for only half of Callanan's original demands.

Lawler privately spoke of candidates as "cream puffs" and "cowards." But on one occasion, the *Globe-Democrat* quoted him as saying, "[The candidates] like to take our money but don't want to act like they know us. They were to be the 'white hats,' and we end up being the 'black hats.'"[9]

It was Lawler, working with Tyus and me, who persuaded Callanan that the coalition would be strengthened considerably by integrating the union membership. He contended that abolishing the color line would also greatly diminish opposition against union-backed candidates in the black wards. Callanan agreed but feared the consequences for his re-election as union boss. Finally, a carefully structured plan was devised and executed to integrate the union.

Lawler, Tyus, and I conducted personal interviews with members and kept notes of their responses. Sometimes we went to the job site and talked to workers in groups of six or seven. Other times we pigeonholed them at union meetings. In due time, we were able to categorically state that the majority of the members would not react adversely if blacks were admitted. One small group was determined in its opposition. A larger number favored integration in various degrees of acceptance and a schedule of phased-in entry. The vast majority of members were indifferent.

In February 1966, a crash program for new members was initiated. A press conference was held to introduce ten black journeymen pipefitters, five black apprentices, and an equal number of new white inductees. It was also announced that I had been hired as educational director of the crash-hiring program.

The most prestigious public relations firm in town, Fleishman-Hillard, was retained to properly promote the occasion. The firm had a monopoly on public relations for the leading downtown businesses. Yet this major breakthrough for blacks in the construction industry was negligibly and negatively covered by the press. For years, the media had attacked construction unions for denying admissions to blacks. For years, they and the federal government had engaged in a battle to force a change in the policy. Now, when the color line in the industry was effectively penetrated, media coverage speculated about sinister political motives, debased the method of selecting the blacks, and ridiculed the fact that only fifteen blacks were admitted. They were unsympathetic, even though Callanan stated that "99 percent of our membership [would] cooperate. We believe[d] our members ha[d] been educated enough."

Ironically, the fifteen represented more blacks than the combined number of blacks in all the other building trade unions. The average annual income of the black journeymen was greater than the top salaries of any top-level black employee working for the city of St. Louis, the state of Missouri, McDonnell Douglas Aircraft, or Emerson Electric.

The media was not alone in its criticism of the selection process. On the day following the announcement, about forty white members lined up in front of the union hall. We thought they were rebelling against the newly adopted policy. The reason an equal number of whites had been inducted was to lessen any resentment among those members whose sons, brothers, and nephews had been on a list awaiting admission. These were the best-paying jobs in the workforce. The pay and fringe benefits were not matched by any other workers. We soon recognized that the assembled members were not protesting the enrollment of blacks into the union; they were demanding that more blacks be admitted so that additional whites would be hired from the list.

The NAACP labor committee also opposed the selection process, which did not surprise me. They requested and were granted a meeting at the union hall. Callanan, Lawler, Tyus, and I listened politely to their concerns. First, they expressed outrage that we did not select blacks who had graduated from O'Fallon Technical Public High School. Second, they decried the paying of Negro journeymen-in-training the same rate of pay as experienced journeymen, alleging it was racial patronizing. Third, they resented that those accepted had been recommended by politicians and other leaders with little knowledge of the construction industry. They expressed indignation that a Negro ex-professional boxer was accepted when others had more education. Fourth, they resented the fact that the union had not negotiated the terms of the integration pact with their organization.

Callanan called on me to respond. I did so by posing to him a series of questions. I asked if union rules required graduation from a technical school, and, if not, how many white members had such credentials? He answered that there was no such requirement, and, since the union had withdrawn its training manual, none had finished at a technical school. I inquired about Negro journeymen-in-training making the same as white experienced workers. He answered that there were only two wage scales authorized by the union bylaws: one for apprentices and another for journeymen. I then asked how many white members were ex-prizefighters. He stated that he loved the sport, and counting both amateurs and professionals, the estimate was fifty. My next inquiry was the clincher: I asked how white members were selected for membership. He stated that all must be recommended by either present members or community leaders who could assist the union in its political struggles.

At that point, I enumerated the sponsors of the fifteen blacks. They were all recommended by important individuals in the black community who represented an awesome array of political power. One each was picked by Frank Mitchell and Nathaniel Sweets, publishers of the *Argus* and *American* weekly newspapers, respectively; one by Jerry Foster, the head of an all-black construction laborers' union; three were selected by Tyus, Goins, and me, who were Democratic ward committeemen. The other sponsors were also in leadership positions.

My closing statement, which also closed the meeting, was that the union should not impose higher standards of admission for black applicants than those established for whites. Larry agreed and thanked the delegation for coming out to express its outrage at the union's selection of fifteen blacks who would earn in excess of twenty-five thousand dollars per year.

Clay campaigning for George McGovern for president, 1972.

CHAPTER

7

JEFFERSON BANK DEMONSTRATIONS

Prior to the 1963 Jefferson Bank protest, St. Louis political and business leaders were hailed in the press for promoting seismic change in race relations. Their radical pioneering, as described in the media, was changing the city into a midwestern mecca for black citizens. But despite its fallacious and phantom national image, it was still a bastion of racial bigotry and a stronghold of intolerance. The bank demonstrations exposed the fraudulent campaign that portrayed the city in a favorable light.

Anatomy of an Economic Murder

Four months before the bank confrontation, I published a statistical document titled "Anatomy of an Economic Murder." It revealed the dismal state of black unemployment. It became the handbook for identifying corporations with discriminatory hiring practices. After years of misleading propaganda, the stark truth became apparent: St. Louis was and would likely remain a fortress of entrenched discrimination. The doctrine of appeasement and accommodation adopted by moderate civil rights leaders was a failure. Unless Negroes engaged in direct-action protest to address the injustices, the status quo would persist.

After the release of the twenty-seven-page "Anatomy," the media and city fathers refused to acknowledge the serious degree of racial exclusion in employment. Instead, they criticized me for the methodology used in obtaining the disparaging information. Both the *Globe-Democrat* and the *Post-Dispatch* labeled the manner used to gather information "unethical." How information was obtained, rather than what it revealed, became the subject of debate. Business and community leaders accused me of fomenting racial disharmony. But they could not refute the appalling statistics that revealed the lack of Negro hiring.

There was nothing complicated, sinister, or unscrupulous about the method used to ascertain the information. Questionnaires were mailed to each large corporation doing business in the city. Eight questions were asked, inquiring as to how many Negroes were employed and what positions they held. The answers documented the severe extent of black unemployment. The report was explicit: 37 blacks were employed in the breweries with a total workforce of 7,325; 69 blacks were employed in sales and office positions at five department stores among 3,107 total workers; out of 1,505 total employees at nine dairies, 51 were black; there were 279 blacks (85 percent in menial jobs) among 1,303 employees at soft drink companies; there were 277 blacks (99 percent in menial jobs) out of 5,133 total workers in sixteen banks; 22 of the 2,141 employees at seven large insurance companies were black; there were 42 blacks out of 2,550 employed at two daily newspapers; and, finally, there were 32 blacks among 1,000 workers at two firms publishing religious periodicals.

"Anatomy" emphasized that blacks spent ten million dollars in 1962 buying automobiles, mostly from five inner-city car dealers, yet no dealers employed black salesmen or mechanics. Two industrial firms employed over 900 workers each, but neither had a single black employee. Utility companies did not hire black linemen, operators, meter readers, or clerks. The few blacks the companies did employ worked in customer relations or as janitors.

The hiring policy at Jefferson Bank was no better and no worse than at other institutions. Most had a propensity for denying equal employment to blacks. Selection of the bank was a decision arrived at by accident. CORE's most menacing problem was to designate a specific bank for direct action. The organization did not have sufficient manpower to challenge the entire industry simultaneously. The dilemma was resolved in early August 1963, when CORE chairman Robert Curtis wrote Jefferson Bank and demanded the immediate hiring of four Negroes. The bank's attorney, Wayne L. Millsap, asserted that there were not "four blacks in the city" qualified for white-collar jobs.

At the next regular CORE meeting, a vote was taken to commence direct action against the bank. On August 29, 1963, the bank filed a petition for injunctive relief, seeking a temporary restraining order to prevent CORE from disrupting the bank's normal business. Judge Michael J. Scott issued the restraining order and set September 26 for a hearing. Named in the restraining order were Bob Curtis, Lucien Richards, Reverend Charles Perkins, Norman R. Seay, Charles and Marian Oldham, Herman Thompson, Walter Hayes, Richard Daly, and myself, both as individuals and as representatives of a class known as the St. Louis CORE.

That same day, Attorney Raymond Howard moved for a continuance. On August 30, 1963, Scott overruled his motion and instructed the named defendants and the class (the members of CORE) not to interfere with the business at the bank by blocking the doors, sitting in the bank, or engaging in other disruptive activities. Later that day, several hundred picketers and a large contingent of uniformed police arrived in front of the bank.

Orderly picketing continued for one hour before a special assistant of the NAACP from New York, Al Williams, suggested that the group defy the court order. Fifteen picketers held a meeting on a nearby parking lot. Only one person prohibited by the court injunction agreed to disobey the order. He and approximately one hundred picketers blocked the front doors and later entered the premises, sat on the floor, and sang freedom songs.

On Saturday, August 31, a meeting was convened at police headquarters to discuss strategies to halt the demonstrations, not to preserve order or prevent the commission of crimes. Participants were Joseph H. McConnell, the executive vice president of Jefferson Bank; Wayne Millsap, attorney for the bank; Chief of Police Curtis H. Brostron; and the Chairman of the Board of Police Commissioners, H. Sam Priest.

Several hours later, Mayor Tucker, aldermanic president Donald Gunn, and Governor John Dalton met with the Board of Police Commissioners for four hours, later publicly demanding swift and retaliatory action against the leaders of CORE. The governor had earlier described the bank demonstration as an act of "lawlessness." Three hours after the meeting, Scott issued arrest orders for twenty-three black leaders.

The order was so preposterous that several parts were later rescinded, and the number cited in the restraining order was reduced. Pruning the list, Scott finally issued writs of attachment for nine people and ordered Sheriff Martin L. Tozer to bring them before the court. Tozer and eight deputies began a late-night roundup of demonstrators on the Saturday before Labor Day. Marian Oldham was the first arrested. While the deputies were searching her home for her husband Charles, she asked permission to freshen up. In the process, she called another CORE member, who alerted the others of their pending arrests. Herman Thompson was the only other apprehended that night. The two public school teachers were taken into custody at about 10:30 at night, handcuffed, and thrown into the police van like common criminals. They remained in the police wagon for three hours as the search for the other seven proceeded.

On Sunday afternoon, the remaining seven demonstrators surrendered. Professional bondsmen signed $10,000 bail each for the release of Marian Oldham, Thompson, Howard, and myself. The minimum bond for any felony offense in St. Louis was $1,500. St. Louis courts customarily released those accused of murder, rape, arson, and bank robbery on $5,000 bond. The four demonstrators were assessed $40,000 for contempt. Charles Oldham, Richards, Curtis, Perkins, and Seay remained in jail until Monday (Labor Day) to protest what they considered a miscarriage of justice.

Conducting midnight raids, handcuffing community leaders, and setting excessively high bail indicated how seriously the white establishment considered the challenge to their system of employment discrimination.

A Lengthy Court Battle Ensues

The legal fight was extensive and expensive, despite the fact that all of the attorneys representing the CORE demonstrators worked pro bono. On September 3, 1963, two days after the nine CORE members were arrested and charged with contempt of court, almost every Negro attorney in the St. Louis metropolitan area was in the courtroom volunteering to represent the demonstrators. Prominent attorneys who joined the defense team included David Grant, legislative research director of the St. Louis Board of Aldermen; Alphonse J. Lynch, head of Lynch and Associates; Margaret Bush Wilson, state president of the Missouri NAACP; Clyde Cahill; Wyvetta Hoover-Young; Billy Jones; Joseph McDuffie; Robert Ratterman, who was white; William Russell; Emanuel Williams; Robert Wilson; and Robert Witherspoon. The trial began in the court of Michael J. Scott before a standing-room-only crowd with the overflow congesting corridors outside the courtroom.

By the end of September, more than one hundred people had been arrested at the bank and booked on charges of trespassing and peace disturbance. During the first week in October, nine others were arrested and charged with violating the injunction. They were immediately taken to Scott's court and charged with contempt. None of the nine had been named in the original restraining order, and none were members of CORE. Attorneys for the defendants filed motions declaring they were not ready for trial but were overruled. The trial commenced and ended in two days. The judge reserved sentencing and remanded the demonstrators to jail.

Jefferson Bank apparently had no intention of eliminating its discriminatory hiring practices. The commission was powerless to effectuate change, even in the face of the bank's stubborn resistance. Highlighting the absurdity of the matter, the commission reported on October 30 that Jefferson Bank had hired five new people—all of them white—since the demonstrations had begun.

Leaders Remanded to Jail

On October 4, the nineteen demonstrators were led to city jail. We were placed in cell blocks with other inmates who were either awaiting trial or had already been convicted of murder, rape, armed robbery, and other assorted crimes. City Welfare Director Chester Stovall pleaded with demonstrators outside the jail to refrain from marching and singing. He feared the activities might incite the hardened criminals within the facility to violent reaction.

Conditions at the city jail were mentally exasperating but physically tolerable—except to James Peake, a paraplegic. He was confined to a wheelchair and forced to occupy a cell too small to accommodate his wheelchair. It was left in the bull pen of the cell block as others assisted him to the toilet or in and out of bed. Peake served fifty-five days under these conditions.

Male CORE members were housed on the third floor, confined to cell blocks for twenty-four prisoners. The cells were approximately six feet by eight feet with a face bowl, toilet commode, and steel bunk beds with thin mattresses—no ventilation, no air conditioning, and no thermostat for regulating heat. Windows were outside the cell areas, and only guards could open and close them. Dust levels equaled those in some coal mines. Insects and rodents were plentiful. The food, served on metal trays in the cells alongside the commode, was bland but edible—not wholesome, not nutritious, simply edible, standard institutional food. There was no room for recreation or exercise. Inmates were permitted to shower once a week. Twenty-four unwashed bodies, adjacent to another cell block with twenty-four additional unwashed bodies, produced a bouquet of fragrances similar to the stench emanating from a pigsty.

Time spent in jail was a mixture of tears, laughter, solace, and reflection. There was much soul-searching and a devoted rededication of commitment to the struggle. Many in the black community reacted with bitter indignation. Hundreds participated in large-scale demonstrations around the city jail to show their deep resentment; the number of marchers at the jail sometimes swelled to more than one thousand.

The Establishment Retaliates

On Friday, October 4, at 4 p.m., demonstrations at the bank resumed, and another fifteen people were arrested. Six juveniles and two adults were released. Seven others were charged with violating the court order.

Louis H. Ford, Ronald Glenn, Benjamin L. Goins, Ian Grand, Taylor Jones, Kenneth Lee, and Roberta Tournour were released on bonds ranging from $1,500 to $5,000. None were members of CORE, nor were they named defendants in the original injunction. Each was gainfully employed and a registered voter. Charged under civil contempt proceedings, their trial started three days later.

On October 8, another large demonstration was held at Jefferson Bank, which resulted in the additional arrests of twenty-one people. Two of those taken into custody were white. The demonstrators were participating in what CORE labeled the "Penny Brigade." Several dozen people with accounts at the bank entered and withdrew small amounts of money without closing their accounts. Potential customers went into the bank asking for change for various denominations of bills. Others requested that pennies be converted into larger coins or bills.

On October 11, CORE's campaign escalated. Demonstrators marched three abreast in the middle of the street, ignoring traffic signals, from Jefferson Bank to police headquarters. They were preceded by detective cars, shunting vehicular traffic aside for the march of several miles.

On Friday, October 12, 250 people demonstrated at the bank. The protest began with pickets circling the bank at the usual 4 p.m. time. Shortly thereafter, fifty marchers went onto the bank property and refused a police order to leave. When placed under arrest, they all lay down and were carried to vans on stretchers. As police removed protestors from the drive-in windows, others quickly took their places on the ground. Officers, finally tired of carrying them away, abandoned the arrests.

Thirty-two protestors were taken into custody, including Alderman Lawrence E. Woodson (D-20th Ward), State Representative Hugh J. White (D-10th District), and myself. The arrests occurred when police filled a large van with demonstrators and attempted to take them to jail. The three of us, along with Richard Anderson, sat on the bumper of the truck and temporarily prevented its departure.

After we were removed by police and arrested, a group of youth lay down in front of the van. Reverend J. W. Nicholson, executive secretary of the Ministers' and Laymen's Association for Equal Opportunity, interceded and persuaded the youth to allow passage of the police vehicles. After CORE permitted the vans to depart, about one hundred protestors followed the arrested demonstrators to police headquarters.

A Cooling-Off Period: A Prescription for Surrender
In the midst of this confusion, the business community began to feel the danger of prolonged demonstrations. In an attempt to reach a settlement, Mayor Tucker met separately on October 12 with bank officials and members of CORE and tried to arrange a truce between the two factions. The mayor's second meeting was with officers of Jefferson Bank. Afterward Tucker announced that he believed significant progress toward a settlement had been reached. The mayor proposed the implementation of his ten-point program, which had been previously developed, and requested a two-week recess of hostilities that he referred to as "a cooling-off" period.

CORE demonstrators at City Jail singing to prisoners, January 18, 1964. Photograph by Renyold Ferguson, MHS Photographs and Prints Collection. © 1964, *St. Louis Post-Dispatch*.

On October 13, Lucien Richards, the acting chairman of CORE, announced the cessation of protest activities and demonstrations for the two-week period. As Richards reported to the media, "We felt we needed time to do some thinking. The point is that on an overall basis we feel we've been very effective. Most banks have attempted to cooperate. Our goal is not to seek revenge or an unconditional surrender at Jefferson Bank."[10] Richards also assured the media and the public that if Jefferson Bank did not hire four Negroes in white-collar positions, the demonstrations would resume with greater intensity than before.

As pressure in the black community grew and the threat of a riot increased, the mayor recommended that two city agencies be created under his stewardship: the St. Louis Council on Human Relations and the St. Louis Commission on Equal Employment Opportunity (CEEO), vehicles for eliminating employment discrimination and resolving the bank dispute.

The CEEO hurriedly convened a session with seven banks, including Jefferson Bank. Its members reached an agreement to extend and implement a fair employment policy. On August 29, the heads of all banks in the city signed the pact, which consisted of ten points:

1) to communicate a written statement of policy on equal employment opportunity to all levels of management within the bank;

2) to publicize their nondiscriminatory policy so that all persons, regardless of race, color, or religion, would know that they would receive equal consideration for employment at the banks;

3) to review the employment records of present employees to determine whether anyone is working below his or her level or is being denied a promotion or transfer because of race;

4) to inform all recruitment sources, both public and private, of the banks' employment policy;

5) to inform schools where Negroes are enrolled of the desire of the banks to employ on the basis of merit and qualification;

6) to request the assistance of the St. Louis Urban League in recruiting qualified Negro employees;

7) to inform the Council on Human Relations and other referral sources in the event that adequate numbers of qualified Negroes are not referred to the banks;

8) to encourage qualified employees to enroll in the American Institute of Banking for additional training that will help prepare them for promotion;

9) to discuss with the Missouri State Division of Employment Security the possibility of establishing training programs for skilled jobs at the banks;

10) to periodically inform the Council on Human Relations of the results of these measures.

The ten-point program was another public relations gimmick. Expecting the two commissions to resolve the problem was ridiculous; they were an integral part of the problem. Both were composed of individuals who owned the corporations responsible for the hiring discrimination. In addition, the two commissions had never conducted an investigation of job discrimination in their several years of existence.

Moreover, the mayor and the two agencies had much gall in attempting to oversee a solution. The city's own record of discriminating was horrendous. Of 12,795 total city employees, 3,333 were Negroes, but 1,000 worked in a single building, the Homer G. Phillips Hospital. Eighty-nine percent (2,932) of Negroes were confined to three departments—streets, hospitals, and parks—that were heavily laden with manual work and offered minimum wages. The other nineteen departments, including large agencies such as public utilities, public safety, and the office of personnel, employed thousands of workers, but only 401 were black. The comptroller, the second most powerful elected official in the city, had a staff of more than 100 workers, only 2 of which were black.

Judge Scott's Pre-Sentence Statement

On October 24 and 25, the court issued its verdict, finding all nineteen protesters guilty. A partial statement, shared by Judge Michael "Dread" Scott before he imposed fines and jail sentences against the nine CORE leaders, read as follows:

> Our Negro citizens are entitled to fair and equal opportunities.
>
> To this end, in our community many things have been done and numerous laws have been passed which are helping to provide those opportunities.
>
> The fact is that all of us in America are members of a minority group. There is no majority group in the United States, and, therefore, adherence to the Constitution and the Bill of Rights becomes doubly important.
>
> This Court takes no sides and no positions with reference to the charges or countercharges with regard to employment policies at the Jefferson Bank and Trust Company. This is a matter for the parties concerned to prove or disprove.
>
> The Court looks with great sorrow and sadness upon this kind of contempt, because it is not in the best interest of the very persons who are involved. Contempt for the law means anarchy and dictatorship.[11]

Scott, who had a checkered history in dealing with Negro defendants before his court, issued such brutal punishment that even many in the power structure were shocked. Scott imposed the following sentences:

First Group:

Marian Oldham	60 days	$500
William L. Clay	270 days	$1,000
Robert Curtis	270 days	$1,000
Rev. Charles Perkins	180 days	$500
Norman Seay	90 days	$500
Charles R. Oldham	90 days	$1,000
Raymond Howard	60 days	$500
Herman Thompson	60 days	$500
Lucien Richards	90 days	$500

On October 25, Scott found the other ten defendants guilty, and they received the following sentences:

Second Group:

Taylor Jones	1 year	$500
Louis Ford	1 year	$500
Ian Grand	180 days	$500
Benjamin Goins	90 days	$500
Roberta Tournour	120 days	$500
Kenneth Lee	60 days	$500
Ronald Glenn	60 days	$500

Third Group:

James Peake	1 year	$500
Michaela Grand	120 days	$500
Danny Pollock	60 days	$500

Each of the convicted defendants was assessed one ninth of the total costs of the trial. Jefferson Bank was refunded $10,000, which it deposited at the beginning of the procedure to ensure that the costs would be covered. After assessing accumulative terms of eight years and two months and fines of $11,000, the court refused to allow defendants to make bond pending the filing of an appeal. The fines were paid by Johnetta Haley, president of the AKA Sorority, which had supported the demonstrators from the beginning.

A joint statement issued by the St. Louis City and County branches of the NAACP called for an impartial legal review of Scott's harsh treatment. There was no discernible logic in the assessing of guilt and dispensing of jail time. Only two of the first nine arrested had entered the bank and sat on the floor. None of the remaining seven took part in blocking the bank doors. The one who entered the bank and sat on the floor blocking the teller cages was sentenced to 90 days and fined $500; two who did not enter the bank and did not block the doors were sentenced to 270 days and fined $1,000 each. Seven of the CORE leaders were convicted of "conspiring with" and "directing" others to violate the restraining order.

Demand That Salary of Alderman Clay Be Discontinued

As an October 25 news article in the *Globe-Democrat* asserted:

> The most severe penalties were assessed against Alderman William L. Clay, 32, and Robert B. Curtis, 27, lawyer and local CORE chairman. Judge Scott sentenced them to 270 days in jail and fined each $1,000."

> A section in the St. Louis city charter discussing qualifications for aldermen specifies that any alderman convicted of malfeasance in office, bribery, or "other corrupt practices or crime" shall thereby forfeit his office.

> The Board of Aldermen, however, has long been the judge of its own members. Criminal contempt is regarded as more serious than a civil offense but something less than an actual crime.[12]

On the same day, the newspaper wrote a scathing editorial advocating my dismissal from the Board of Aldermen:

> Of the nine found guilty yesterday, none is more so, nor his actions more reprehensible, than Alderman William Clay.

> This man, this public official, who has so contemptuously disregarded a court order in a city in which he is an elected leader, has forfeited any claim to public office.

> We urge the body to consider what can be done to cast him from their midst.[13]

But the law was clear and unequivocal, according to the city counselor. He ruled that only the voters of the Twenty-sixth Ward could make the decision—and then only by recall petition—for me to vacate my aldermanic seat.

More embarrassing to my opponents was the fact that I received my salary each day while in confinement. The city counselor ruled that the salary of an alderman was an annual stipend not dependent on attendance.

On November 16, there was another effort to punish me. The *Globe-Democrat* suggested that the Board of Aldermen dock me ten dollars for missing the previous board meetings while in jail. The Board refused to consider the matter, as it routinely excused all aldermen who were absent.

Enacting Civil Rights Legislation from Jail

Who would have believed I was so legislatively adept that I could pass a major civil rights bill in the Board of Aldermen while confined to city jail? But strange things do happen. In absence, I achieved that great distinction. The media had made me a despised elected official in white political circles. The steady drumbeat of adverse publicity and the constant impugning of my motives framed the choice for voters in such stark terms as to blur the realistic analysis of issues. Voters either opposed me and my "gang of hooligans" or supported my radical, intemperate campaign to change long-standing social conditions.

While I was confined for fifty-five days beginning January 15, 1964, the Board of Aldermen considered a bill to establish a fair housing law. The outlook for passage was doubtful. The issue was one of grave concern for white politicians because the vast majority of white voters believed that blacks should be contained in ghetto neighborhoods. White aldermen who personally supported the public accommodations bill feared voter retaliation if they supported open housing.

While other ethnic groups have been able to grow and mature in their ghettoes and then assimilate into the larger society, it has been different for blacks. Many whites surmise that blacks have a manifest destiny to reside there. The justification for this is indicative of a much broader psychology commonly held by a substantial number of white Americans—that most blacks prefer to live together. Assuming that freedom of choice favors slum living is the epitome of cynical derision. It is a bizarre notion implying that blacks have a different lifestyle, their own unique customs, and even special foods and delightful music. Therefore, separation from the rest of society, even if mandatory, is appropriate.

There were sharply divergent views among the citizenry and their elected officials. The head count in the Board of Aldermen revealed that the bill would lose on a tie vote. At a Democratic caucus, Grant summarized the politics confronting a tie vote. He said, in a very calm voice, that on a tie vote the measure loses. Pausing briefly, he facetiously predicted that the courts would soon release me on bail and that my vote would pass the measure.

Alderman Joseph W. B. Clark reminded his fellow Democrats that I was the "best claim artist in town" and said I would take credit for the bill's passage when released. The argument influenced several to change their votes, and the bill passed without the privilege of this "claim artist" voting for it. Grant laughingly told the story many times.

I also made several key political decisions shortly after incarceration. I learned from my friend and business partner Richard Anderson that the candidate for Democratic committeewoman of the Twenty-first Ward, June Dugas, was withdrawing. Apparently, her husband was very unhappy with her involvement in politics. I had encouraged her to file as Goins's running mate. Anderson informed me that his half sister, Jacqueline Butler, lived in the ward and was very active in church and community affairs. Butler agreed to seek the office of committeewoman if her husband was in agreement. Several days later, she and Dugas went to the Board of Election Commissioners, where Butler filed for office and Dugas withdrew her candidacy.

Bail and Jail

On November 1, all nineteen CORE defendants were released on bail after the Missouri Court of Appeals issued writs of habeas corpus, pending review of their case. The court set a hearing for November 12. The appellate court fixed bonds for the defendants at $51,000, ranging from $1,500 to $5,000 individually. Two and a half months later, on January 15, 1964, the appeal was rejected. Lawyers for the defendants requested the simple courtesy of bail while appealing the lower court's decision. The plea was turned down by the State Court of Appeals, the Missouri Supreme Court, and the Federal District Court. Denied bail, the nineteen leaders were sent back to jail while the federal court considered granting a writ of certiorari for their release.

On February 7, 1964, appellants petitioned the U.S. District Court of the Eastern District of Missouri for a writ of habeas corpus. It was denied. The court determined that we had not exhausted state remedies. Subsequently, the U.S. Eighth Circuit Court of Appeals determined in March that we had exhausted all state remedies and released us on bail pending application for a writ of habeas corpus. On the forty-eighth day after the petition for bail had been filed, the order of release came from the three-panel U.S. Court of Appeals, instructing Scott to free us until an appeal to the federal court was heard.

After fifty-five days in jail, Curtis, Seay, Peake, and I sported beards that had been grown in defiance of jail rules. CORE demonstrators had served a combined total of 565 days. Negroes became more determined to oppose the harsh treatment of the demonstrators. The showdown with the power structure at the bank had become the fountainhead in a drive for black political and economic equity. Police-state measures, used by the power structure to penalize CORE protesters, unified the black people. The venom of the banking industry was released with full force. CORE issued a memorandum stating, "The use of the courts for intimidation, the use of political prisoners as hostages, a well-managed public relations campaign in the news media, and, finally, mass arrests, are clear examples of a carefully coordinated display of naked power."[14]

In February 1967, the U.S. Supreme Court refused to review the case, and we were returned to jail. Justice William O. Douglas was the only dissenting vote. For the three years we were at liberty awaiting the decision, the city experienced a period of genuine peace and launched a campaign of real racial progress in employment. After the initial start of the protest and the convictions, the community had undergone a radical change and witnessed a lessening on the part of the white establishment to seek further punishment of the demonstrators.

Some major businesses had either hired blacks or were interviewing them for job slots formerly off-limits. By April 1964, newspaper reports identified 1,300 blacks working at department stores, hospitals, and insurance companies in positions of new job classifications for their race. Eight hundred of them were employed in white-collar jobs and managerial positions in the banking industry alone.

CORE was no longer livid about the harsh sentences and publicly expressed satisfaction with the progress in the hiring of Negroes.

CORE demonstrators demanding equal opportunity employment in front of Jefferson Bank, January 16, 1964. Photograph by Jack January, MHS Photographs and Prints Collection. © 1964, *St. Louis Post-Dispatch*.

The business community was swept up by the new atmosphere of racial harmony. The Urban League was swamped with requests to refer qualified Negroes.

It was a time of authentic cooling off while electrifying results were being ascertained. The warring factions re-evaluated the situation and allowed born-again, reformed businessmen to make amends for past indiscretions. However, there were exceptions to the new mood of peaceful coexistence. Recalcitrant adversaries such as the irascible owners of Jefferson Bank, the obstructionist editor of the *Globe-Democrat*, and the uncontrollable Judge Scott continued their vendetta against CORE. The bank was still alleging that qualified Negroes were unavailable to fill vacancies. The *Globe-Democrat*, in characteristic bombast, leveled attack after attack against the civil rights activists.

Scott, however, ordered us back to jail. This time we were confined in the city's medium-security facility, a much more modern place.

Inmates slept in dormlike rooms with no more than twenty to a section. There was a large cafeteria with decent food and a commissary for toiletries, candies, and other snacks. The facility was clean and air-conditioned, visiting hours were liberal, and there was ample space for conversing. Best of all, it was possible to shower on a daily basis.

Being handcuffed before leaving the courtroom was only the beginning of the humiliation. Being forced into a police patrol wagon with eighteen others and driven like herded cattle to a drab jailhouse cell did not begin to explain the full range of indignities involved in such an escapade. Being fingerprinted, strip-searched, and sprayed with DDT to kill lice and other antisocial pests merely scratched the surface of the emotional degradation that agonized the prisoners.

Judge Assailed over Jailing of Demonstrators

Tension, bitterness, and resentment in black neighborhoods were growing at a greater pace now than when the demonstrators had first gone to jail. Doctors, ministers, laymen, educators, and fraternal members redoubled their efforts in picketing the bank and demanded unconditional release of the prisoners. Some civic and political leaders predicted rioting. More important, they believed it was imminent. The powers-that-be immediately recognized that they had entrusted the fate of the city into the hands of an intractable, irascible judge. City fathers did not relish a confrontational showdown with the black community and attempted to quietly convince Scott of its serious repercussions.

Scott apparently believed the fantasy promulgated by the media that he was the protector of law and order and that respect for the dignity of the court was the highest mission in the land. Contrary to the advice of those who planted the distorted notions in his head, Scott deemed it compulsory to remand the demonstrators to jail. Despite the pleas from city officials, business magnates, religious leaders, and legal authorities, he insisted that the demonstrators serve the remainder of their sentences.

Group of civil rights leaders waits for hearing, March 8, 1967. From left: Danny Pollack, Norman Seay, Michaela Grand, Lucien Richards, Clay, Charles Perkins, Robert Curtis. Photograph by Lou Phillips, MHS Photographs and Prints Collection. ©1967, *St. Louis Post-Dispatch.*

The black community proved to be equally as unyielding as Scott in its insistence on releasing the demonstrators from jail. Within a matter of hours, the community responded swiftly and effectively to Scott's latest intemperate judicial edict. Huge protest demonstrations were initiated around the security facility. Under the leadership of Percy Green and Ivory Perry, nightly demonstrations were staged at the judge's home, where large crowds witnessed the burning of Scott in effigy.

After quiet persuasion and diplomatic pressure from the business community, Scott reluctantly agreed to offer parole, providing that CORE members publicly apologized. But the wording of the apology was so odious that men and women of integrity, honor, and pride could not possibly entertain the thought of uttering it. Judge Scott's demand for a public apology was viewed by CORE as repudiation of the organization's basic principles. The linkage of freedom with apology was reprehensible. No one should have been surprised that those deeply committed to justice and equity would summarily reject such a proposition.

The public statement Scott mandated as a condition of parole demeaned those steeped in Gandhian philosophy. Lying prostrate, pleading forgiveness for demanding equal rights, was too vexing to countenance. Goins was never a part of the civil rights struggle and was probably not familiar with the concept of passive resistance and civil disobedience. At the time of his arrest, he was campaigning for public office. His civil rights altruism was short-lived. It started with his first demonstration at Jefferson Bank and ended twelve months later with his election as committeeman of the Twenty-first Ward. He had never participated in a sit-in, walked a picket line, or challenged discrimination before the bank demonstration. Neither did he engage in any direct-action protest after his release.

Goins, Glenn, and Lee apologized. Glenn and Lee, in their early twenties and the youngest of those arrested, had already served fifty-five days of their sixty-day sentences and so had only five days left. Goins had thirty-five days remaining. Unwittingly, the two youngsters were used to shield a deal that Goins had worked out with Governor Warren E. Hearnes for his release. Those who apologized had their own reasons.

Norman Seay and Lucien Richards served the remainder of their 90-day sentences without apology. So did Roberta Tournour, who completed her 120 days. Curtis and I had already served 105 days of our 270-day sentences and paid $1,150 in court costs. Jones had served 120 days and paid $605 in court costs. We were in no mood to capitulate to the diabolical forces dictating the policies of race relations. We announced that there would be no freedom without dignity. We argued that the judge and the power structure owed the black community an apology for using the instruments of government to foster the continuation of institutionalized racism. Refusing the judge's offer to apologize exacerbated the highly explosive situation. Heightened demonstrations and community pressure forced the judge to reverse his vindictive stance.

Curtis, Jones, and I refused to apologize, refused to crawl out. We strutted out peacock-like, as proud, conquering heroes, our backs erect, our heads unbowed, and our dignity intact.

The Meaning and the Aftermath of the Bank Protest

From the very beginning of the demonstrations, the landscape of the civil rights movement in the city underwent radical change. The parameters of the relationship between the white establishment and the black community were expanded to include young black leaders who had become legitimate spokesmen. The realignment of forces caused a change in the basic metabolism of the body politic. The passive, condescending behavior of established Negro leaders with whom the power structure customarily dealt was replaced by an aggressive, uncompromising—and in many cases angry—new black leadership.

It is doubtful that white and black leaders immediately grasped the impact of this new dynamic. Obviously, the white power structure and the old-guard black political and civil rights leadership did not comprehend the significance of Negroes defying a court order, the willingness of hundreds to be arrested, or the demand to withdraw tax money from Jefferson Bank. They certainly did not understand the resolve of CORE demonstrators to serve their entire sentences rather than apologize.

The political scenery of St. Louis was transformed in cathartic fashion by the bank protest. New black leaders challenged the absurd concept that white elected officials could barter for the expansion of Negro rights better than they could. Black leaders who continued to believe in this perverted logic were faced with serious challenges to their right to represent. The election of blacks to positions of ward committeemen and -women, state representatives, senators, aldermen, and school board members in the following months and years was the direct result of the struggle at Jefferson Bank.

Victory at the Jefferson Bank and Trust Company etched in stone a significant place for black people as participants in determining the future of St. Louis. The dramatic struggle for job equity capped the Negro community's effort to earn respect and influence policy.

The bank altercation served as a pivotal turning point in exposing blacks to the tangible benefits of protest demonstrations. It was responsible, in large measure, for lifting from the shoulders of blacks the burden of their political impotence. No longer were those entrapped in the sordid environs of the ghettoes content to let white outsiders—or self-serving Negro insiders—decide what was good or bad, what was or was not in their best interests.

At the conclusion of the bank protests, four facts were readily apparent to those who impartially critiqued such incidents: 1) the conviction and incarceration of the nineteen Jefferson Bank demonstrators had been a miscarriage of justice; 2) Judge Scott had made a mockery of the due process procedure of the judicial system; 3) vindictive retaliation against the demonstrators by firmly entrenched white political leaders and powerful business interests had intervened and exerted undue pressure to deny CORE defendants a fair trial; and 4) determined black activists risked jobs, careers, and personal liberties to achieve equal employment opportunity for Negro people. Not readily apparent during and after the bank confrontation was the reason for the more militant degree of black activism. It took some time before the power structure realized that its overreaction to the situation had awakened a sleeping giant in the black community. Despite the great odds faced by an economically powerless black community, in the aftermath of the bank protest the generally accepted system of racial apartheid in St. Louis was abolished, and the city's white leadership was forced to deal with a tougher, more community-oriented cadre of independent black leaders.

Excessive use of force encouraged the involvement of Percy Green, Ivory Perry, and other like-minded young persons to resist such high-handed tactics. Young activists with potential honed their leadership skills during the bank protests and joined forces with other youngsters equally committed to vigorously championing the cause of political and economic liberation of Negroes.

The confrontation at Jefferson Bank was the cause for the dramatic changes in the economic and political status of black St. Louisans. The picket lines manned by doctors, lawyers, and other professionals, the boycott of downtown businesses by ministers, the letters advocating more demonstrations by jailed CORE members, the burning of Judge Scott in effigy, and the endless demands for equal job opportunities were signs of new black politics.

Twenty-five years after the conflict ended, Norman Seay appropriately gave credit to the activity at the bank for the great improvement of blacks in St. Louis. He said, "The Jefferson Bank Demonstration has been the most powerful catalytic civil rights action to improve the quality of living for African Americans in the history of St. Louis."[15]

CHAPTER

8

WARREN E. HEARNES: MY CHOICE FOR GOVERNOR

Warren E. Hearnes was the second white knight to enter my life. We met in 1960, a year after my election to the Board of Aldermen. Joe Ames, secretary treasurer of the American Federation of State, County, and Municipal Employees (AFSCME) Local 410, introduced us at a swimming party in his backyard. After a brief but meaningful conversation, I agreed to endorse Hearnes for secretary of state. Ames, a close friend of Jordan Chambers, explained that my decision must not be discussed with anyone until the next day because Hearnes was scheduled to meet that night with Chambers, who was the most influential black politician in Missouri. Ames explained that if word got out that Hearnes had approached me first, it would be impossible for him to get Chambers's support. It was a matter of pride, respect, and deference. Hearnes met with and secured the backing of Chambers and went on to win the nomination and election as one of Missouri's youngest secretaries of state.

Three years later, I had dinner with Ames, Oldham, and Hearnes. Chambers was deceased. The get-together was to discuss the race for governor. Hearnes's chief rival was Hillary Bush, who was sponsored by the powerful Central Trust Bank of Jefferson City. Challenging Democratic Party leaders for the nomination, Hearnes was hailed in the media as a white knight wearing a "white hat." The cabal, consisting of bank owners in alliance with businessmen, party leaders, and some labor leaders, had autocratically imposed its handpicked choices for governors, state assessors, and state treasurers on the party for more than twenty years.

Weighing the pros and cons, and being the rebellious new entrant in politics, I agreed to support the antimachine Hearnes. In return he promised to appoint blacks to the Board of Police Commissioners and the Board of Elections. Their appointments would have been the first for our race. He also committed to placing a black in charge of the state license office in St. Louis and to integrating the Highway Patrol.

A month before our meeting, Bush's campaign manager had rebuffed me twice, insisting I talk to Weathers and Dwyer and work out an arrangement for my endorsement. That was the preferred brush-off when candidates did not want to alienate chief backers. How ludicrous! Weathers and Dwyer were supporting Seay, whom I was challenging for Twenty-sixth Ward committeeman. Why would I endorse a candidate who refused to discuss issues?

My long-range agenda called for gambling on neophytes such as Hearnes and rising to a power convergent with theirs. I believed the forty-one-year-old Hearnes was tough enough to persevere in the trenches of Democratic warfare and young enough to reach real power while still receptive to new ideas. It was obvious that I would not be able to penetrate the inner circle of the established Democratic Party. Party bosses Dwyer, Weathers, Michael Kinney, James McAteer, and others were not going to enthusiastically relinquish power. Therefore I was compelled to seek alliances with other aspiring politicians. Hearnes fell into that category.

Some blacks labeled Hearnes a racist and vigorously opposed his candidacy. They were in no mood to forgive him for prior racial remarks opposing civil rights legislation. They cited his infamous "black bird, white birds sitting on separate tree limbs" speech delivered on the floor of the legislature. It was uttered as he literally scorched the U.S. Supreme Court for its 1954 decision declaring separate but equal educational facilities "inherently unequal." Hearnes argued that separation of races by color was a designation by the Creator.

I refused to heed warnings of Hearnes's capacity to denigrate black folk. I was the only black elected official in St. Louis who naïvely endorsed Hearnes. He put together a tough, well-organized campaign committee that tapped many resources opposed to the Central Trust Bank and Hillary Bush. Hearnes's support group included disillusioned ward leaders who had been ignored when patronage was doled out, dissident young Democrats, good government antimachine forces, and bank officials denied deposits of state funds, and he had the overwhelming support of the St. Louis and Kansas City media.

In an upset, Hearnes defeated the party regulars in the primary. But his vote tally in the black community was dismal. Some black wards defeated him by margins of 4–1. The only black ward that came close to carrying him was the Twenty-sixth Ward, where he lost by 42 votes. In 1960 Governor Dalton carried the Twenty-sixth Ward by 3,131 votes, but Hearnes, his choice for governor, losing it four years later by 42 votes was a net loss of 3,173 votes for the old guard.

In the Twenty-first Ward (approximately 55 percent black), Hearnes carried the lead by 805 votes (Hearnes, 2,713, to Bush, 1,908). Both Goins and the incumbent white committeeman, Morrell, endorsed him. Hearnes lost every black precinct and won every white one. In five all-white precincts, he received in excess of 1,500 votes. Goins received only 136 of the total 2,276 votes cast in the same precincts for his committee position.

Hearnes Reneges on Promises

During the first six months of Hearnes's administration, it seemed that he would erase the image of former Missouri governors from rural areas. He immediately took a progressive stance in regards to promoting civil rights legislation and supporting the passage of public accommodations and equal employment practice laws. Both became laws. He also pumped new life into the State Commission on Human Rights by increasing its budget by $116,000, which allowed for an increased number of employees to process cases.

The rift between Hearnes and me developed shortly after he won the general election. It was obvious that he did not intend to keep his commitments. He privately told his friends that I had double-crossed him. The same tactic was standard procedure whenever politicians intended to renege on campaign promises. In a fashion endemic to the politicians who wear white hats, by inference and innuendo I became a threat to the continued dominance of the Democratic Party. Party leaders claimed that blacks suffered many of their problems because there were too many Clays dictating party positions and not enough of us reaching out to achieve party harmony.

Governor-elect Hearnes announced his list of honorary colonels. It was a tradition established in southern states to bestow honor on major contributors. The conspicuous absence of my name was a personal affront. My ally Callanan, who had contributed more than $300,000 to Hearnes's campaign coffer, was angry. Placing a call to Hearnes, Callanan was convinced that the decision was politically astute. He was told that I was the leader of the notorious civil disobedience bank protest, and it was unwise and indefensible for Hearnes to name a colonel who was a jailbird. Larry bought the story lock, stock, and barrel.

After returning the telephone receiver to its cradle and forgetting that Goins had been named an honorary colonel and had also been arrested, tried, convicted, and sentenced in the same demonstration, Callanan explained to Tyus and me the wisdom of the action. Smiling, I reminded Callanan that my time in jail for disobeying a court order for contempt was less onerous than serving a term in the penitentiary for labor racketeering. Larry, smiling, agreed. He had served a prison term for racketeering and had also been appointed a colonel.

Callanan placed a second call demanding, in his familiar undiplomatic style, a more logical reason for omitting my name. The next day, I received a telegram naming me an honorary colonel for the state of Missouri.

The honeymoon with the governor did not last long, as we witnessed the reversal and evasion of pledges that would have advanced the cause of Negroes. Hearnes refused to appoint a black member to the police board. He appointed a black Republican to the election board who was recommended by a white union leader who opposed Hearnes's candidacy in the primary.

Integration of the Highway Patrol had to wait several years and occurred only after tremendous pressure was applied by black members of the legislature and the federal government. Even then only one Negro was hired during Hearnes's eight years as governor. The governor established a new state license office in an inner-city black neighborhood, appointing a black woman, Beatrice Hatton, as director. Hatton was a forceful, spellbinding stomp speaker who in 1948 had the honor of introducing Harry S. Truman at a campaign rally in St. Louis. Hatton's counterpart, Georgia Buckowitz, a white woman, was named to run the main license office in downtown St. Louis. Although the new ghetto facility handled twice as many license transactions and grossed thousands of dollars more in revenue, the governor paid his black administrator $7,000 a year less than he paid his white one.

Several weeks after the inauguration, Goins and I arranged a meeting with the governor at the state capitol. During the meeting, I asked Hearnes about his promise of employment for me. I had resigned my position with AFSCME to devote all of my time to my bid for ward committeeman. After election, the law required my resignation from the Board of Aldermen. The committeeship was a nonpaying position.

The governor informed me that he had arranged for Goins and me to work for the highway department, inspecting axles at a truck checkpoint about forty miles from St. Louis. The salary was $800 monthly, and coveralls and gloves were provided free by the state. The offer was demeaning and contemptuous. I told him that my educational background and work history prohibited my performing any task not utilizing my qualifications.

Hearnes continued to disrespect the intelligence of black citizens. In 1966 the Jefferson Bank demonstrators had been out of jail for two years on writs of habeas corpus; when the U.S. Supreme Court refused to hear our appeal, we were ordered back to jail. A group of distinguished black leaders approached Hearnes, requesting that he pardon the demonstrators. Empowered by the state constitution to pardon murderers, rapists, armed robbers, and other felons, the governor argued that he did not have power to pardon civil rights demonstrators involved in peaceful protest. Representative Elsa Hill requested that state attorney general Norman Anderson issue a clarifying opinion. Anderson delayed issuing the opinion until the demonstrators had served the balance of their time.

By the 1968 election, blacks had become dissatisfied with Hearnes's leadership. Bob Curtis, one of the Jefferson Bank demonstrators, ran against Hearnes in the Democratic primary as a protest candidate. Spending less than five hundred dollars, the militant civil rights attorney garnered more than 50,000 votes. Without any ward endorsements and less financial support, he won all of the black precincts in Kansas City. In St. Louis, most black officials did not campaign for Hearnes against Curtis.

Hearnes's assault on minority rights continued throughout his term of office. In Washington, D.C., I constantly fought off his efforts to undermine federal legislation enacted to provide benefits for the poor and minorities. The governor demonstrated his lack of compassion for the needy by opposing all Great Society programs established to abolish poverty and to eradicate obstacles to equal opportunity. He fought against legislation to provide equal employment opportunity, legal aid to the poor, Job Corps training for disadvantaged youth, the Human Development Corporation (an umbrella agency for anti-poverty programs), Aid to Dependent Children, and various government self-help programs.

On April 10, 1969, President Richard M. Nixon announced the closing of fifty-nine Job Corps centers. The training facilities were successful educational programs designed to teach vocational skills to impoverished youth. One school that closed was the St. Louis facility for young women. In a series of meetings, I convinced the Department of Labor to authorize a new $3.5 million Job Corps center in my congressional district. Funds were approved by Congress, and a site selection committee was appointed. Hearnes opposed the center and, on three separate occasions, vetoed the sites, returning millions of dollars to the federal government.

In 1970 Congress was considering the Family Assistance Plan, which included a training program paying a cash bonus of $30 per month for each enrollee, $750 in annual food stamp assistance, and provisions for day-care centers that would have made it possible for welfare mothers to work. Hearnes was a leader in opposition to the legislation.

Governor Warren E. Hearnes in 1968.

In the midst of the great civil rights struggle to end legal seg-regation as public policy in the country and the tremendous resistance from recalcitrant southern governors to extend equal rights to Negroes, Hearnes joined the Southern Governors' Conference. The organiza-tion was the epicenter of racial bigotry and a chief advocate of opposi-tion to laws and court orders to desegregate society. It provided an official forum for ideological zealots to espouse their warped concepts of "justice for all" in a democracy. They adamantly opposed the exten-sion of legal rights to black citizens. In joining the conference, Missouri shared the ignoble distinction of carousing with Mississippi, South Carolina, North Carolina, Georgia, Arkansas, Louisiana, and Virginia—states whose policies on behalf of the poor and black people were notoriously negligent.

Numerous acts defined the governor as unsympathetic to Negroes' right to participate in meaningful elective office. In 1972 he was involved in behind-the-scenes maneuvering to destroy a congressional district where it was possible to elect an African American. He was party to masterminding a proposal to divide the black population into three congressional districts. With the help of Margaret B. Wilson and the NAACP national office, I filed a lawsuit, and the courts ruled in favor of preventing the diminution of minority voting rights.

Hearnes's true conservative color was revealed when Republican vice president Spiro Agnew was indicted on criminal charges of extortion and corruption. Hearnes, a Democrat, accepted the role of national co-chairman of Agnew's legal defense fund.

In 1974, Hearnes announced his candidacy for U.S. senator. Adversely affecting the outcome of the election was a grand jury investigation into Hearnes's financial affairs. The federal government had embarked on what I considered a witch hunt. I was receiving similar treatment at the hands of the government. I knew the anguish he suffered in confronting the vast array of power available to his adversary, the U.S. government.

The 1976 Democratic primary for the U.S. Senate was a three-way race between Representatives James Symington, Jerry Litton, and Hearnes. Litton, an eight-year member of the House, won the election, but he, his wife, and his two children were killed on election night in an airplane crash. Subsequently, Hearnes was picked by the State Democratic Committee over State Treasurer James I. Spainhower to replace Litton as the Democratic candidate. He was defeated in the general election by Republican John Danforth. Many elected Democratic officials believed that, because of the government persecution, Spainhower would have been a much stronger candidate than Hearnes.

Hearnes was a victim of prosecutorial overzealousness. He found his public life hauled before a grand jury on trumped-up, politically motivated charges and became the focus of unreasonable, unscrupulous, and unfavorable newspaper attacks. A grand jury of his peers (too late to salvage his campaign) found insufficient evidence to issue an indictment.

In 1978 Hearnes ran unsuccessfully for state auditor. He was disappointed, bitter, and heartbroken when the general election returns were posted. He lost to his Republican rival, James F. Antonio, by 58,577 votes. Hearnes announced that he would not seek public office again. The ex–army officer, ex–state representative, ex–secretary of state, and ex-governor took a job as director of the Legal Services program in Sikeston, Missouri. How ironic—as governor, he had opposed all anti-poverty programs, even vetoing the Legal Services program. He opposed the government providing legal assistance to the poor and, on several occasions, vetoed Missouri's participation in the program. Unemployed officials and government-sponsored employment programs make strange bedfellows.

Racial Politics of White Democrats

Hearnes was not the originator or the architect of the policy adopted by Democrats that effectively ostracized Negroes from the party's inner councils. His attitude differed very little from that of other Democratic leaders, nationally and locally, in the perception of blacks in politics. In years past, Negro political pioneers had suffered the same disappointments and rejections from both parties as black leaders did in the last half of the twentieth century.

If there was a new black politics, the old, traditional white politicians were seemingly indifferent to its meaning. White Democrats, like Republicans who had received the majority of black votes for almost one hundred years, refused to heed the admonitions voiced by avant-garde black leaders. Democrats, too, devised numerous tactics to avoid recognizing and respecting the legitimate concerns of African Americans. They established rules and procedures for ignoring, opposing, and undermining the pursuit of African Americans for economic and political justice.

The strategy for effectively continuing the exploitation of black voters encompasses 1) the belief that African Americans have no alternative, since Republicans are not serious about soliciting their votes; 2) the notion that the safe way to maintain black support is to avoid racial controversy—refuse to discuss or speak out against racial injustice and leave that responsibility to black elected officials; 3) the illusion of caring for black people while advocating the repeal of minority rights; 4) the support of ceremonial resolutions honoring black heroes while also voting to reduce funding for education and Head Start and voting against affirmative action; and 5) the attack on black causes and black leaders whenever it benefits white Democrats in their bid for election.

The clever stratagem even provided a plausible explanation of Democratic candidates going down in defeat. Instead of admitting that the majority of white voters had rejected them, they vociferously proclaimed that the turnout in black precincts had been extremely low.

A. J. CERVANTES: GIFTED, INNOVATIVE POLITICIAN

Alphonse J. Cervantes was the most colorful political knight I ever was privileged to meet. His flair, style, humor, and flamboyant exploits compare in many aspects to those of New York's Fiorello LaGuardia, Detroit's Coleman Young, and Chicago's Richard Daley. Cervantes was a builder of organizations, businesses, cities, recreational resorts, and political alliances. He was an insurance broker, real-estate developer, and taxicab owner. He had a gift for innovative ideas. His effervescent personality dominated the St. Louis political scene during the twenty years of his reign. My friend Mickey McTague once remarked that Cervantes "breezed upon the field of politics with gusto and eternal optimism, amidst a flurry of bitter opponents and skeptics." His business partner, Joyce Littlefield, said Cervantes "had no time for grudges or vindictiveness. He could laugh at himself."

Cervantes Becomes Mayor

In the 1965 Democratic primary for mayor, with major support from the black community, Cervantes defeated three-term mayor Raymond R. Tucker. During the campaign, the *Globe-Democrat* pointed out to its readers why Cervantes should be defeated. The newspaper described his three biggest supporters as reprehensible characters. The paper wrote in an editorial:

> A most frightening aspect of Mr. Cervantes's candidacy is the caliber of unsavory backers. Among such choice characters are John L. "Doc" Lawler, Second Ward committeeman, boss of the Steamfitters' union, and henchman of Larry Callanan, who served a prison term for labor racketeering. Another is ex-Alderman William L. Clay, Twenty-sixth Ward committeeman and rabble-rouser, who went to jail as a result of his activities in the wretched Jefferson bank demonstrations.[16]

Louis Buckowitz, committeeman of the Tenth Ward, Lawler, and I provided the margin of victory for Cervantes. The plurality in my ward was twice what Lawler produced and two and a half times that of Buckowitz.

Several factors figured prominently in Cervantes' ability to beat the incumbent mayor. The influx of blacks immigrating from southern states increased the minority population to 40 percent, and many of them were in no frame of mind to forgive Tucker for destroying their homes in the Mill Creek area. The program described as "Negro Removal" was considered an unconscionable transgression on the property rights of black home owners. However, in terms of political assessment, it greatly expanded the political base of our people. The forced exodus from the Mill Creek area pressured more whites to move to the suburbs, making a realignment of political power only a matter of time.

Before then, 90 percent of all blacks were neatly concentrated into four compact and contiguous political wards. After the city took their property by imminent domain and forced them out, they were now the predominant voters in seven wards (Fourth, Fifth, Eighteenth, Nineteenth, Twentieth, Twenty-second, and Twenty-sixth). They constituted from 25 to 45 percent of the voters in the Seventh, Sixteenth, Seventeenth, Twenty-first, Twenty-seventh, and Twenty-eighth wards. The 100,000 Negroes registered to vote were a force to be reckoned with.

In the 1965 Democratic primary, Tucker lost to Cervantes by 14,442 votes. In the ten black wards—even though Tucker had the endorsements of four black committeemen of delivery wards—he was trounced at the polls. Overall, Cervantes compiled a 9,000-vote majority in the black areas. Troupe of the Fifth Ward gave him a 1,900-vote plurality; Goins in the Twenty-first Ward delivered a 1,200-vote plurality; Tyus of the Twentieth Ward added another 1,900-vote plurality; and my ward gave him the largest plurality: 2,888 votes.

Weathers and Dwyer, who endorsed the mayor, provided him 447- and 262-vote pluralities, respectively. Rump groups in their wards, headed by Hugh White and Arthur Kennedy, opposed them. Once again the hospital issue dominated an election, resulting in the chastisement of a white politician who did not understand the deep reverence blacks held for the institution.

A year before Mayor Tucker was preparing to seek re-election in 1964, rumors surfaced that he planned to close Homer G. Phillips Hospital (HGP). The mayor denied having suppressed a survey report praising Phillips and criticizing the white-run city hospital. His denial was not well received because, just prior to the accusation, Tucker's director of health and hospitals forced HGP to abandon a privately financed program for granting internships. The move reduced the number of interns at HGP from several dozen to one. The handwriting was on the wall. The mayor's press releases denying closure were read with jaundiced eyes.

Politicians continued to misread the mood of black voters as it related to the value and respect they held for HGP. As a result, they consistently paid a high price for the mistake. The drumbeat for saving the hospital was deafening and staccato-like. Those who marched to a different drummer were out of step and eventually out of office.

The community was on the warpath. Tucker's most trusted black confidants could not quell the uprising: In only a few days more than 50,000 signatures were collected in petitions opposing the effort to close HGP. When the mayor was presented with the signatures, he gave no assurance of keeping the hospital open. His noncommittal position convinced black voters that Tucker's re-election would mean closing the facility.

Cervantes boisterously gave assurance to keep HGP open and reaped the benefits from a community desperately in need of health care.

Cervantes and Black Leaders
My relationship with Cervantes was warm and cordial but at times combative and confrontational. We were friends in the sense that we respected and appreciated each other and perhaps shared a likeness in our egotistical, stubborn ways. Cervantes initiated many programs beneficial to my constituents. The bond that tied us together involved his

sincere effort to advance the cause of Negroes despite opposition from powerful forces in city politics. Sometimes, however, we disagreed about what was in the best interests of the black community.

Cervantes' administration had positive attributes. He was the first mayor to give the blacks that he appointed the authority to run their programs and control their budgets. Many whom he appointed were personally brought into his camp by Tyus and me. They did not know

Mayor Alphonse Cervantes and Clay, undated.

him and had no reason to support his candidacy. The majority of black elected officials supported his opponent. In each of the wards where this happened, we organized and supervised independent groups that either beat the regular organizations or seriously neutralized their ability to deliver overwhelming margins.

Every politician in town except Cervantes recognized the role I played in his election. The news media showered me with credit for an impressive effort in his victory. Typical of the acknowledgment was an editorial appearing in the *St. Louis Defender*:

> In a magnificent display of raw power, Bill Clay, the Democratic committeeman of the Twenty-sixth Ward, emerged from last Tuesday's primary election as the number one delivery politician in the city of St. Louis.

> Committeeman William (Bill) Clay of the Twenty-sixth [Ward] who became the target of the *Globe-Democrat*, *Post-Dispatch*, and the *Argus*, proved his ability to deliver in a crucial election. His ward organization gave A. J. Cervantes the biggest majority of any ward in the city of St. Louis.

> The prowess of the organization built by Clay in the Twenty-sixth Ward brings back to memory the heyday of the late Jordan W. Chambers.[17]

Shortly after winning the mayoral contest, Cervantes hailed his victory as an upset and a mandate. An upset, yes—he had upset the favorite candidate who had the support of both major newspapers, all television and radio stations, the leading black weekly newspaper, and a majority of the ward organizations. A mandate, no—it was the efficiency of producing votes by the few supporting organizations that provided the victory. We supplied the muscle. Our people were not enamored with Cervantes but were motivated more by resentment of Tucker. We got them to the polls.

Mayor Cervantes announced in 1966 that Anthony Sansone, his campaign manager who had recently been appointed committeeman of the Twenty-fifth Ward, would seek the chairmanship of the Democratic Central Committee. He then proceeded to twist arms in soliciting votes for his choice. The strong-arm tactic alienated some of his chief supporters. Louis Buckowitz was appeased by his appointment to the mayor's cabinet and supported Sansone. Lawler, Goins, and I had no intention of surrendering our power. We objectively analyzed the situation and concluded that it would be detrimental to the party. Fearful that too much power would be vested in the mayor, some committeemen drafted Lawler to challenge Sansone.

The battle was necessary to preserve party integrity. Friends opposed friends, and, in some cases, relatives disagreed with relatives. The outcome was close. Twelve black committeemen and -women, including Goins and me, supported Lawler, who won by one vote. Lawler ran only to stop the mayor's power grab. Eight months later, he resigned and the Central Committee elected a compromise candidate other than Sansone.

Clay Calls for Economic Summit

Four months after Cervantes was sworn in as mayor, I wrote him a letter asking for a summit conference to discuss the problem of unequal job opportunities for Negroes. I asked the mayor to institute "immediate measures" to deal with the severe joblessness. The record was clear. Only 3.6 percent of the Negro labor force were working as professionals or technicians. There was one white doctor for every 691 white persons in the metropolitan area, but only one doctor for every 3,750 Negro persons, and one white dentist for every 1,322 white persons, but only one Negro dentist for every 9,677 Negro persons. There was also one white policeman for every 277 white persons in the city of St. Louis, but only one black policeman for every 1,923 Negro persons. I asserted that the shortage was because Negro professionals, unable to find employment in St. Louis, had moved on to other cities.

The economic statistics cited were startling. The 1960 U.S. Census revealed that 65 percent of all Negroes in St. Louis had earnings of less than $4,000. One of every three Negro families had earnings of less than $2,000. It showed that 19.8 percent of white males earned $5,000 to $6,000, while only 11.4 percent of Negro males earned the same; 12.9 percent of white males earned $7,000 to $9,999, while only 1.6 percent of Negro males earned the same. Most amazing was the fact that only 414 Negro males in St. Louis earned more than $10,000 in 1959, compared to 40,247 white males.

At a meeting of fifty Negro leaders summoned by Cervantes to the mayor's office, I was elected chairman of a nine-member committee to seek improvement of economic conditions for Negroes. The *Globe-Democrat* issued its expected tirade against my selection. In an August 28, 1965, editorial, it wrote, "Clay has gone about building a shoddy political base by mixing gutter politics with sidewalk demagogy." It further stated that "Clay's most notable attempt at securing jobs produced a contempt of court conviction, a $1,000 fine, and 270 days in jail." The following week, on September 3, the newspaper wrote another editorial, stating:

> The mayor began the whole endeavor on the wrong foot by inviting fifty-three Negroes, excluding business and labor leaders who must provide the training programs and the entrance to apprenticeship. [A] nine-member committee . . . compounded the mayor's folly by naming the racially incendiary William L. Clay as chairman.
>
> Clay is not only anathema to the business community; he is a divisive element in the Negro community—for instance, in the NAACP.[18]

In accepting the responsibility of chairman, I stated, "It is agreed that many solutions to unemployment call for the use of federal administrative powers, but local responsibility and action cannot be dismissed. The Negro is not the only victim of unemployment. The Negro is afflicted and crippled, but the total community is affected." I went on to outline a program for a Minority Affairs Department equipped with staff to accomplish results in at least eight areas, including establishment of a food and clothing bank, the elimination of all vestiges of discrimination in employment, and negotiation with labor leaders and businessmen to include Negroes in the skilled labor force. In spite of the opposition, the committee continued to function as a sounding board for the improvement of job opportunities, and the business and industrial community continued to hire Negroes in professional and white-collar positions.

Bad Guys Also Wear White Hats

The shoddy treatment afforded my older brother, Irving, was a contentious issue between Cervantes and me. Irv was a career city employee in the recreation department; his field of pursuit spanned twenty-one years as a merit system employee who never leaned on politicians for promotion or other personal favors.

Jim Heath, the commissioner of recreation, took a job in upstate New York, leaving the position of commissioner vacant. My brother, who was Heath's second in command, passed the competitive examination and finished number one on the civil service list to fill the vacancy. Under normal circumstances there would be no doubt about his elevation to commissioner. But these were not normal times.

Louis Buckowitz, as the director of parks, recreation, and forestry, was the appointing authority for the job. His negative attitude toward my brother might have been in retaliation for the role I played in defeating his wife during the 1959 election for the school board. But the incident involving my brother only fortified his reputation as an individual harboring racially intolerant habits.

Cervantes claimed he had met several times with Buckowitz but could not persuade him to change his mind. That scenario was unlikely in view of the fact that the director served at the pleasure of the mayor. The city charter clearly states that no reason is necessary to replace a cabinet member. In this instance, everybody would have understood replacing an insubordinate appointee. Only the will and wisdom of Cervantes stood between my brother's elevation and Buckowitz's stringent and adamant position. My brother remained number one on the register, and the position of commissioner remained unfilled. Buckowitz refused to appoint him. Cervantes refused to bite the bullet. I refused to capitulate.

More than a year after Cervantes' election as mayor, my brother was still number one on the civil service list to fill the vacancy of commissioner of recreation. Buckowitz was still adamant; Cervantes was still coy.

Mayor A. J. Cervantes, undated.

But a little levity sometimes has a way of resolving the most complex problems. One evening, while several of my allies were dining at a popular hangout for elected officials, Buckowitz approached the group, inquiring about our health. As the five of us began to eat our salads, Callanan, in a loud voice, told Buckowitz to get his carcass away from the table. Buckowitz irritated Callanan even more when he engaged in his routine verbiage about unqualified "nigras." Callanan lost his temper, and Buckowitz almost lost his life. Grabbing him by the throat, and throwing him upon the table (food and drinks splattering everywhere), Callanan choked a commitment to appoint Irving Clay out of "little Buckowitz."

For once in his life, Buckowitz honored an agreement. The next day, my brother was named to the position of commissioner of recreation. To my knowledge, that was the first time in Irv's career that political "muscle" was used to assist his upward advancement on the civil service ladder.

Poelker Defeats Cervantes

Comptroller John H. Poelker defeated Cervantes in the 1973 Democratic primary by a margin of 5,601 votes (Poelker, 48,941, to Cervantes, 43,340). In Cervantes' eight years in office he helmed three important projects. The first was the impressive convention center that he led the fight to build. The other two were related to his Hispanic heritage—the Spanish Pavilion and the *Santa Maria* featured at the 1964 New York World's Fair. Both the pavilion, hailed as the "gem of the fair," and the replica of Christopher Columbus's boat were deemed natural tourist attractions for the city. Although both turned out to be financial failures, Cervantes was not a failure.

He was able to awake a sleeping giant in his program to rebuild the downtown area, which generated the impetus for revitalizing the rest of the city. For years the city reaped the fruits of the building boom that started during his first administration. But the mayor also had a kind of courage other elected officials did not demonstrate. In 1971, when the debate about establishing a day honoring the assassinated Dr.

Martin Luther King Jr. was opposed by a majority of whites, Cervantes ignored their questionable reasoning. He led the fight and signed the bill making St. Louis one of the first cities to observe Dr. King's birthday as a legal holiday. Cervantes was also successful at running a city in such a way as to make the total community, including the common folk, feel a part of government. He gave the average person a sense of belonging. His office was open to any citizen who had an idea or a complaint, or just wanted to say hello.

CHAPTER

10

BARRIERS OVERCOME IN ELECTING A BLACK
U.S. CONGRESSMAN AND A BLACK CITYWIDE OFFICIAL

I n 1967 a coalition of thirteen black legislators, fifty-seven Republicans, and nine white Democrats from the rural area voted to establish a district that would make it possible for a Negro in the St. Louis area to be elected to Congress. The unusual coalition of inner-city blacks, rural whites, and suburban Republicans held strong to protect its self-interests. The newly drawn congressional districts provided representation in the cotton-driven, agricultural economy of the "Bootheel" section of the southeastern part of the state, maintained a substantial number of Republican voters in the suburban area of St. Louis County, and created a black-majority district located mostly in the city of St. Louis.

Democrats (who controlled both houses of the legislature) and Governor Hearnes, a Democrat, opposed the redistricting proposal. They filed a lawsuit supporting a plan to place the black population in three separate districts. However, the U.S. Supreme Court thwarted the will of the Democrats and ruled that the district drawn by the legislature was legal. The court ordered it to be the boundaries for the 1968 election.

Rejection of the Democrats' scheme put a temporary end to the racial numbers game in redistricting that had been played by both parties since the turn of the century. It was tradition every ten years for the legislature to create three congressional districts in the St. Louis metropolitan area, minimizing the Negro population in each.

According to the Bureau of the Census, the newly created district was 54.3 percent black, 45.3 percent white, and 0.4 percent others. The median educational attainment was 10.7 years. (The state average was 11.8.) The median income was $8,485, which was $423 lower than the state average. The median income for blacks was $6,930. The new district consisted of all wards in the city north of Forest Park, Mill Creek

Valley in the city's midtown, as well as Washington and St. Ferdinand townships in the county. Most of the 250,000 black city residents were in the district.

In early 1968, while driving to the office, I heard on the car radio that the congressional incumbent of twenty-two years, Frank Karsten, would not seek re-election in the newly drawn district. I immediately placed a call to my wife and then to Leroy Tyus. Both expressed their support for my candidacy, and the campaign was launched. Tyus was a quiet, effective politician who was more comfortable in the back room making deals than he was out front issuing statements. He was committeeman of the largest delivery ward in the city.

I made several dozen calls to the media and key supporters such as Pearlie Evans, Gwen Giles, Ann Voss, Committeeman Franklin Payne, Nat Rivers, Frank Mitchell Sr. (publisher of the *Argus*), and Sonny Hawkins of the *Defender*. Their commitment threw me into the lead for the position. Within hours my group had locked up support from the most important sources in the black community. I owned a printing press, and by nightfall thousands of handbills on the street declared, "Bill Clay is ready—are you?"

The news media announced other potential candidates, including six whites. Four were considered major candidates (two committeemen, a state representative, and a state senator). Milton Carpenter was considered the front-runner and possessed an excellent resume: He was former city comptroller, state auditor, and state treasurer.

Although I was on the Pipefitters' payroll as educational coordinator and Frank Karsten was a product of the union, I felt compelled nevertheless to make this decision independent of union leaders Larry Callanan and John Lawler. I did not want to chance anyone talking me out of it. In a rush to claim the rail position in the congressional race, I made the decision to run without consulting them. Lawler was already being quoted on the radio as saying that Karsten rushed his decision and that the labor leaders would go to Washington, D.C., to try to convince him to change his mind.

For the previous five years, Tyus and I had developed a close relationship with the Pipefitters' union, spending many hours plotting campaigns. My unilateral decision to file was not viewed as a coalition effort, but as a Bill Clay project. Callanan was not opposed since Karsten refused to reconsider his decision. But he was neither impressed nor enthusiastic. I knew that he did not want to deny me, his strongest political ally, the opportunity of going to Congress. The position would strengthen the alliance between the union and the black community and considerably increase its influence.

Callanan called a meeting the next morning with Tyus, Webbe, Lawler, and me. He opened the meeting by assessing the chaotic condition caused by the unexpected retirement of Karsten. Predicting that at least five other Negroes would file, he cast doubt on the chances of anyone being elected in such a free-for-all. Then, characterizing Carpenter (who had not filed) as the possible winner, he admitted that there was no love between them. He also said he had no reason to oppose him. Having spent the previous night mulling over the situation, he decided the best course for him was to take a position of neutrality. At that point, he reached into his desk drawer and pulled out a check already made out to the Clay for Congress Committee.

Handing me the check in the amount of five thousand dollars, he said, "I am not supporting anybody in this race, and this is positively all the money you will receive."

True to Callanan's assertion, there was a flurry of activity among politicians considering the replacement of Karsten. Two other blacks announced that they would run: Joseph Clark, a city alderman, and Ernest Calloway, the president of the NAACP and a Teamster official. A third black, James Troupe, a committeeman, state representative, and official of the steelworkers' union, had already filed for the position before the court approved the black-majority district. Representatives Ray Howard and Fred Williams also indicated an interest.

Consensus on a Black Candidate Impossible to Reach

To reach consensus on a black candidate, a meeting was arranged early in the campaign at a swank hotel. In attendance were ministers, newspaper publishers, professionals, community activists, businessmen, and politicians. Each aspirant was convinced of his right to seek the office and, based on the contribution of each to the struggle for black advancement, expected the support of the grassroots community. Three hours of feinting, sparring, and jabbing resulted in no decisive knockouts. All four candidates insisted on remaining in the race. The session concluded with an agreement that the group would reconvene in two months. In the interval, endorsements secured by the candidates would be weighed and a decision reached at the next meeting.

Troupe and I, as committeemen, had our own ward endorsements. Calloway had the support of Committeeman Weathers. Clark did not have the endorsement of his committeeman, Payne. For five weeks the tempo of the drama increased as politicians tried to solidify their support. McNeal, who had announced his retirement from the state senate, was approached about being a consensus candidate. He refused, based on his health status and his age of sixty-five years. He stated that the power in the U.S. Congress was predicated on seniority, and he was too old to arrive in Congress as a freshman. That logic was already tilting the scales in my favor. I was thirty-seven years of age, Calloway was fifty-nine, Troupe was fifty-eight, and Clark was fifty-two.

At the second meeting, I emerged as the choice in most categories. I had been endorsed by four of the seven black wards (by Payne, Tyus, Goldston of the Nineteenth Ward, and my own). I also had the unconditional support of white committeeman Matt O'Neil of the Twenty-second Ward and the tacit support of committeemen Doc Lawler of the Second Ward and James Barnes of the Third Ward. Most black pastors announced their support for my candidacy. A majority of the community activists were already working on my campaign. Equally as important, forty-two candidates who were seeking to unseat incumbents in local races endorsed me. Two unions, Local 5 of the Seafarers' International Union and Local 160 of the Leather and Luggage Workers' Union, came out for me. Five of the seven Negro weekly newspapers— the *Argus*, the *Defender*, the *People's Guide*, the *Crusader*, and the *Mirror*—were supporting me. The *Argus* wrote a few weeks later, "The

St. Louis Argus recommends William Bill Clay for Congress because his portfolio contains outstanding credentials. . . . [He] is a civil rights and political activist. He organized and led the fight for racial justice in this city when others thought there was no hope."[19]

Four of the major white contenders, including Ed Roach, committeeman of the First Ward, withdrew on the same day after meeting with leaders of the Democratic Party. Each endorsed Carpenter. The strategy assured that Carpenter would be the only viable white candidate in the race. His one serious drawback in the black and liberal white community was that he was the owner of a Howard Johnson restaurant in the center of a black community and did not allow blacks to enter the premises. It was the same restaurant where Ray Howard and I had been arrested for attempting to be served. The Carpenter family went to court seeking an injunction to stop peaceful demonstrations to change the restaurant's discriminatory policy. This incident further infuriated Negroes, who were excited about voting against him.

In July, Weathers issued a statement saying:

When there were seven whites and four Negroes in the race, any one of [the Negroes] had a good chance. But on June 14, when the field narrowed to but one serious white candidate, the whole picture changed. The new picture revealed a massive thrust of white-power politics. This can only be met now by a greater thrust of massive black-power politics. We must now join forces to defeat this conspiracy with total black support for but one of ours.[20]

After the consolidation of white elected officials behind Carpenter, an effort was initiated to do the same in the Negro community. Weathers, who was supporting Calloway, held a series of meetings in his home in an effort to reach a consensus candidate and bring the community together.

Subsequently, Clark withdrew but refused to endorse any candidate. Troupe withdrew, throwing his support to me, but it was too late to remove his name from the voting machine. Calloway remained in the race although it was apparent his campaign had not caught fire. I stated that "if Calloway were really interested in unity and in the political progress of the Negro community, he would withdraw from the race even if it meant losing his job with the Teamsters' union."

Gwen Giles, my campaign manager, was a very forceful, articulate spokesperson. She took a public swipe at Calloway for trying to undermine my campaign, saying, "A conspiracy is afoot in this community to keep Bill Clay from getting elected to Congress. Calloway and [Harold] Gibbons, head of the Teamsters, are involved in the conspiracy to defeat a Negro." She further stated that "Gibbons and Calloway are in error when they say that Carpenter would be better for this community than Clay." Our views differed as to what were the critical issues facing the district. Calloway favored strict gun-control laws to combat the rise in violent crimes. He said that the first step in ending poverty was to provide decent jobs. Carpenter based his campaign on law and order. He advocated "taking the shackles off of the police and putting them on the violators." My platform called for a $2-an-hour state and federal minimum wage, a thirty-five-hour workweek, and full Social Security at sixty years of age.

Calloway won a backhanded endorsement from the *Post-Dispatch*. In an editorial that taxed the intellect of its readers, the newspaper stated in summary that Negroes had a right to be represented in Congress and had the right to decide for themselves who should represent them—and the majority seemed to want Bill Clay to be their representative. But then the editorial proclaimed, "Ernest Calloway is highly respected in St. Louis, yet the practical fact is that he is running second to Mr. Clay in Negro ward support. Every one of the Negro committeemen is supporting the younger Bill Clay. Although our own choice would be Mr. Calloway, we respect the right of the Negro community to choose for itself."[21]

Goins Files for Sheriff

When it looked as if the black community was coalescing around one candidate and developing total energy to elect its first African American congressman, Goins announced his support of Calloway and declared his candidacy for sheriff. Weathers and other black elected officials regarded the maneuver as a plot to muddy the waters and assure the loss of the congressional seat for a black. The five black ward committeemen were aware of his previous conduct in similar situations. Several years prior, Goins had solicited and received from them a commitment to run for the office of clerk of criminal corrections. After two weeks, he was persuaded by white politicians not to seek the position. In exchange, his ward gained three low-paying jobs in the clerk's office. On another occasion, he bolted ranks with black leaders by refusing to support a black for the office of license collector. In that situation, he was promised the position of chief deputy in the same office in return for his support of the white candidate, John O'Toole. O'Toole lost the election, and the job for Goins never materialized.

Goins, without consulting other black politicians and without any pledged community support, filed for sheriff. To indicate that his candidacy had substantial backing, he alleged support from five unnamed white ward leaders. They remained unnamed even after he filed and during the campaign.

His precipitous act prompted black committeemen Weathers, Tyus, Troupe, and Payne and I to issue a sharply worded press release attacking his ill-advised candidacy. In part, the statement read:

> Our prior decision to unanimously support a Negro for a citywide office was aborted by [Goins's] action. Goins's selfish, premature, divisive act may have seriously hampered the chances of a Negro winning citywide office. Consideration by us of several highly qualified Negroes . . . was callously disregarded by Mr. Goins. His personal ambitions place the hope of Negro unity in a precarious position.[22]

Several weeks before the election, the black committeemen reluctantly hammered out an agreement to support Goins and me. It eliminated the rift that possibly could have divided the Negro vote and allowed Carpenter to win.

A Threatening Black Candidate

A lesser candidate who had no chance of shaping the outcome of the election was Elsa Hill, a black state representative. I was directly responsible for her election to the state legislature. She was my candidate from the Twenty-sixth Ward. Her four-year tenure of office was quite stormy for me and members of the Twenty-sixth Ward organization. She was a high-strung, emotional, and sometimes abrasive individual. However sincere she was in her efforts to represent constituents of the district, it oftentimes appeared otherwise.

I personally had no real problems with the manner in which she handled her legislative duties. But many within the organization disagreed with her. Under pressure to replace her in the legislature, I attempted unsuccessfully to make her aware of the situation. Apparently, our conversations reaped little reward.

To keep peace in the group and to allow her to save face, I offered her a job at city hall that paid more than that of state representative. She rejected the offer and threatened to support my opponent for Congress if I did not endorse her for re-election.

I decided to support Nathaniel Rivers, one of the most trusted and faithful precinct captains in the organization, against her. Rivers defeated her by a vote of 1,985 to 709. It was the beginning of an extended confrontation with Hill. She not only ran for re-election but endorsed my opponent. Her central theme was that I held the title of the city's "biggest Uncle Tom." One distributed pamphlet said, "Clay instructed [Hill] to vote in the Missouri House for a congressional redistricting plan that would have reduced chances of electing a Negro to Congress in the First District."[23]

Her bitterness did not end with my victory for Congress. She filed a lawsuit challenging the election and also went to Congress opposing my seating. In the five succeeding elections, Hill filed against me for Congress. She usually got between 5 and 10 percent of the vote. In the 1976 primary, I received 29,094 votes to her 574. Her campaigns were never taken seriously by anyone except my opponents, although the media usually saw fit to quote her diatribes.

Twenty-sixth Ward elected officials, 1970. From left: State Representative Nathaniel Rivers, Alderman C. B. Broussard, Committeewoman Ida L. Harris, and Committeeman Clay.

Contest between Two Unions

Weeks after Callanan's declaration of neutrality, Webbe devised a plan to nudge him into opening up the purse strings of the union's Political Action Committee (PAC). If it worked, I would be unbeatable. I was the candidate with the best name recognition, the most support among black voters, and the best organizational skills. To exploit these assets to their fullest, adequate finances were needed.

Callanan was a proud person with a big ego. His pride had been fractured by my independent action of filing without his blessing. Webbe, a friend of us both, devised a scheme to massage his ego and to facilitate release of the unlimited PAC funds. His brainstorm called for prodding Callanan's biggest rival in the labor movement, Harold Gibbons of the International Brotherhood of Teamsters, into directly challenging the Pipefitters. The two union Goliaths were long-standing personal friends who fiercely and frequently clashed in political contests to determine who was kingpin. Callanan resented the generous media treatment accorded Gibbons, who was often described as a "white hat" to highlight the differences between him and Callanan.

Webbe speculated that the fastest, surest way to Callanan's endorsement was through his deep-seated urge to embarrass Gibbons. He arranged an off-the-record session with a reporter from the *Globe-Democrat*. They agreed that the conversation was printable but that the source was not. Skillfully, Webbe spoke in laudatory language of the qualities of Calloway and why the Teamster candidate would defeat Clay. He played up the fact that Gibbons was a foxy political manipulator who viewed the campaign as a contest between two unions fighting for political supremacy. Webbe revealed that Callanan, in a telephone conversation, had asked Gibbons to pressure Calloway into withdrawing so the Negro community could unite behind my candidacy. Allegedly, Gibbons told him that a small union like the Pipefitters' should spend its time increasing membership instead of dabbling in serious politics.

When the reporter called Gibbons for a quote to add credibility to the story, he unwittingly fell into the trap. He stated that Calloway would win hands down and the Teamsters would rally their forty-three thousand members, including seven thousand Negroes, behind his campaign. The Pipefitters had one thousand members, including thirty-nine blacks. The taunting remark and the front-page story of the *Globe-Democrat*, written by Jack Flach, was titled "Teamsters to Fight in First District Democratic Race" and caused Callanan to abandon his position of neutrality.

The *Globe-Democrat*, a morning paper that Callanan detested, hit the streets at about 10 p.m. By midnight Callanan was on the phone arranging a meeting at the union hall. The next morning, Callanan was in rare form. Cursing, shouting, and pacing the floor in one of his famous tirades, he said, "Who do these punks think they are? I know more about this game than all those b———s put together. When I finish, everybody in this g—d— city will know who makes things happen."

In a loud voice, he summoned Ed Beck into the office. Beck was the check writer for the political campaign fund. In an even louder voice, he said, "Write Clay a check for what he needs now and for whatever he needs on a daily basis."

In 1968 inflation had not set in. It was possible to purchase a brand-new Cadillac DeVille for $5,000. Could you imagine how much printing, canvassing, telephoning, newspaper ads, and radio time could be bought with the funds from the Pipefitters' money machine? Neither could Gibbons, Calloway, Carpenter, or the *Globe-Democrat*. Fortunately, they were not aware that that amount was at my disposal.

Over coffee and rolls the morning after Callanan was jostled by Gibbons, my opponents—the editor of the *Globe-Democrat*, suburban Democrats, Calloway, and Carpenter—were doomed. The race was over. They just did not know it. The most uninformed and misinformed of the coup d'état were the so-called expert political analysts. Unaware of the ramifications of Callanan's decision, they continued to predict my loss until the votes were counted on election night, August 6, 1968.

Lawler realized that he would not be able to deliver his predominantly white ward for me against Carpenter. Because of my reputation as a strong opponent of discrimination and the racial fallout of the Jefferson Bank demonstrations, white voters were not inclined to cast their votes for me. Therefore, Lawler endorsed Harry S. Leahey Jr., a white candidate who was not seriously campaigning.

The maneuver paid off at the polls. In his ward, Carpenter received 974 votes to Leahey's 688 and my 451. It was a victory for me. Leahey's total vote in the district was only 1,526 (45 percent of it came from Lawler's ward). In the other white areas, Carpenter was beating Leahey 20–1 and me 11–1.

The outcome showed me, the victor, with 23,758 votes. Carpenter had 16,927; Calloway, 6,405; Leahey, 1,526; and John J. Relles, 1,258. Troupe, who withdrew from the race too late to get his name off of the machine, had 3,186 votes.

Naming the First Black Citywide Officeholder

My opponent in the general election was Curtis Crawford, a well-liked black attorney who at one time was the assistant circuit attorney for the city of St. Louis. The debate in the community was extensive and intense. Churches invited both of us as guest speakers. We made the rounds to the schools, block units, and senior citizens' homes. Conversation in the bars, poolrooms, and PTA meetings buzzed with speculation. No issue or election in recent history had inspired the St. Louis black community like this. The thought of a black man standing on the floor of the U.S. Congress, articulating the dismal life of ghetto residents in the St. Louis metropolitan area and being able to effectuate a change for the better, gave new meaning and an exhilarating sense of pride to many who had despaired.

Crawford, a former Democrat who had switched parties to make the race, believed that the Democrats would nominate a white person. In that event, he speculated (probably correctly) that he would be the overwhelming favorite of the black community. He advocated self-help projects for Negroes and a reduction in federal expenditures, closely following the Republican Party's national campaign platform. I continued to promote the agenda proposed in my primary contest—racial equality and workers' rights.

In the general election, I received 79,295 votes to Crawford's 44,316. Most of his votes (21,011) came from the heavily Democratic white precincts in St. Ferdinand and Washington Townships, areas that had not elected Republicans in decades.

After the primary, the Democratic Party was in a position to reward St. Louis blacks by the appointment of its first black to a citywide office. It was quite a struggle to extract that small measure of equity from those who had benefited tremendously from Herculean efforts by black voters on their behalf. Common sense and fair play should have dictated long before that blacks serve at the highest level of elective office. But old prejudices and racist practices are hard to dispel. It was no different in the effort to name the first black citywide official.

Occasionally, there is poetic justice in the field of politics, and seeking it sometimes make for strange bedfellows. Goins became the first

Official portrait of Congressman Clay, 1992.

black citywide official not because he had a strong base in his own community, not because he was well respected by his peers, and not because he had spoken out forcefully on behalf of his people. He was chosen in spite of and because of these impediments.

He succeeded because a few black elected officials, although not in agreement with his philosophy, properly understood that his advancement would be a victory for our community. He was the only black whom the white political establishment would tolerate in breaking the color barrier. His condescending demeanor was not offensive to them, and, certainly, his elevation posed no threat to their continued dictation of politics in minority communities.

Few people, black or white, are privileged to sit at the table and negotiate, manipulate, and influence the final decision of who will or will not be appointed to public office. Only seven people have firsthand knowledge of the deals put together that resulted in the naming of Goins as the first black citywide officeholder in St. Louis history. Tyus and I shared that honor with Hearnes, Lawler, Callanan, Webbe Sr., and Roddy. Goins was not in the room and had no knowledge that such a meeting was taking place.

We agreed to support Goins after it was made clear that no other black was acceptable to the white power brokers in the room. However, we felt the black community deserved better treatment than to have an individual of Goins's caliber pawned off on it. Others, like Webbe and Lawler, did not comprehend our great antagonism toward Goins. They, like most whites, appreciated Goins's shallow interpretation of the civil rights drive, encouraged his program of cautious attack on racial bigotry, and laughed behind his back at his general ineptness.

In August 1968 at the Democratic National Convention held in Chicago, word came that Phelan O'Toole, clerk of the courts for the city of St. Louis, was dead. Two weeks prior Hearnes had won the Democratic primary to be re-elected governor. The right to appoint a replacement for clerk was in the governor's purview. Arguments about O'Toole's successor were reduced to a debate of race and retribution. Callanan was in favor of Roddy, a longtime union supporter and old-line Irish politician. Tyus, Lawler, and I pushed for the appointment of a black.

Tyus and I contended that with the Irish holding nine of the thirteen citywide elected positions, time was past due for a black to assume a responsible position. We recognized the debt that Hearnes owed the Pipefitters. But Hearnes, Lawler, and Webbe also knew the obligations that the union and the Democratic Party owed the black community.

We figured Hearnes could not deny his most trusted black supporter this appointment. We reasoned to ourselves, "So what if the first black was not ideal? The object was to get our foot in the door."

Neither Tyus nor I was opposed to Roddy. But it was manifestly clear that unless the Democratic Party began to share power more equitably with a large emerging bloc of black voters, there would be trouble in the party. Blacks were demanding quid pro quo concessions from politicians. Young blacks, especially, were becoming very pragmatic, loudly expressing their resentment toward the policy of exclusion.

After an hour, an agreement sanctioning Roddy's appointment was reached. The commitment was made to fill the next vacancy for citywide office with a black whom the governor would appoint after consulting with black leaders. If no vacancy occurred before the next election, Democrats, led by those in the hotel room, would sacrifice one of the present Irish officeholders for the sake of party harmony.

With that commitment in hand, none of us expected that the climax would present itself within weeks. In October, License Collector Joseph T. "Juggie" Hayden died.

Lawler, Roddy, and Callanan were on board in support of Goins. Webbe fully supported Goins. Tyus and I insisted there be no change in the agreement. As the drama unfolded, the only suspect was Hearnes. True to his reputation, he attempted to place a fly in the ointment. He arranged for a luncheon of black committeemen at a fancy Italian restaurant in the area of the city commonly referred to as the Hill. A neighborhood inhabited mostly by Italians, its restaurants are noted for their good food, great wines, and clandestine political gatherings. Some of the greatest decisions by wheelers and dealers have taken place over pasta and Chianti in these quaint eateries.

Hearnes was angling to get out of his commitment. He set the stage by personally telephoning each black committeeman prior to the luncheon, attempting to play one against another by capitalizing on our internal division. If the governor could persuade at least one to offer a name in opposition, he could have accused the blacks of not being united. This was the customary rationale used for not sharing power with blacks, the obvious assumption being that whites are always united and show solidarity.

But the ruse did not work. Black committeemen had already met at the Chase Park Plaza Hotel following a reception for Vice President Hubert H. Humphrey, who was campaigning for the presidency. At that meeting, it was unanimously agreed upon to petition Hearnes to appoint Goins. I was authorized to send a telegram to the governor stating our position. The telegram read, "The appointment of Bennie Goins to the position of license collector before the November elections would bolster the Democratic campaign in midtown St. Louis and possibly mean victory for the party at all levels, especially in the governor's race." There was tension and apprehension about the appointment. Goins was the only black committeeman who trusted Hearnes. The rest doubted that the governor would keep his commitment.

At the meeting with the governor, Weathers offered Goins's name. Tyus, Payne, Troupe, and I spoke in support. Lawler, Webbe, and Roddy concurred in our selection. Hearnes appointed Goins in mid-November, after the election.

Weathers and Tyus concluded that we probably overstated the power of our unity in convincing the governor to appoint Goins. We learned later that some white Democrats were arguing just as passionately for Goins. They alleged that I would have to share center stage and political power with Goins, who could be trusted to counter any aggression against the Democratic Party.

In true fashion, Goins gave the credit for his appointment to white politicians. The *Globe-Democrat* stated that "Goins credits Lawler,

Berra, and St. Louis Revenue Collector John K. Travers with influencing Gov. Warren Hearnes to make [him] the first black ever to hold citywide office." Goins stated that "several months before that appointment, Doc opposed [him] for sheriff in the 1968 primary. [He] th[ought] he felt after that it was time a black had a citywide office."[24]

CHAPTER

11

INFLUENCE OF WOMEN ON MY POLITICAL CAREER

The four most important women in my life—my mother, wife, and two daughters—were the sources of strength, encouragement, and inspiration in my career. Without my mother, I would not be. Without my wife, I would not be who I am. Without my daughters, there would be no pressing need to celebrate any accomplishment. The women in my family have instilled in me a system of values and concerns that seeks justice for even the least of my fellow citizens. Because of them, I have engaged in a struggle to improve the quality of life for the many who have been abandoned, ignored, or discarded.

My mother, née Luella Hyatt, was one of eight children born into her family in Black Jack, Missouri, a suburb of St. Louis City. She was denied an education because St. Louis County did not provide schooling for its black children. At age five, she moved into the city to stay with an aunt and completed Lowell Elementary School in the Baden area. Eleven years later, the Missouri Supreme Court ruled that any district providing public high school education to whites must also provide it to blacks. Rather than integrate the schools, St. Louis County arranged to pay the city of St. Louis to educate their high-school-aged blacks at the all-black Sumner High School. It was years later before black elementary school children were provided education in the county.

My mother married young, giving birth to seven children—four girls and three boys. She was a proud black woman who adored the role I played in trying to right the many racial and economic wrongs existing in society.

My wife, the daughter of Gerald and Helen Johnson, was one of three children. Our marriage produced two girls and a boy. She always encouraged my participation in politics, nurtured my career without necessarily agreeing to every step of it, and cared for me when I was battered and bruised by the opposition. She served as a beacon in a lighthouse, keeping me on course. When I was lost in a sea of self-importance, Carol was always there to bring me back to safe harbor and solid ground. She stood by me in business, civil rights, and politics, and especially those times when I went to jail.

Clay flanked by daughter Michele (left) and wife Carol.

My daughters, Vicki and Michele, rejoiced in the excitement, regretted my many hours away from home, and tolerated my single-minded stubbornness of purpose. Like most kids, they could not explain the crazy world I chose to live in but sensed my crazy reasons for making the choice. From the early ages of three or four years, both participated with Carol and me in many picket lines and demonstrations.

It is impossible to personally acknowledge and individually thank the other beautiful women who played meaningful roles in enabling me to reach the pinnacle of success. Each performed a critical part in my career development and upward mobility. Without their significant contributions, I would probably still be driving a bus for the St. Louis transit system or collecting debits for a weekly insurance company. It was their untiring participation and unswerving loyalty in the political battles that changed the social, economic, and political fabric of life in St. Louis for the better.

Role of Women in a Male-Dominated World

Women in politics were always relegated to performing menial but important tasks. They were expected to host teas, stuff envelopes, make telephone calls, and canvass precincts. Although these chores provided the glue that cemented victorious elections, it was the men who basked in the sunshine of triumph and received the medals for orchestrating the campaigns. Women served as storm troopers for men who hogged the spotlight, rode the lead limo in the ticker tape parades, and received the public accolades.

Once electioneering ceased, so did the importance of women in the male-dominated political circles. They were shunted aside and figuratively placed in mothballs to be reactivated in time for the next election. Their reward for heroism above and beyond the call of duty, if any, was usually some insignificant, low-paying job at city hall. More often, it was merely a meaningless title such as chairman of the women's division. Their male counterparts even lacked the sensitivity to refer to them as chairwomen or chairpersons.

The appointment of a few women to panels, boards, and commissions by Presidents Roosevelt, Truman, Eisenhower, and Kennedy was the extent of their recognition. Despite the cosmetic overtures, the historic reality was that women were commonly excluded from effective governmental participation until the emergence of the crusade to eliminate racial and gender discrimination. Only then did women, white or black, assume leadership roles in proportion to their numbers in society and parlay their recognizable skills into political actuality.

Only in rare circumstances were women permitted to hold public office. In most instances, the few who did replaced their husbands who had died while in office. By replacing their deceased husbands, they were temporary stand-ins or protective guardians of the position. Party bosses appointed the female survivor as a ploy to stymie intraparty struggle among opposing factions. It gave party bosses ample time to make deals for a candidate in the next regularly scheduled election.

This was the acceptable way of political life in America until the civil rights movement of the 1950s. Many strong-minded, dedicated women participated in marches, picket lines, and demonstrations, demanding equality for blacks and giving rise to the fight for women's rights. Motivating factors in the development of the women's rights movement included the noble deeds of Autherine Lucy at the University of Alabama; Rosa Parks on a bus in Birmingham, Alabama; Daisy Bates at Central High School in Little Rock, Arkansas; and Angela Davis's confrontation at the University of California–Los Angeles; as well as the killing of Viola Liuzzo on a lonely road in Alabama. Because of the civil and women's rights movements, the parameters of constraint placed by men on women in politics, business, and religion were decisively shattered and discarded.

The boldness, creativity, and aggressiveness of the leaders in this new crusade gave courage, encouragement, direction, and incentive to other movements. Oppressed groups, normally passive and definitely fearful, picked up the banner of equality and joined in a marathon race for recognition and equity. Inspired by the civil rights movement, large numbers of morally concerned people began to protest against the war in Vietnam, the assault on the environment, and sexually oriented discrimination in employment.

Women in St. Louis, as in other large metropolitan areas, were the victims of massive employment discrimination. Until the mid-1960s, city business leaders—and the city government itself—played to the hilt a game of sexist policies. To paraphrase W. C. Handy, "white women with their diamond rings and black women with their store-bought hair" were equally victimized by male chauvinistic practices. Distinction between women and men in politics was a nationwide scandal. Until World War II and the employment of women on a massive scale in defense plants and factories, females were not admitted into most cocktail lounges unaccompanied by male companions. They were excluded from certain jobs and usually relegated to the lowest-paying, most menial types of work. Women were expected to be seen and not heard.

Until DeVerne Calloway was elected to the state legislature in 1962, women generally did not hold important government posts. In the city, Leonor K. Sullivan, who replaced her husband in Congress, and Mrs. Edward Baumgartner, appointed by Mayor Tucker, were the exceptions. Typical of the treatment suffered by women was Mayor Joseph Darst's 1954 appointment of a black woman, Olivia Calloway, to the St. Louis Board of Education. She would have been the first black to serve in that position. Several days after publicly declaring the appointment at a press conference, the mayor reversed his decision and named a black male dentist, Dr. Edward Grant, to the position. Male politicians maintained that no pressure was applied to scratch Calloway's appointment. However, at the time of the announcement, a St. Louis daily newspaper quoted an influential black male politician as saying, "She ain't gonna stay there."[25]

The excuse given for Mrs. Calloway's resignation was that she held a job in the circuit court that required her to record tax monies collected by the state and due to the school system. The appearance of a conflict was as good as any "unreasonable" excuse to shelve her appointment. The simple solution would have been to change her work responsibilities in the probate office, which employed more than one hundred persons.

The election of DeVerne Calloway, the wife of Ernest (no relation to Olivia), was the beginning of a drive to place women in high office. I did not support her candidacy. However, I believe my decision to endorse a black female for the office stimulated other male politicians to ask Mrs. Calloway to file. Initially, Al Wallace, a patronage worker for Dwyer, was slated for the position. I did not welcome the prospect of him defending our interests in the legislature. For years he had carried water on both shoulders in matters relating to race and, in most instances, had sided with the power structure in attempting to frustrate legitimate advancement for our people.

I counseled with Attorney James Bell, and we reached an agreement to support his good friend Ida L. Harris for the seat. It was apparent to those knowledgeable about campaigns that Harris would defeat Wallace by a large margin. Dwyer, Weathers, and T. D. McNeal found DeVerne Calloway to be a candidate of enough quality for competition. She defeated Harris by fewer than fifty votes and served for twenty years with distinction and honor.

Women and the Twenty-sixth Ward Organization

I often asked why the abilities of women were not used more broadly and what their extensive involvement would mean. After due deliberation, I answered those questions by analyzing other organizations and reached the conclusion that women made the difference in terms of which groups were superb, average, or mediocre. I foresaw women producing the best political machine there was. During the initial stages of developing the Twenty-sixth Ward organization, it was a common sight to see our headquarters filled with fifty or sixty females addressing, stuffing, and sealing envelopes, manning telephones, and giving instructions to male workers under their supervision.

In the Twenty-sixth Ward, women received the same consideration as men. Despite the unfortunate taboos, women in our club formed a powerful cog in the group's machinery. I always felt that they made better politicians than men. They had the finesse, temperament, and determination for the business. The patience, perceptiveness, and perseverance that they possessed were critical factors in stimulating a community and enticing individuals to vote. In the Twenty-sixth Ward organization that I built, women made the best precinct captains and the best vote organizers.

I was befriended by extraordinary black women. They plunged into the midst of campaigns with vigor and excitement. Their effort and leadership ability made it possible to transform a despaired, frustrated, and apathetic community into one of hope and aspiration. These ladies were proud, eloquent, and compassionate, but above all possessed an indomitable spirit for social, racial, and political justice. Ethel Jones, Addie Rice, Magnolia Dease, Myrtle Dearing, Jerri Easter, Zelda Hudson, and Marian Oldham—the list of heroic fighters for political justice has no bounds.

My dealings with supporters, both men and women, were based on their contributions to the development of a strong, enviable organization. Those who made significant contributions were rewarded in kind. Unlike other groups, we valued and rewarded females for their accomplishments. I established a rule of thumb for others to follow that women would be rewarded commensurate with their services. In my organization, they got the better jobs at city hall. They were encouraged and supported in their efforts for public office. Contribution, not gender, decided the bounds of limitation in this field.

Articulation of that standard made me an instant idol for women who had the know-how to cultivate supporters and organize people. When word of our policy circulated, women seeking a meaningful role in politics came to our headquarters in scores. Many flocked to us, bringing experience gained in the trenches of other political organizations. Originally, the Twenty-sixth Ward consisted of twenty-six precincts. Eighteen of the precinct captains were faithful women, dedicated to the ends advanced by the organization. The Twenty-sixth Ward became the largest, most respected, and most feared delivery ward in city politics, as these women melded their talents with those of seasoned males such as Lee Lloyd, John Curtis, and Nat Rivers. The maturity of several Dining Car Porters trained in the A. Philip Randolph organization and the energy, drive, and determination of young civil rights activists also played a pivotal role.

One example of the kind of votes we were capable of delivering is the 1960 general election for president of the United States. Several wards in North St. Louis produced similar results; the Twenty-sixth Ward had some of the best. In that election, John F. Kennedy received 8,739 votes to Richard Nixon's 2,143. Kennedy won the state of Missouri by less than 9,000 votes. I was correct in my initial assessment. Without the assistance and hard work of females, I would never have succeeded to the extent I did. From the very first questionable days of my involvement in the process until my triumphant victory for Congress, my biggest supporters came from the ranks of women. They provided the vote pluralities and kept the campaigns in focus. As far as I was concerned, women were entitled to exceptional benefits for their extraordinary political labors.

Naming a District Director

In 1972 I hired Pearlie Evans to replace Walter Lay as my district director. Lay, a former member of the state legislature, had been a good political operative but refused to quit his job in the private sector to devote full time to my congressional office. Evans, a talented, educated, and experienced person, was what I needed to effectuate a positive relationship between constituents and my faraway presence in Washington, D.C. She had received her bachelor of arts degree in sociology and political science from Lincoln University and her master's degree in social work from Washington University. At the time, she was serving in the Cervantes administration as commissioner of social services. Having worked in several private-sector social programs dealing with ghetto residents, she had the credentials I was seeking to manage my office.

Evans was a very good political strategist who had the talent to get maximum efforts from volunteers. There was no question in my mind about her ability to coordinate and improve the efficiency of the office.

Pearlie Evans, district director for Congressman Clay, in 1987.

Her connections with grassroots groups, sororities, and the middle class made her a great asset. She had a realistic grasp of the problems of my low-income constituents and a deep-rooted association with key white groups in the district.

I first met Evans in 1965. I had known of her through others who were close to my political activities. One in particular was Arthur Kennedy, who had joined with us in electing A. J. Cervantes mayor. He was the leader of the rump group in the Fourth Ward and ran against Dwyer for committeeman. In that campaign, Evans had been very active, but I had not personally met her. After the election, the new mayor informed me that there was a vacancy in his administration for the position of commissioner of the Division of Social Services. I invited Pearlie to lunch and offered her the position. But this highly intelligent, proud black woman was too committed to her career of helping ghetto residents to even consider the offer. Her work at the Fellowship Center and Plymouth House directing children, adults, and seniors in community activities was the alpha and the omega in her life.

Even though the commissioner's pay was twice what she was earning, it took two more lunches to convince her that in this new position she could do greater good for a greater number of welfare recipients, including the ones she was presently serving. She did accept the position in Cervantes' administration and performed well.

One of my most exasperating confrontations with black men occurred when I announced that Evans was taking charge of the district office. Again, the ugly head of sexism reared. No sooner had the ink dried in the newspapers announcing my selection, than a group of my very close friends asked for a meeting with me. I was flabbergasted to hear them object to her because, as they stated, "they would not deal with a woman in such a position." They were adamant about not working with a woman who would be considered a peer. The tone of their conversation was threatening and objectionable. As usual, I welcomed the challenge and met it head-on. The problem was theirs, not mine, and I accepted it in that vein. They were advised to do what they thought best. I assured them I would definitely do what I knew to be best.

The meeting was probably the shortest I ever attended. I declared the finality of my decision and informed the men that they would deal with her or with no one. I opened the door, walked out, and left them to make their own decisions. It really did not matter to me. After that explosive session, their differences with Evans were resolved, and in subsequent years they looked to her for advice and counsel on many matters, especially in the area of the census and redistricting, where she became an expert.

Ruth Porter for State Legislature

In 1966 Ruth Porter filed for state representative against incumbent Harry Raiffie in a seat covering the West End section of town. Porter was a prominent housing specialist and civil rights activist who had earned her political and civil rights spurs in the ghettoes of Chicago, fighting Daley's machine politicians and skirmishing with absentee landlords who gouged their tenants while refusing to repair their properties.

Raiffie, who had represented the heavily populated Negro district for several terms, lived outside the city limits and the district's boundaries. He and his brother were the owners and suppliers of pinball and cigarette machines to numerous retail stores and cocktail lounges in the Negro community.

Porter was a friend of Gwen Giles and one of my favorite people. She was married to Bill Porter, a vice president in charge of special promotions for Anheuser-Busch. As a leader in organizing the Woodlawn Neighborhood Association, she had been instrumental in guaranteeing that residents of the rehabilitation program surrounding the University of Chicago would not be forced out of their homes by the city agency sponsoring a massive land-clearance program.

Porter and I became friends soon after she moved to St. Louis. She had the idea that our city was ripe for a housing enforcement group similar to the one she had helped establish in Chicago. I was in business at the time and had excess rental space in my office complex. For the exorbitant sum of $25 per month, including utilities and janitorial services, my partner, Richard Anderson, and I provided her with office space. That was the beginning of the Freedom of Residence organization (FOR), which today continues to fight housing discrimination based on race and sex. She was also an active participant in the West End Community Conference.

In the campaign to unseat Raiffie, Porter waged a vigorous and valiant effort. Her defeat by forty-nine votes cannot be blamed on the method in which she conducted that campaign. It was more attributable to the system and a series of events beyond her control. The committeemen who controlled the political machinery in the district supported the incumbent. Our organization in the Twenty-sixth Ward endorsed Porter, but we covered only 20 percent of the district.

Two factors beyond Porter's control affected the negative outcome. First, Beatrice Hatton, a well-known political ward heeler, endorsed Raiffie. She was known in the community as a "fire and brimstone" political stump speaker who had had the privilege of introducing President Harry S. Truman when he visited St. Louis during his 1948 election campaign.

Second, Louis Ford, a well-known civil rights personality who had demonstrated with Dr. Martin Luther King, Stokely Carmichael, James Farmer, and John Lewis in the South, filed for the same seat. He was a bona fide candidate who had earned meritorious medals in the trenches of battle in Alabama, Mississippi, Georgia, and Missouri.

In discussions, I advised him against such a move. It was my opinion that although he was imminently qualified and certainly had paid his dues, his presence on the ballot would only lead to splitting the black vote and thus assuring the re-election of Raiffie. Ford was a personal friend whom I admired. I never told him that he did not have a right to run. I only reminded him that Porter had the organization and the public support. It was my contention that he was in the wrong race at the wrong time.

In promoting his candidacy, Ford was able to convince fellow civil rights operatives to come to St. Louis and campaign for him. Comedian and activist Dick Gregory, a hometown hero; James Meredith, the first black student admitted to the University of Mississippi; Joan Baez, the popular folksinger; and Mahalia Jackson, the great gospel singer, sponsored a fund-raising benefit on his behalf. His effort produced 374 votes. Porter tallied 858 votes to Raiffie's 907. There were four other candidates in the race.[26]

Porter was not a person who easily admitted defeat. After analyzing the returns, she filed in the general election as an independent candidate. The incumbent decided to withdraw, recommending Hatton as his replacement. Porter was successful in blocking her nomination by the Democratic committeemen in the district. Raiffie then rescinded his letter of resignation.

In the general election, Raiffie was victorious again, defeating Porter by sixty-eight votes.[27] Her campaign caused anger and consternation among some Democrats and led to the passage of a state law forbidding candidates who lose in primary elections from running as independents in the general election for the same office.

The first woman assessor for the city of St. Louis, my dearest friend, Gwen Giles, was appointed because of my efforts. She was also the first black woman elected to the Missouri senate. She was my protégé, who had managed several of my congressional campaigns. The first black woman elected citywide to a county office in St. Louis, Billie Boykins, also came from the Clay camp. The election bids of successful candidates for the school board (Anita Bond, Adella Smiley, and Joyce Thomas) were vigorously supported by the Twenty-sixth Ward organization. Gwen Reed's election to the Junior College District Board was orchestrated in a meeting that I convened. Elsa Hill, a Twenty-sixth

Clay and campaign manager Pearlie Evans in 1991.

Ward precinct captain, was elected to the Missouri legislature. Ida L. Harris, my longtime committeewoman, was named vice chairperson of the city's Democratic Central Committee because Tyus and I were able to line up the votes.

In my sixteen elections to Congress, women managed all of my campaigns: Pearlie Evans, who was the district director of my congressional office; Gwen Giles, former state senator and former assessor of the city of St Louis; Doris Moore, an administrator in the public school system; and Gwen Reed, a public school teacher. They performed the task of organizing the campaigns with class and professionalism.

John Bass, Clay, and Clay's campaign manager Gwen Reed in 1998.

However, the fight to eliminate sexism in American society is not over. Some women, even in 2004, are still being held hostage to primitive mind-sets. Unfortunately, in some circumstances, women who feel they have reached professional status in the new millennium find themselves relegated to the same old roles as men envisioned for them in the 1950s and 1960s. The struggle for equality of the sexes must continue until every vestige of discrimination based on gender is eliminated.

CHAPTER

12

THE POLITICS OF SELF-DESTRUCTION

For a number of years, black St. Louisans were victimized by internal political disputes between bickering black elected officials. The division stymied efforts to aggressively challenge uncaring, absentee white representation and to effectively address pertinent community issues. Before strategies could be formulated and executed to increase black political influence, it was necessary to contend with internal guerilla warfare from an assortment of black nihilists, hustlers, and obstructionists who possessed a mentality anathema to the emerging militant mood engulfing African Americans. They served well the forces that kept blacks politically and economically subservient.

People dedicated to racial advancement and committed to performing the tedious work required to enhance political strength were replaced by a group of political parasites willing to circumvent the process. They ushered in an era of regressive activity that impeded the progress of black people. In their thirst for power and recognition, everything was for sale. Brazenly commercializing politics in our community, these political pimps flagrantly merchandized the black vote to the highest bidder, callously disregarding the consequences.

Negroes Ambivalent on Issues

The attitude of political scamps was similar to that of the freeloaders who pimped the civil rights movement. Many who ridiculed the marchers, demonstrators, and protestors were the first to make reservations at fine restaurants and hotels when the establishments dropped racial barriers. They were the first to apply when corporations began hiring Negroes in management, sales, and clerical work.

These individuals never attended political or protest rallies, never donated to black candidates, and never spoke out against racial injustices. But after sacrifices were made, community spirit was elevated, and precinct organizations formed, the parasites offered themselves as candidates for public office. Citing credentials of attending prestigious universities and hobnobbing with social elites, members of the right fraternities, and private clubs, some actually believed that the people who had developed organizations to challenge institutional racism owed them support in their political pursuits. Their expectations usually meant financing approximately 90 percent of the campaign expenditures, convincing other elected officials to endorse them, and placing at their disposal hundreds of people obligated to the activists' political machinery.

Twenty-sixth ward Young Democrats for Clay, 1970.

Without exception they received a rude awakening. Meetings with my top advisers and me left some bitter and disillusioned but educated to the reality of hardball politics. We were not impressed by their résumés or portfolios. As a result, these overly ambitious Negroes—who watched the picket lines from a distance, debated the feasibility of boycotts, and opposed affirmative action as unfair to whites—became outspoken enemies of my "tough love" brand of politics.

Some of the disillusioned joined the political nomads who sashayed aimlessly from ward to ward, attacking aggressive legitimate black leaders while substituting illogical rhetoric for sound, sensible judgment. The misguided charlatans were agents paid by the establishment, in some cases to confuse the issues and to sow seeds of dissent. They were professional community destabilizers who were comfortable in their idiotic crusade. They seemed to feel safe, serene, and content in playing the role of surrogate for elite power forces bent on denying us our basic rights of citizenship.

The obnoxious and undisciplined gypsy vagabonds were accepted and promoted as leaders by the white community. But no matter how excessive the media attention to their disruptive exploits, the roving bands of Philistines were unable to win respect in their own communities.

Stratification of Black Leadership

Disharmony among leadership led to a delay in the extension of rights for black citizens. The stratification of leadership was generally confined to four basic opposing groups: 1) the politically and entrenched old-guard Negro leaders; 2) the ambitious, free-swinging young turks; 3) the naïve and pathetic status quo defenders; and 4) the destructive and disoriented nihilists.

The old guard consisted of pioneers in the struggle for civil rights. They had spearheaded the assault on racial injustice for decades, often jeopardizing their own lives, security, and economic stability. They were usually identified with organizations such as the NAACP, the Urban League, the National Council of Negro Women, and the

A. Phillip Randolph Institute. They pursued racial change primarily through lawsuits, appeals to the moral conscience, and development of alliances with other marginalized groups.

At the other end of the spectrum were the young turks. The old guard genuinely feared that the robust, abrasive behavior of these young and impatient activists would interrupt the drive for the elimination of segregation and discrimination.

Rivalry between the young activists and the older, well-established Negro leaders divided the community. Old-guard politicians rejected direct action as a major tactic in achieving rights and feared that the militant approach to confronting and addressing racial inequities would be counterproductive. Reconciliation of the dispute was virtually impossible. Older, more respected leaders who had courageously pursued justice and equality in very perilous times were ignored or ridiculed by youngsters engaging in a new thrust for the attainment of rights. Pleas for moderation by stalwarts of the NAACP and the Urban League often resulted in a loss of respect and credibility for them in the new, inflamed atmosphere. Some, unfortunately, were condemned as accommodating racists and vilified as apologizing for racism.

Another group consisted of those who were satisfied with the status quo. They fell into a category not akin to the others. In contrast to the conservative leadership of the old guard and the militant leadership of the young turks, the status quo seekers possessed a different, bewildering mentality about the purpose of leadership and what was expected of it. In my opinion, they possessed an inferiority complex, believing that only whites were capable of leading. They were willing to endure second-class citizenship without complaint. The group had no concept of or appreciation for the struggle for equality. They never made waves or rocked any boats. The manipulators best described their mission as a "credit to their race."

The fourth group was the nihilists. The nihilists were extremists, motivated by an envy of successful blacks and driven by a greed for monetary compensation. My irritable, ill-tempered reaction to these phantom politicians came as no surprise. My reputation of not treating fools politely was well known. My anger toward them was impossible to conceal. Their kowtowing, head-scratching behavior in protecting advocates of racial inequality was nauseating; the nihilists shamefully denigrated the struggle for equal rights. Their appeasing rhetoric put them at odds with other black leaders and a majority of black people.

In their effort to quell the effectiveness of black achievement, Democrats, Republicans, businessmen, and socialites discovered the Achilles' heel of gullible Negroes. They found it easy to persuade some to oppose pertinent black issues and yet look like heroes. The magic formula was to wine and dine them at exclusive country clubs or fancy restaurants. Bankers, publishers, and merchants exerted more influence on them through their diets than sources within their own community. Somehow, sipping cocktails with the oppressor was preferable to eating hamburgers with the oppressed. Dining on pheasant under glass with one who would eventually brutalize black people took priority over confronting racist policy. Being pleased to be in the company of civic leaders was as idiotic as pretending to savor the distinctive quality of vodka and caviar.

The 1972 Democratic primary race for public administrator manifested the debilitating role that nihilistic politics played in stemming the tide of racial advancement. Sorkis Webbe, a Lebanese first elected in 1963, announced he would not seek re-election as public administrator. Lebanese constituted less than 1 percent of the population but had three citywide officeholders. Blacks, more than 40 percent of the population, held one citywide office.

Ten black committeemen met to agree on a replacement. Goins objected to all proposed candidates and refused to place a name of his choice into consideration. The damage was major. White Democrats were willing to cede the position without a contest. They contended that passage of the office without engaging in a bitter primary fight or witnessing a divisive struggle among Negroes would avoid negative fallouts in the general elections for president, governor, and other statewide offices.

In an effort to reach consensus, Weathers offered the name of Lawrence Albert, a well-liked businessman and civic leader who had a closer relation to Goins than to any of the other committeemen. He was a childhood friend, active in all of Goins's campaigns, and had raised substantial sums of money for him. When Goins vetoed Albert, we were convinced that a hidden agenda existed.

Charles Deeba, a Lebanese, filed for the office. A white committeewoman from South St. Louis also filed. Fearing that Deeba might be unpopular in some white wards and that the committeewoman might siphon off enough votes to enable Albert to win, our opponents found it expedient to split the black vote. A black deputy constable with ties to Goins and the Lebanese filed for the position. So did an unknown black, Willie Smith. Roscoe McCrary, a perennial black candidate, also filed. But his candidacy was more threatening to whites than blacks. In biennial election campaigns, McCrary usually received more white votes than black because of his Irish-Scottish name.

The effect was predictable. Albert's campaign was shot down before it got off the ground. Deeba won with 26,761 votes. The four blacks in the race (Albert, R. C. French, McCrary, and Willie Smith) received a total of 27,891 votes, or 1,130 more than Deeba.

The negative activity of the nihilists did not end with the Deeba incident. Goins played a role in foiling the ambitions of a black candidate seeking elective office in a predominantly black judicial district. Michael Calvin, a young black lawyer, filed against the incumbent magistrate Oliver Collins in the city's far North Side. He assembled his supporters, young lawyers, neighborhood leaders, block unit chairmen, and activists. With the assistance of other black elected officials, he waged a creditable campaign. Goins launched a countercampaign on behalf of the incumbent. He and Third Ward alderwoman Delores Glover supported Collins and sent their precinct workers to campaign on his behalf. The activity was so brazen that two of their major players rebelled. Rep. Russell Goward of Goins's organization and Glover's committeeman, Freeman Bosley Sr., split with them and endorsed Calvin.

Calvin and many volunteers went door to door to spread the word of his candidacy. Despite the efforts of the nihilists, he won the magistrate position by a slim margin.

For the nihilists, 1972 was a banner year in their effort to deny blacks more political offices. In expanding guerilla activity, they sabotaged the appointment of a black judge and the election of a black woman as Democratic state committeewoman. In addition, they engaged unsuccessfully in a plot to destroy the majority black congressional district.

In a united front, blacks from Kansas City, the southeastern part of the state, and St. Louis offered significant possibilities for major government appointments. The alliance formed to 1) preserve the majority black congressional district in St. Louis; 2) support Representative Orchid Jordan of Kansas for Democratic national committeewoman from Missouri; and 3) back Circuit Judge Theodore McMillian for the St. Louis Court of Appeals or for the Missouri State Supreme Court.

Bruce Watkins, head of Freedom, Inc., of Kansas City; Negro leaders in the Bootheel section of the state; and the ten black city committeemen agreed to the plan. Goins, present at the meeting, later denied giving his support to Jordan. Troupe and Tyus held a press conference, explaining what was at stake in Goins's failure to cooperate. They charged him and white Democrats with conspiring to abolish the black majority congressional district. Goins denied the accusation, but Troupe alleged that "Goins's divisive efforts to become the political boss" led to his desire to "kill any effort to retain the First Congressional District."[28]

Electing a Black Citywide Official

Goins's appointment as the first citywide officeholder was a cakewalk compared to the obstacle course encountered in the election of the first black to a citywide office. Few, politically knowledgeable or otherwise, were aware of the details surrounding the colossal task of electing John Bass as comptroller.

Goins, following his appointment in 1968, had been elected in 1972 without serious opposition. But in St. Louis, re-election to county office is usually automatic for incumbents. Defeat in primaries is a rare occasion. In general elections between 1950 and 1968, only one Republican had won a citywide contest, and it was not to head a patronage office.

The election of a Negro as city comptroller was in sharp contrast to the appointment of a Negro license collector. It required greater planning, more shrewdness, and enormous plotting, cajoling, temporizing, and finessing. Above all, it necessitated the soft-pedaling of issues offensive to influential politicians with overly sensitive egos. The plan to accomplish that goal was conceived over two martinis and one scotch on the rocks. At Slay's restaurant, a popular hangout for politicos, the strategy was mapped out while eating lunch. Tyus, Webbe, and I fantasized that we constituted the nerve center of the new political movers and shakers in city politics. Our conversation zeroed in on the next election in March 1973 and who should be the candidates for mayor and comptroller. At first a black mayor was discussed. But Poelker, the incumbent comptroller of eighteen years, had announced his intention to challenge Cervantes. A viable candidate for mayor was possible but not feasible. Poelker's move left a vacancy that would be easier to win.

Because ward leaders were divided over Poelker's replacement, no candidate had a lock on the nomination. The race was an open invitation to several ambitious individuals and promised to be a Democratic donnybrook. Several known politicians had considered and rejected the idea of running. Finally, Tyus said that it was as important for a black to sit on the Board of Estimates as in the mayor's office. The three-member board consisting of the mayor, comptroller, and president of the Board of Aldermen controlled the budgetary expenditures and tax rates for the city.

Successful elections are won because 1) a candidate is able to galvanize a large bloc of supporters; 2) a reasonable amount of money is available; and 3) a sufficient number of political leaders are in support. All three factors are not necessary in every election, but if all three are missing, winning is almost impossible.

Our problem was to find a candidate who would be overwhelmingly acceptable to the black community and who would be able to garner enough white votes to assure election. Tyus offered the name of John Bass, a former school administrator who was presently serving as city welfare director in the Cervantes administration. The comptroller was the second highest official in city government. The office handled all city finances and supervised all of its property and assets and their disposition. The city charter concentrates enormous fiscal and administrative powers in the office.

Webbe facetiously mentioned Fred Williams, a complex personality first elected to the Missouri House in 1968. He constantly strove for recognition and yearned for respectability. He received the former, but somehow the latter always escaped him. After a few laughs and another round of drinks, the conversation got down to serious business. Bass's chances were thoroughly analyzed. We admitted that his position in Cervantes' cabinet posed one notable problem. What effect would it have on securing support from those endorsing Poelker for mayor? Would it be viewed as a ploy to entice potential voters in the black wards to support Cervantes? Should he resign his position in the cabinet before filing?

Clay, Pearlie Evans, John Bass, and Leroy Tyus, undated.

The second problem was more complex. The leading white candidate was almost certain of getting solid support in the South Side wards if no other white filed. That made it necessary for us to consider another white candidate with name recognition and political status.

The third and perhaps most critical problem was in rallying maximum support in the black community behind a single candidate. Warring factions in North St. Louis had reached a senseless level of internal fratricide. Unity around any issue or any candidate seemed improbable. Factions were constantly at loggerheads over candidates and issues.

Before we could approach other leaders and discuss the situation, word of our plan leaked to the press. We were accused of trying to force a handpicked candidate down their throats. Goins stated outright, "Bass is not my candidate."[29] Howard was more strident, asserting, "I'm not sure Bass has any charisma or appeal. You can't go around talking to South St. Louisans and say that you handled the welfare budget for a few years, so you are qualified for the comptroller's job."[30]

Webbe's denial of an agreement to promote Bass's candidacy somewhat cooled down the wrath of the nihilists. But suspicions lingered. A statement by Calloway, a guru in the eyes of many blacks, lowered the screams of opponents when he said that regardless of who broached the original idea, the ultimate end was beneficial. Calloway convinced Goins that he was the only Negro with credibility in the white sector and that he could become a kingmaker if successful in shepherding Bass to victory. Webbe supported Calloway's contention and persuaded Goins to take the lead in developing the South Side campaign for Bass.

John Roach, alderman of the Twenty-eighth Ward, negated the need to file a second white candidate. His entry represented white liberals and gave them an alternative to voting for an African American. Raymond Percich, a political gadfly in the bonnet of established politicians, also filed. He had spent most of his political life criticizing Democratic officeholders and attacking the patronage system.

Webbe's function was to secure Bass's endorsement from three white wards and to raise money from labor unions. Tyus, Goins, and I were responsible for collecting on numerous political IOUs, calling on people to redeem their promissory notes. Those reluctant to endorse a black were encouraged to divide their support among the white candidates.

In November, I easily defeated Richard Funsch in the general election for Congress (90,149 to 53,860). The next day, we moved my entire operation into a headquarters for Bass. The campaign manager, telephone bank, furniture, canvassers, and paid staff all migrated to the new location. Tyus assigned his key personnel and patronage workers to the campaign. The two of us assumed the responsibility of mobilizing the black community. Goins agreed to escort Bass to the white ward meetings and introduce him to the committeepeople in South St. Louis.

Webbe secured the three white ward endorsements. The black community rallied to support Bass with both money and volunteers. White liberals supported Roach. Organized labor and machine politicians were split between Roach and Percich. The daily newspapers disagreed on the two major white aspirants. One supported Percich. The other endorsed Roach. Black officials solidified efforts behind the candidacy of Bass.

Bass won with 42,074 votes to Roach's 28,449 and Percich's 27,192. Goins and Bass campaigned tirelessly in white areas; however, the results were not encouraging. Bass received 27,609 votes in the ten predominantly black wards, 4,039 votes in the seven wards that were middle income, 6,030 votes in the racially mixed wards, and only 3,404 votes in the six predominantly low-income white wards.

Defeat by Gerrymandering and Other Scurrilous Schemes

The origin of the word "gerrymander" comes from an 1812 conflict between legislators in Massachusetts while attempting to draw legislative districts. The proposed boundaries of one looked like a dragon or a salamander. Governor Gerry favored the odd-shaped district. The art of drawing similar districts eventually became known as the gerrymander. Gerrymandering legislative districts and purging the registration rolls of eligible black voters have been the most common means of denying representation to Negroes.

In my 1972 race for Congress against Richard Funsch, a white GOP opponent, the Democrat-controlled St. Louis Board of Elections arbitrarily disqualified 16,000 black voters by erasing their names from the registration books. The precipitous action took place just prior to election day, forcing me to seek injunctive relief from the courts.

Presenting a unique opinion, the judge ordered election officials to keep the polls open all night, if necessary, to allow the stricken sixteen thousand an opportunity to requalify and to vote. It was a cumbersome procedure. The voters were forced to go downtown to the election board and get recertified. This process consisted of approximately four to five hours of waiting in line, completing forms, and then returning to the precincts, where they had to wait until the official records were returned from the election board. Some did not get to vote until midnight. In some areas, the polls remained open until after 1 a.m.

In 1971 and also in 1981, after the national censuses, I was forced to petition the federal court to redraw the congressional map. In both instances, it was a Democratically controlled state legislature that attempted to abolish the seat I represented. This was despite the fact that, as committeeman of the Twenty-sixth Ward, I had delivered more votes for Democratic candidates running statewide in ten years than 99 percent of those representing other political entities. Despite the fact that in 1981 I was the senior member of the Missouri congressional delegation with the highest percentage voting record for the Democratic Party's platform, my district was targeted for elimination.

The architect of the proposal to target the First Congressional District on each occasion was Robert Young, a Democratic state senator from St. Louis County. In 1971 he was vice chairman of the Senate Reapportionment Committee and plotted with fellow Democrats to create a district to enhance his personal chances of election to Congress. The scheme necessitated the transfer of large numbers of blacks to establish a district at least 60 percent white and based mostly in St. Louis County.

The nefarious escapade to destroy the black district was joined by the divisive nihilists and some black politicians. It was rumored that they were backing the proposal offered by Young. A similar map was introduced in the House. Both maps divided the black vote into three congressional districts, creating a district for Young that was approximately 25 percent black. The rest of the black voters would have been distributed between congressional incumbents Leonor Sullivan and James Symington.

The *Argus* reported that a group of black politicians had devised "a clandestine plot to defeat Clay for re-election." One attempted to pass a bill that would have jeopardized the chances of a black being elected in the First Congressional District. According to the *Argus*, "his efforts to aid Senator Young were defeated by the other black members of the House." The scheme was halted in its tracks when the *St. Louis Sentinel* reported that "an ally of Goins was working to pass a bill in the House of Representatives, which would have made the First Congressional District predominantly white and favored State Senator Robert Young, who was an avowed aspirant for the congressional post held by Clay."[31]

The newspaper also reported that a black legislator's support of the redistricting bill was given in exchange for an appointment of a black to the State Parole Board. The bill passed the Senate but was rejected in the House. The federal courts ended up drawing a map that protected the black majority. It was a galling experience to watch black leaders willingly exchange a congressional seat for a position on the parole board. It exposed the pettiness and ignorance prevailing among the reactionary groups. The *Sentinel* ridiculed the plot, writing:

> Behind-the-scenes maneuvers designed to defeat Congressman William L. Clay in his bid for re-election w[ere] reportedly shaping up in the latest tug-of-war among black political leaders; central in the maneuvering has been the name of City License Collector Benjamin Goins, who has been repeatedly reported in a power struggle with Clay. According to reports, the strategy that emerges is for the filing of a strong white candidate in the First Congressional District to run against Clay. This is to be coupled with the filing of a black candidate for the same seat. Rep. Clay's district is now nearly half-and-half racially since the redistricting.[32]

The New Democratic Coalition (NDC) of metropolitan St. Louis charged that the redistricting measure that passed the Senate was a "blatant gerrymander" against myself and the Negro population of North St. Louis.[33] The NDC further adopted a resolution accusing Young and the Democratic-controlled Senate of spearheading the attempt to obliterate the majority minority district.

Although Young had never spoken out on issues of importance to the black populace and had never voted in favor of legislation beneficial to the black community, he actively sought to increase the number of black voters in a district specifically designed for him. The legislation passed 22–12 in the Senate. It left the First Congressional District with 155,000 people in the city (mostly black) and 312,000 in the suburbs (overwhelmingly white). Democrats believed that as long as black voters did not constitute more than 25 percent of a district, their overwhelming support of Democratic candidates assured that the districts would be safe havens for white party candidates.

Rep. James Troupe led the fight against diluting the effect of the black vote. The House, following his urging, refused to concede to the Senate and drew a district more favorable to black interests. The two bodies were unable to reach agreement, and my supporters filed suit in the U.S. Federal Court. A three-judge panel consisting of H. Kennett Wangelin, Floyd Gibson, and William Becker drew congressional boundaries almost identical to the House version.

The scenario was replicated in 1981 when the state of Missouri lost a congressional district due to a new census count. By this time, Young, a member of Congress, still maintained considerable influence in the state senate, where he had served for twenty years. His plan, agreed to by the Senate, was to abolish the black-majority district and disburse black voters among two districts represented by Richard Gephardt and himself. Both districts would have been predominantly white and overwhelmingly Democrat.

A committee of "100 for Fair Representation in Congressional Redistricting" was established under the leadership of Chairman Margaret B. Wilson and Presiding Officer Larry Williams. In a meeting called by the committee and attended by more than eight hundred people, Reps. Quincy Troupe, Fred Williams, and Elbert Walton were charged with blocking the appointment of two blacks, Dr. William Harrison and Leroy Tyus, to the reapportionment committees scheduled to redraw state senatorial and house districts. They recommended to Governor Christopher Bond the appointment of two St. Louis County whites. The committee demanded an explanation as to why the three legislators were working "so diligently to undermine the efforts" of other black political leaders to preserve the congressional district and two senatorial and nine house seats currently being held by blacks.

Wilson, the state NAACP president, expressed shock and disbelief that members of the legislature could be so naïve as to think that the community would permit personal vendettas and petty politics to

Attorney Margaret Bush Wilson, James Bush, City Treasurer Larry Williams, Public School Executive Charlene Jones, and Dr. Lawrence Nicholson.

threaten the political interests of black people. She said, "Banks, Williams, [Quincy] Troupe, and Walton's decision leaves us in a situation where state House and Senate seats will be drawn by panels which are all white."[34]

The federal courts, however, disagreed with the Democrats and drew a district that preserved the possibility of a black being elected. There was nothing surprising about the attitude of Democrats. They had opposed the original creation of the black-majority district. No thanks to Democrats in the senate, I won the party nomination and re-election to Congress without much effort.

The efforts of Young and his cohorts in the state legislature vividly displayed the dilemma facing both blacks and whites in the Democratic Party. Blacks who had been loyal supporters of the party were considered by white candidates as necessary appendages to a political structure meant to provide the grist for keeping white Democrats in power. Other than that, black people had no political raison d'être. The laissez-faire attitude convinced some blacks that they had no compelling reason to vote and, consequentially, they should stay at home on election day.

Nihilists: The Threat to the Well-Being of Black St. Louisans

I never disguised the scorn I harbored for the contemptible activities of the black nihilists. In terms of philosophy, ideology, and integrity, the group of political nomads was light years from where a majority of blacks stood. I cringed every time I watched them play the buffoon for unsavory characters attempting to reverse the hard-earned gains of the civil rights movement.

The nihilists were anathema to the new militant mood engulfing black Americans. On questions of racial advancement, they were passive almost to the extent of timidity. They were ambivalent, constantly in flux, and mostly in confusion. Leaders such as Ernest Calloway, Marian Oldham, and Frankie Freeman thought they could wean them away from their harmful mind-set and eventually develop them into credible spokespersons for our people. They failed in the effort.

The community was upset and disturbed by the constant competition between the two sides. In September 1972, a unity meeting was
held at a midtown restaurant where both Goins and I agreed to work
"shoulder-to-shoulder" on behalf of our respective districts. Goins stated,
"As the chairman of the First Congressional District, and as license collector, I feel that this meeting between Bill and me is the new breath
of life needed."[35] In the hourlong meeting, we agreed that our first initiative would be to unite in an effort to reach the nearly 40,000 unreg-
istered but otherwise eligible voters in North St. Louis. After laying out
our strategy for working on registration, I said, "I'm sure that Ben and
I, along with the other responsible leaders of our community, can work
in unison and on behalf of those we represent." [36] Goins added that it
was the first time he and I "had ever sat down and made peace."[37]

Goins, Webbe, and Teamsters Reach Out for Power and Control

The rivalry between North Side politicians had reached a dangerous
and destructive level in May 1972. During the Democratic caucus to
select national convention delegates, Tyus joined forces with county
committeepeople and elected the entire slate of delegates.

In August, shortly after the primary election, Tyus and I were
invited to a meeting at the Teamsters' council house. Chairing the session was Dick Kavenner, an influential leader of the Teamsters union.
We were informed that Tyus would have to step down as chairman of
the First Congressional District and give the position to Goins. Webbe,
who was also present, identified the votes of committeepeople he and
Kavenner had corralled. The list constituted a majority, but most of the
votes came from white committeepeople in suburban townships that
represented less than 10 percent of the district's population.

The law was clear. If a ward or township had at least one
precinct in the district, it was entitled to cast two full votes at the organizing meeting.

Tyus and I strenuously opposed the maneuver. We argued that
the majority of black elected officials in the majority-black congres-

sional district were supportive of Tyus. Our objections went unheeded. As a last resort, Tyus proposed to withdraw and to support Weathers, who was considered the dean of black politics. The proposal was rejected.

For the next two weeks, we continued to promote Weathers as the best alternative. At the organizing meeting, Ray Howard nominated Goins. In his presentation, he chose to describe Weathers—his original political benefactor—as old, decrepit, and out of touch with the new black politics. He suggested that Weathers should retire and leave the running of political affairs to the young, intelligent, and dedicated. Weathers was on the executive boards of both the NAACP and the Urban League and had raised more money for civil rights causes than anyone in the city. His commitment to racial equality had never been questioned in such harsh, personal terms. His pride and ego were hurt by the attack. Howard's display of insensitivity, ingratitude, and irascibility guaranteed that he would suffer political discomfort in years to come.

The Goins-Howard faction elected Goins as chairman, all the officers of the district, and all members to the state committee. Only four of twenty-four whites voted for Weathers. In return, Goins did not name a white person as an officer of the district or as a delegate to the state committee. But most of his white supporters were not disturbed by the omission. They celebrated, carnival-like, the event of an impertinent African American congressman being put in his proper place. After the meeting, Dr. Milton Greenberg, white committeeman of Creve Coeur Township, said, "They went along with Goins because Congressman Clay didn't confront them in his decision to support Senator McGovern for president. He made his deal, so now we make ours."[38] Dr. Greenberg's reasoning sounded precisely like the medical writing on one of his prescriptions: impossible to understand. Mary Madeson, a white committeewoman from Hadley Township who had supported Goins for chairman, was even more incoherent. She blamed Goins's failure to include whites in his slate of officers on me. She stated, "This oversight of the largest voting area [St. Louis County] in the First Congressional District is going to make it difficult for myself and other white committeemen to sell the congressman."[39]

CHAPTER

13

BRUISING 1974 CANDIDACY FOR CONGRESS

From the first days of my entry into politics until my retirement from Congress in 2001, elements within the St. Louis power structure waged a war to diminish my influence and destroy my career. Members of the business community, in every election, sought individuals to oppose my candidacy and made lucrative offers of financial campaign assistance. The 1974 election was a reflection of the others, except it was much more intense. My opponents in business and the media again envisioned the possibility of defeating me. A highly qualified black candidate, Clifford W. Gates, filed for office. His credentials were impressive: He was the owner of the largest black real-estate company in town, board chairman of the only Negro-owned bank, former member of the St. Louis Police Commission, and former president of the Urban League.

Gates repeatedly said that if he decided to run, he would not necessarily be obligated to the "special interests of the white business community." Despite his denial of being encouraged by downtown businessmen to seek the office, the *Post-Dispatch* reported on May 17, 1974, that "[at] least two other black leaders were approached by business leaders [before Gates agreed] to run against Clay. Harold Antoine, head of the Human Development Corporation, and William Douthit, executive director of the St. Louis Urban League, acknowledged that they were approached by a business group."[40] The *People's Guide* was even more direct, stating on April 10, 1974, that it had learned that Gates "had been offered a substantial amount of money to challenge Clay."[41] My position was that anyone had a right to run for whatever office he or she chose. I was confident that Doris Moore, my campaign manager, and our organizational operatives would be adequate to handle the situation while I remained in Congress four days a week working to save the poverty program and finalizing legislation for pension reform (the Employee Retirement Income Security Act, or ERISA).

The Fraudulent Campaign Promise

Despite Gates's denial, persistent rumors circulated about the obsession of the downtown business crowd with financing campaigns against me. The business tycoons soliciting candidates were constantly boasting of their desire to defeat me. Candidates have been routinely enticed by them to file for Congress in the First District, only to be disappointed with the scant level of support received.

Authoritative sources revealed the ordeal of one individual who gullibly swallowed the propaganda. The story goes that he envisioned an enriching campaign based on the much-publicized rumor of "promised" contributions to oppose me. Supposedly, he was promised $250,000 if he ran. As a clever entrepreneur, he envisioned the normal 10 percent commission off the top for his services; the rumor in political circles, at least, was that he intended to fare very well in pursuit of his "forty acres and a mule." After filing for Congress, it was said that he called a meeting with his alleged backers. It took place in one of the newly constructed high-rise buildings in beautiful downtown St. Louis. His opening statement thanked everyone for their promise of financial commitments, and he proceeded to outline a budget for the $250,000.

When finished, the chairman of a major bank board outlined the method of financing the campaign. He deleted the $26,000 rental and utility costs for a headquarters because a large realtor was to provide ample space on a heavily traveled street without charge. A major printer doing business with the campaign backers would donate the $35,000 in printing. A newspaper delivery service company would donate $20,000 for door-to-door distribution of at least three leaflets. The $37,000 in postage for two mailings would be a joint venture; several businessmen agreed to run the envelopes through their stamp meters. An outdoor advertising firm would donate the billboards at no cost. Headquarters furniture, typewriters, automobiles, and telephones would be leased and

paid for by several of the leasing companies. Manpower would be provided by giving some of their employees paid leaves of absence to work
on the campaign. Vehicle rentals and other necessities would be
absolved in a similar manner. They then suggested that small fund-
raisers given by the candidate's committee would be good for encouraging citizen participation and would also raise enough to cover miscella-
neous expenditures.

At the conclusion of the meeting, a bewildered, confused, and
disillusioned candidate for Congress knew he had been outfoxed by the
shrewdest politicians in town. He left without a cent in cash and had
to pay $6 of his own money for parking in the building's garage.

**Clay/Goins joint campaign for re-election, 1974. From left: State
Representative Raymond Quarles, Clay, John Bass, unidentified,
Benjamin Goins.**

Goins and Clay Campaign Jointly

According to the most knowledgeable political professionals, Goins's chances for re-election were in serious doubt. Webbe, Berra, Gibbons, and other white politicians assessed his chances of winning South Side wards as dismal. In a meeting with several statewide and citywide elected officials, they prevailed on Tyus, Weathers, Payne, and me to forget our disagreements and combine our efforts for the good of the party. In consideration of their deep concerns, we agreed, and I took a lead role in campaigning for Goins in the portion of the city that was in the First District.

Most of my top advisers and longtime supporters vigorously and vocally followed my lead. Some, however, refused to endorse or campaign for him. But Goins and I printed literature for joint distribution in the city. We established a telephone bank together. We engaged in a joint effort to raise money. Along with Bass, we promoted "An Evening of Entertainment" fund-raising benefit featuring Redd Foxx at the Powell Symphony Hall.

Media Assault on Clay's Character

The campaign was filled with fallacious accusations and exaggerated untruths. The *Globe-Democrat* exhibited its usual excessive and brutal form of reporting. Typical editorial and news headlines intended to undermine my campaign were: "Gates Calls Clay Hypocritical," "The Unrepresentative Mr. Clay," "Clay Backers Split on Gates's Candidacy," "Hoodlums Support Clay," "Feet of Clay," "Alderwoman Claims Life Threatened," "Clay's Vicious Tactics," and "Clay's Staff Assistant Also Defended Drug Traffic Kingpin." The content accompanying the headlines was a diatribe of slander and smear, more sinister than in any previous campaign.

For two years, the newspaper had vilified my character almost daily. The FBI, Justice Department, Drug Enforcement Agency, and Internal Revenue Service conducted investigations of me based on fabricated news items appearing in the *Globe-Democrat* and the *Wall Street Journal*. The governmental lawlessness and prosecutorial witch-hunting were partially a result of my being placed on President Nixon's list of

240 Americans he named as "enemies" of the country. I was disappointed that my name was included while such known enemies of democratic liberties and constitutional rights as J. Edgar Hoover and Spiro Agnew were omitted.

Padding my congressional payroll, accepting kickbacks, peddling narcotics, double-charging for travel, and misappropriating campaign contributions were only a few of the reckless criminal charges leveled against me by the media and government agencies. Considering the attacks, I could not afford to take Gates's filing lightly. He was a successful entrepreneur with important connections in the white power structure. The *Globe-Democrat* endorsed him early and intensified its vendetta against my type of uncontrolled and uncontrollable leadership. Gates was also endorsed by N. A. Sweets, publisher of the weekly *St. Louis American*, who declared in a front-page August 1, 1974, recommendation that "Clay's strength in his strongest wards has deteriorated. It could be a horse race to the wire. We hope Gates wins in a photo finish."[42]

The local CORE leaders, Kermit Guy, Henry Thomas, and Solomon Rooks, issued a sharply worded statement endorsing Gates and telling me "to shape up, or . . . be shipped out."[43] The three claimed they were angry because I refused to debate Gates. The accusation was true in a sense. The *Post-Dispatch* reported that I had charged that "G. Duncan Bauman, publisher of the *Globe-Democrat*, [was my] real opponent. [I] called Gates a front and . . . challenged Bauman to a debate."[44] ACTION, an activist civil rights group, took exception to CORE's position. George Johnson, vice chairman of the group, issued a press release urging the black community to "ignore CORE's rhetoric. For CORE to publicly attack an active politician who has paid sacrificial dues in the interest of human rights is definitely insane."[45]

The committeewoman of Normandy Township, Helen Gerleman, endorsed Gates. The Twenty-seventh Ward, under the leadership of Alderman Milton F. Svetanics Jr. and Committeeman Allan Mueller, also voted to support Gates. Committeeman J. B. "Jet" Banks of the Nineteenth Ward had trouble deciding whom to support. He was quoted by the *Post-Dispatch* as saying he "might work on behalf of Gates, possibly as campaign manager."[46] I was unimpressed and unconcerned about the biennial threats of the paper tiger of the Nineteenth Ward. Perhaps the most influential business tycoon in town, Lief J. Sverdrup, chairman of the board of Sverdrup & Parcel and Associates, who normally donated to Republican candidates, was the first contributor to Gates's campaign. Gates's first campaign report to the clerk of the U.S. House of Representatives showed Sverdrup as donating one third of Gates's funds. Other big Republican contributors included Walter King, president of Curlee Clothing Company; James B. Abernathy, real-estate broker; Ethan Sheply, vice president of Boatsman Bank; John H. Lashly, corporate lawyer; George Linne, president of Killark Electric; Joseph Vatterott, real-estate developer; M. R. Chambers, chairman of Interco; and Johnny Londoff, automobile dealer.

I called on U.S. Attorney Donald J. Stohr to investigate Sverdrup's illegal contribution. In citing an opinion issued by Henry R. Peterson, assistant attorney general, architects and engineers doing business with the federal government could not contribute to federal candidates. The *Post-Dispatch* covered the story, quoting me as saying, "The conflict of interest is very obvious in view of the fact that Sverdrup has a substantial number of federal contracts. My opponent should have known better than to solicit or accept a large contribution from a firm having earned millions of dollars from government contracts."[47] Sverdrup had to admit his mistake, and Gates had to refund the contribution.

John D. Schneider, a devout Catholic I respect very much and a prominent Democratic state senator elected in the county part of the district, also came out against my candidacy. He stated that "he would oppose renomination of [me] and Symington because of [our] refusal to support legislation that would stop abortion."[48]

Another powerful force indirectly gave support to Gates. The week before the primary election, Cardinal John J. Carberry, archbishop of St. Louis, wrote a pastoral letter "urg[ing] Catholics to inform themselves of candidates' positions on [abortion] and to vote in Tuesday's primary."[49]

My opponent had garnered an impressive array of support, but I was not helplessly or hopelessly without major backers. I received the endorsement of thirteen of the fifteen Democratic city ward organizations and six of the Democratic county townships. The fifty members at a meeting of the First District Democratic Committee unanimously endorsed me for re-election. The very powerful Missionary Baptist Ministers' Union of Greater St. Louis, an organization of 125 ministers representing 85,000 parishioners, endorsed me. I had the editorial endorsements of the *Defender*, the *Post-Dispatch*, and the *Argus*.

The greatest, most ridiculous, most painful, and almost humorous accusation against me in many years was one implying my involvement in the importation of a hit man. The media reported the absurd, trumped-up charge that a hit man had come from California to kill my opponent. News stories provided the grist for the sordid and ridiculous rumor: Gates reported to the police that he feared for his life. A black female alderwoman allegedly overheard two people in a cocktail lounge discussing the details of the planned assassination. She informed the *Globe-Democrat* instead of the FBI. Later, she alleged that she had been threatened by former state representative John Conley, a convicted drug trafficker who was free on appeal bond.

The *Globe-Democrat* informed the federal crime task force by way of a sensational front-page scoop, mischievously identifying the convicted felon as a close ally of mine. The alderwoman was first quoted as saying that she thought my name was mentioned when Conley threatened her for not endorsing me. The crux of the story was as such: Did I or did I not put up the money to bring in the hit man? The alderwoman never said that she had heard my name mentioned.

She gave the location of the alleged conversation but was blurry as to the description of the phantom assailants. The law-abiding woman had reason to personally dislike me. Several years prior, in a similar political battle, I had tagged her with a nickname that clung like white on rice and crippled her political effectiveness. Since that time, the endorsement of candidates by this public servant whom I had labeled a "political zero" ceased to be taken seriously.

Apparently, the radio, television, and newspapers were not concerned about their excessive reporting. After a week of the story circulating around the country and becoming more distorted, I announced a press conference to be held at Lambert–St. Louis Airport. The media was informed of my scheduled arrival, the conference was set to last thirty minutes, and I intended to board the next plane back to Washington, D.C. Local TV, radio, and newspapers and a few national media organizations attended.

My opening statement categorically denied the accusation and cast aspersions on the credibility and sanity of the charging party. I also engaged in a lengthy dissertation outlining my rise up the political ladder from total obscurity to become one of the most influential politicians in the state. Next, I explained that much wisdom and skill were required to accomplish such feats. I said that if brains, intellect, and good judgment had gotten me where I was, why would anyone suspect that I would be dumb enough to import a hit man to kill my harmless opponent?

My closing statement was classic Bill Clay. I said, "With the high rate of unemployment for hit men in the First Congressional District, why would a gifted politician like myself give the job to someone from California?" That concluded the press conference and ended the overly dramatic news coverage of the hit man incident as a major campaign factor.

Police Officers Stationed at Polls

The decision by the St. Louis City Board of Elections to assign policemen at each of the 184 precincts in the city's portion of the First Congressional District was sharply criticized. The Board of Police Commissioners voted unanimously to station officers at the polling places. Attorney Frankie Freeman, a member of the U.S. Commission on Civil Rights, expressed serious concern in a letter dated July 29, 1974, to T. D. McNeal, president of the Board of Police Commissioners. She said that only one of two situations precipitated such action:

1) only in an election in which two major contenders are black could conditions be created for potential trouble, or 2) the presence of the police was intended to intimidate voters. In the first case, it is my opinion that the proposed action of the police department is unwarranted. In the second case such action would be illegal.[50]

Attorney Margaret B. Wilson said, "There appears to be a suggestion that something is unusual about the North Side that requires a massive infusion of police. I don't understand the reasoning, and I don't think a climate should be created when none exists."[51]

Without doubt, one of the nastiest, most reprehensible media attacks of any political campaign was launched by the *Globe-Democrat* on the day before the August 1974 Democratic primary. In a front-page editorial endorsing Gates, the newspaper ran a photo of me and two individuals who had extensive criminal backgrounds. The caption above the photo read "Hoodlum Associates of Congressman Clay," and the headline above the editorial was titled "Hoodlum Support for Clay." The impression created was that mobsters were playing a major role in my campaign. However, deep in the article it was mentioned that the photo was taken seven years earlier. Four hundred similar photos, selling for $1.50 each, were taken at a Christmas dance fund-raiser. One individual in the picture had been dead for three years, and the other had been in prison for the past two years. The editorial stated, "This newspaper is convinced that William L. Clay's tenure in Congress has been a disgraceful affront to all the citizens."[52]

After the polls closed and the votes were counted, it became obvious that the *Globe-Democrat* had very little influence in the First Congressional District. I defeated Gates by almost 20,000 votes. In the predominantly black inner-city precincts, I beat Gates 10–1. In the Twenty-sixth Ward, I won by a vote of 2,929 to 231.

Shedding crocodile tears and licking its wounds the day after the election, the *Globe-Democrat* editorialized, "There can be nothing but a taste of ashes over the victory of William L. Clay, the racist incumbent of the First District."[53]

Threat to Kill Bond Issue

On the night of my victory, I issued an ultimatum to the business community and city fathers. During a live interview on the local CBS radio station, conducted between the sixth and seventh innings of the National League pennant-bound St. Louis Cardinals baseball game, I stated that unless 50 percent of contracts awarded from a $109,385,000 bond issue went to black contractors prior to the November election, we would defeat the bond issue. At the time, black contractors were receiving less than 1 percent of all city contracts.

The powers-that-be went bananas. As usual, certain elements in the black community were called upon to rebut what they considered to be my irresponsible tirade. Within hours, leaders of the Urban League and the NAACP decried my pronouncement. Several members of the black press followed suit in criticizing my action. The *Globe-Democrat* and KMOX editorialized against it. Goins appeared on radio and television, opposing the demand as radical and unnecessary. Immediately, some of his followers stated, "We told you so."

I held steadfastly to my demand for 50 percent, and for two weeks I allowed my critics to vent their anger and frustration. Psychology was on my side. I knew that the more they spoke, the more support for my position would develop. How could it be intelligently and honestly argued that 50 percent of the people are entitled to less than 1 percent of tax-supported contracts?

I returned to St. Louis from Washington, D.C., and called a meeting of those who were responsible for organizing the opposition to the bond issue. I invited sixty-two people; more than one hundred came.

I deliberately invited those who had attacked my position. Those opposing my demand presented the expected arguments about polarizing the community, doing more harm than good, not having enough qualified black contractors, and a litany of other disparaging remarks. For a brief period, I imagined I was at a Ku Klux Klan pep rally—until it dawned on me that many of the anti-quota people had been attending Klan meetings for years under the guise of dialogue groups.

Dialogue groups[54] were established in the early 1960s by a downtown business group called Civic Progress. They were designed to bring black and white leaders together and to prevent the kind of violent racial eruptions in St. Louis that were taking place in most other metropolitan centers. But, in time, they became an effective mechanism for establishing a safety zone between the victims of injustice and the victimizers. Until recently, the dialogue committees met weekly to discuss racial issues. The term "dialogue" was a misnomer because it implied discussion between two or more people; the only people talking were the blacks. The leaders of Civic Progress did all of the listening and received enough information to effectively develop strategies to offset any serious challenge to the welfare of the downtown business interests.

When my turn came to speak at the meeting, I stated, "If you believe that demanding 50 percent of the contracts is unreasonable, unfair, disruptive, [and] racist, what percentage do you recommend we take back to our constituents?" There was silence. Calloway then spoke. He said that blacks accounted for 42 percent of the total population and that we should demand no more. The group agreed, and a committee was appointed to work out the details. Mayor Poelker supported the 42 percent and assigned Gwen Giles, executive director of the city's Civil Rights Enforcement Agency, to monitor all contracts on the convention center.

Before the project was completed, 27 percent of all contracts were awarded to black contractors. Although the goal of 42 percent was not reached, minority participation increased by 26 percent, and the principle of equitable contract awarding was concretely established for tax-supported building projects. It was a major advancement for minority contractors.

Despite the turmoil and controversy surrounding my politics, I not only survived but also prevailed in most of my initiatives. One newspaper reporter described the situation in very straightforward terms. Jake McCarthy of the *Post-Dispatch* wrote:

> Clay's popularity seems to be riding high despite the publicity barrage against him. At a recent dinner sponsored by the St. Louis chapter of the National Association of Social Workers, Clay arose to introduce the principal speaker,

Congresswoman Barbara Jordan of Texas. As he went to the rostrum in the Khorassan Room of the Chase-Park Plaza Hotel, the full house gave Clay a standing ovation. One Clay associate noted accurately enough that this was an assemblage of middle-class black and white social workers and their spouses, not a band of precinct workers from Clay's Twenty-sixth Ward.[55]

Uneventful 1976 Campaign for Congress

The 1976 campaign for Congress lacked the excitement of my previous elections. James "Pal" Troupe, who had originally filed for Congress in 1968 but withdrew in my favor, decided to make another run for the position. His campaign consisted of a series of press releases attacking my record, but it suffered from inadequate funds and no visible campaign organization. What made the election eventful were the demise of Troupe as a political player and the rise of two new, spirited, young ward leaders.

I sponsored a fund-raising event at a midtown hotel on a Sunday afternoon the day before the deadline to file for office. One individual showed up at the very end of the affair and explained that his tardiness was due to a family squabble at a cookout. He said that there had been a long discussion about the feasibility of his uncle filing against me for Congress. I was flabbergasted because I did not expect to be challenged.

Immediately, I invited several key players to my hotel suite to plan a strategy. Troupe, a Democratic ward committeeman, had to be challenged. We decided that Louis Ford would be a good candidate for committeeman and had an excellent chance of winning. Leroy Wilson then mentioned that Billie Boykins would make a good candidate for committeewoman. He went to her home and brought her back to the hotel. She agreed, and the two of them filed for office the next day. The result was the election of Ford and Boykins as the Democratic committeepeople in the Fifth Ward. Troupe not only lost his committeeship but also was beaten badly in the race for Congress.

Fund-raiser at the Chase Park Plaza Hotel, 1970.

CHAPTER

14

BAIT YOUR HOOK WITH A SNAKE TO CATCH A BASS: BASS'S CAMPAIGN UNDERMINED BY BLACKS

The most reckless exploit with the most devastating impact on black political advancement in my entire career was the defeat of John Bass for re-election as comptroller. His election four years earlier set the tone for our reaching political manhood in St. Louis. The comptroller sits on the Board of Estimates, and the Board of Aldermen cannot spend any tax money without the recommendation of the Board of Estimates. The comptroller personally approves all city contracts and has a voice in how the city spends its taxpayer-generated revenue.

Bass used the power of that office to increase tenfold the number of black contractors doing business with the city. He stood like a giant in keeping Mayor Poelker from closing HGP Hospital, the source of primary health care for indigent patients.

His re-election bid was undermined by a cadre of black officials collaborating with Democratic officeholders. Goins, Howard, and Fred Williams, in plotting Bass's defeat, issued press releases questioning his competency, character, integrity, and suitability for public office. They hammered away at Bass's credibility with demeaning statements. When asked if he was going to support Bass, Goins said, "I'm endorsing him, but that's as far as I'm going." Williams stated, "Bass is a man of lackluster performances. [Bass's] one dubious achievement—raising property taxes to the maximum limit—singles him out as the most ineffectual comptroller in the history of the city of St. Louis."[56]

Meanwhile, whites consolidated their support behind Sheriff Percich for comptroller and entered into an arrangement for Goins to replace him as sheriff. The chief duties of the office were to act as bailiff in the courtroom and to transport prisoners from jail to court and back. A sheriff without arrest powers impressed some as being more important than a comptroller with purse power. The *Post-Dispatch* wrote that

"Goins and several other black political leaders would reject the write-in efforts in return for being allowed to select the new sheriff if Percich is elected comptroller."[57]

The plot thickened when Goins was publicly mentioned to replace Percich as sheriff. The media commented that Goins would be able to run for Congress without jeopardizing his position as license collector. The elections for Congress and license collector were decided at the same time. The sheriff's election was held two years afterward.

Promoters of the Machiavellian scheme were unexpectedly aided when city voters passed a ballot referendum spearheaded by the Republican Party that called for an audit of all county offices. The state's Democratic auditor, George Lehr, conducted the audit, in which the comptroller's office was severely criticized. The office, which for twenty years had been run by the recently elected Mayor Poelker and touted by the media for its efficient, progressive operation, was singled out for harsh criticism. Bass was basically prohibited by law from replacing the merit system employees who managed the office and continued to use the procedures put in place by his predecessor, which had been hailed as innovative and progressive.

Percich Elected Comptroller

Two years before Bass's re-election bid, five white ward leaders were supported in citywide elections by black committeemen in exchange for their commitments to support Bass for re-election. Four of them reneged on the promise and supported his opponent.

In fact, every white elected official except one endorsed Percich, even though over the years he had established a reputation for accusing Democratic officeholders of incompetence, malfeasance, and, in some cases, corruption. He often ran for public office on a platform of abolishing patronage, reducing the size of the Board of Aldermen, and merging the city with the county. These issues ran counter to the agenda of regular Democratic politicians who depended on patronage as the basis for their ward organizations. But in the racially polarized atmosphere, a white candidate anathema to the well-being of other white politicians was preferable to a black incumbent who protected their basic interests.

Negroes were generally appalled when Mayor James Conway stated his intention to close HGP Hospital. They were more shocked that the black leaders who supported him had tacitly accepted his insensitive position. Criticisms of them were both stinging and tempered. They were chastised in the harshest of terms and accused of being more interested in patronage jobs and personal enrichment than in the welfare of their impoverished constituents. Without specifically naming anyone, I said, "You've all seen *Roots* on television, where they talked about house niggers and field niggers. Well, we have some house niggers in this town, and some of them made a deal to trade the comptroller's office for the office of sheriff."[58]

The admonishment touched a raw nerve. Banks, Goins, Calloway, and several black ministers took offense, demanding a retraction. I declared that the accusation was against those who had schemed to undermine Bass's campaign, and "if the shoe fits, wear it." But politics is politics. Bass was sacrificed by fellow Democrats and targeted for defeat by the local media. Adverse news coverage and invidious sniping by black officials resulted in his loss.

Percich defeated Bass by 3,500 votes. The black community was outraged. C. B. Broussard, a Democratic Party member who had helped lead blacks from the Republican Party in the 1930s, was a well-respected community leader and a member of the Board of Aldermen. He was "deeply disturbed" by Bass's defeat, stating, "There seems to be substance to the allegation that some members of the Central Democratic Committee conspired to defeat Bass."[59]

Four days after the primary, I called a meeting in Bass's headquarters. In attendance were Reverends Ralph McDaniel, James Cummings, William D. Edwards, Willie J. Ellis, J. H. Oxley, Wormley, and Kaufmann of St. Phillips Lutheran Church. They joined Bass, Tyus, and Pearlie Evans. I outlined my reaction to the election in a lengthy and caustic statement. The following excerpts are from my remarks:

It is that time to put our foot down with the Democratic Party. For too many years, we have been responsible for keeping them in office with our overwhelming vote margins on the North Side. . . . Only one white leader endorsed Bass, and he did not work for his election.

I personally don't care whether the Democratic or the Republican candidate for mayor wins. Both have publicly stated they will work to close Homer G. Phillips Hospital—so either way we lose the hospital that provides care for the black indigent.

We need to mobilize our community in an effort to put together a write-in campaign to re-elect Bass. It is going to be a difficult . . . task, and, in all probability, he will not win. But we need to show the Democratic Party that if [they want] our continued support, they must fight for it.[60]

Following my remarks, Reverend James Cummings, pastor of Lane Tabernacle AME Zion Church, took the floor and gave an impassioned speech. In part, he stated, "In reading the novel *Roots*, the first thing a Mandingo warrior learns is never to fight another Mandingo. As ministers, our destiny is always in the hands of God. We don't have to win. We want a piece of dignity—and when John Bass was dehumanized, it was occurring to all black people."[61]

Rev. J. H. Oxley stated:

What I am hearing is a power play—I am glad to hear Clay and Tyus say we are not adhering to the philosophy of loaves and fish. We are always looking for something. Our bellies lead us instead of our dignity. For thirty-five years, I have never received anything but checks from black people and have never been one to sit back and let white people make decisions about me.[62]

The ministers agreed to devise a plan expressing outrage at Bass's defeat. Two days following the meeting at Bass's headquarters, fifty-five ministers met at Lane Tabernacle AME Zion Church and endorsed the write-in ticket. The organizers were joined by community business and professional leaders.

However, the meeting was not peaceful, and the endorsement was not unanimous. Several ministers disagreed about the strategy that

Leroy Tyus, Clay, Doris Moore, and John Bass in 1982.

the black religious community should employ in reacting to losing its highest-ranking black elected official. A few ministers expressed doubt about the strategy of a write-in campaign. But their objections did not deter or dampen the enthusiasm of the overwhelming number of black ministers who endorsed the write-in slate.

Two black ministers, Melvin Smotherson of Washington Tabernacle Church and Richard Fisher of Metropolitan AME Zion Church, opposed the write-in campaign. Rev. Smotherson said, "I'm sick and tired of the constant fighting on every front. I demand a retraction of Clay's 'house nigger' statement. We would be up in arms if anyone else had said it."[63]

Three other ministers who demanded a retraction were John W. Heyward, pastor of Union Memorial United Methodist Church,

Rev. Daniel Hughes of Eastern Star Baptist, and John Doggett, United Methodist district superintendent. However, they did not go so far as to refuse to support the write-in ticket.

I refused to apologize or retract my statement, saying instead, "When Frederick Douglass, W. E. B. DuBois, and Alex Haley apologize for using the term 'house nigger,' then expect to witness my retraction."

Two nights after the ministers announced support of the write-in ticket, another group of black ministers decided that a better way of teaching white Democrats a lesson was to support the Republicans. They endorsed the two Republican candidates: James Stemmler for mayor and Alderman Leonard Burst for comptroller.

Rev. R. J. Ward resisted joining the move to vote Republican. He stated, "I am not anti-Banks, anti-Payne, or anti-Clay—I'm a Democrat, and I want to be part of a reconciliation."[64]

Clay and Bass Announce for Mayor and Comptroller: A Crusade for Dignity

On March 9, more than five hundred people crowded into the Bass headquarters to evaluate election results, assess the feasibility of retaliating against the Democratic Party, and consider a write-in campaign.

The following night an even larger crowd met as Bass and I announced our candidacies. Addressing the audience, we were on the same wavelength in explaining the reason for the write-in. Bass stated, "We want to restructure the party and strengthen it." I called the campaign "a crusade for dignity—a crusade to reform the party we have been a part of for forty years."

Prominent religious, business, community, and civic leaders formed a committee to elect us. Nettie Cunningham was appointed chairperson, Tyus co-chairperson, and Mary Brewster treasurer. Wayman Smith III became the campaign manager. Pearlie Evans was named director of political strategy.

There was substantial political support for the write-in. The *Argus* reported that 2,500 people attended a Clay-Bass write-in rally at the United Auto Workers hall. Although the newspaper did not endorse me,

Alderman Steve Roberts, unknown, Senator Gwen Giles, Clay, Alderman Wayman Smith, and Constable Leroy Tyus.

it endorsed Bass and gave editorial justification for the validity of the write-in campaign: "To lose black representation on the city's [Board of Estimates] is a serious matter. The current write-in campaign at least demonstrates that this black community will react to such monumental losses and will not retreat to a cave and lick our wounds when betrayed."[65]

The write-in campaign drew bitter criticism from blacks who had supported Conway in the Democratic primary. Goins described it as "emotional and [it] does not reflect long-range planning. Just because you lose doesn't mean that you get out of the party."

The *St. Louis American* lamented the write-in with the words "Losers, weeping, seek Democratic split." The article was titled, "Three-Ring Political Circus Has Race for Mayor in a Turmoil." It referred to supporters of the write-in as being "sufficiently trained to jump when Clay cracks his whip."[66]

J. B. Banks, one of the most vociferous critics, joined the chorus of attacks, describing me as a self-serving politician "who puts pride as the highest prize rather than serving the best interests of the community." He alleged that I was vindictive because of a wounded ego and accused me of "putting the whole black community up for auction." Banks further stated, "Bill Clay seeks the mayor's post without a platform, promise, or commitment to the voters. . . . He has not brought any federal jobs or appointments to his district, except for personal gain. The black community has a right to expect leadership with foresight [and] upward mobility, not marginal or blurred vision."[67]

Calloway referred to the ministers who supported the write-in slate as "a motley crew of black ministers."[68] He blamed black Democratic politicians who supported the write-in for engaging in "politics of defeat and frustration" and attributed Bass's defeat to my ineptness as his "chief strategist." He also praised Goins's campaigning for Bass in South St. Louis during the first election, alleging that that was the reason Bass won.

This was a brash misrepresentation of Goins's role in Bass's 1973 election and a distortion of the relationship between Cervantes' mayoral campaign and Bass's efforts to be re-elected. Calloway was wrong on each assertion. First, I was not Bass's chief strategist, though I did provide maximum support. Second, Goins's escorting Bass around the South Side was an exercise in futility. Third, in his re-election campaign, Bass lost every white ward, receiving the same number of votes in those areas as four years prior. If Goins had been so influential in the white area, why did he lose every white ward by lopsided margins in his own race to replace Percich for sheriff just thirty days after Bass's loss?

Calloway's biased review gave credence to Weathers's assertion that "Calloway had never overcome his humiliating defeat for Congress at the hands of Bill Clay." Instead of asking why only one white Democrat endorsed Bass, Calloway attempted to place the blame for his defeat on the low turnout in Negro precincts.

An open letter to the *Argus* from one community leader, businesswoman Nettie Cunningham, stated, "Observe very carefully the viciousness and the swiftness with which the white press and white politicians and a few subservient Negroes have combined their forces to attack Representative Clay for daring to join with John Bass."[69]

My response was consistent with the history of my long battle with the Democratic Party. I stated, "We are not partners [with Democrats]. We are cannon fodder. We get the votes for them, and they take the victory, the glory, and the power. If we don't demand what's rightfully ours, we won't get it."[70]

Media distortion in analyzing the write-in alleged that Bass's and my protest action was unpopular, ill advised, and soundly rejected by black voters. Prophets of doom and gloom in some segments of black leadership attempted to describe the write-in as a failure. Deeming 17,000 citizens handwriting our names on a voting machine roll of butcher paper a failure was absurd. The procedure was outrageously cumbersome. Large stand-up voting machines were used, enclosed by a draw curtain to provide secrecy. In order to vote, it was necessary to manually pull the write-in slide panel, open one slide for mayor and one for comptroller—then write the names of Bass and Clay with a special felt-tip pen. Holding one lever while pulling another to open a small slot to write names on a roll of white butcher paper was a complicated procedure even for a contortionist.

Our opponents, not so much prophetic as pathetic, proclaimed that the write-in set blacks back twenty years. Others, more farsighted and more committed to progressive black politics, contended that blacks won a significant victory. The venture dispelled the myth that our people, regardless of the issue, had no alternative but to vote the Democratic ticket.

The *Globe-Democrat*, in an editorial the morning after the election, boasted:

> Conway and Percich walked away with the election, easily putting down the blustering write-in effort mounted by Rep. William L. Clay and Comptroller John F. Bass. If Clay intended to teach the Democratic Party a lesson, he winds up wearing a dunce cap. With 16,542 votes he cannot take much satisfaction from finishing behind Republican James A. Stemmler, who got only 16,877 to Conway's 69,677.[71]

The *St. Louis Argus*, which endorsed Bass but not me, had an opinion contrary to the *Globe-Democrat*. On April 7, 1977, it wrote:

> The write-in was an important step and gesture for St. Louis politics. A black man took a controversial stand against both the party machine and mainstream black politicians—the first step of its magnitude in St. Louis history. Whether he won or not, Clay's bid for mayor should be the needed fuse for black involvement in top government positions.[72]

The official tally by the St. Louis Board of Elections showed Conway losing to me in the ten predominantly black wards, 13,253 votes to 8,668 votes. In delivery wards where black leaders endorsed Conway, Bass and I ran exceptionally well. In Goins's Twenty-first Ward, I beat Conway by 212 votes. In Howard's First Ward, I won by 140 votes, and I lost Bank's Nineteenth Ward by 165 votes. Bass won eight of the ten black wards, with 11,180 votes to Percich's 2,958.

On election night I did something uncommon in St. Louis politics. I went to Conway's headquarters, shook his hand, and congratulated him. The only time this happened in my forty-two years of elective office was after my first election to the Board of Aldermen in 1959. The incumbent, Bill Brady, whom I had defeated, had entered our headquarters and congratulated me. Before I left Conway's headquarters, I jokingly said that I would have received 25,000 more votes if it "had not snowed heavily on the North Side and the sun had not shined brightly on the South Side."

White Democrats Displeased

White Democrats were horrified that blacks challenged the party in such a bold manner. The majority of white elected officials claimed they did not know our constituents were disgruntled. Alderman Martie Aboussie arrogantly reflected the mind-set of many white Democrats, saying, "The Democratic Party has been good to black people."[73]

The issue prompting the write-in was the indignation of black people toward white voters who customarily oppose qualified black candidates. Bass was not defeated because he lacked experience or competence. He lost because he adamantly supported his belief that all people, including blacks, deserved equitable representation and opportunity to engage in government policy-making. His rejection was part of the continuing saga to deny blacks a place at the table of political respect. Suggesting that powerless blacks were engaged in a power struggle was a cynical distortion of reality. Admittedly, there was a struggle between black leaders, particularly those associated with the Goins and the Clay factions.

White leadership has an uncanny talent for using disagreement among blacks as an excuse to dodge issues of racial unfairness. They skillfully divert attention from a conflict between the black and white races into a struggle for power between powerless individual blacks. The media and white Democrats, using their vast resources, effectively confound and successfully confuse the bottom-line issue: Democrats oppose the right of qualified blacks to hold important elective positions.

Absurdly, the media made it seem as if Bass and I were running against other black candidates. Conway and Percich were never called upon to respond to charges leveled by our supporters. News accounts featured only the rebuttal of black officials who had supported Conway in the primary and conspired with Percich in the deal of his replacement as sheriff.

The publisher and staff of the *Globe-Democrat* orchestrated the public effort to divert attention from Democrats organizing to defeat a black officeholder. The newspaper published an article titled, "Write-in Move Called a Clay-Goins Power Struggle." Two white politicians, Alderman Aboussie and Treasurer Berra, were quoted. Both ignored the basis for the write-in while supporting the concept of a power struggle. Aboussie said, "Every time Clay gets beat[en] and gets his back against the wall, he yells and screams. I don't think Clay is a real leader in the black community." Berra, in the same article, said, "Goins put short pants on Clay. This is the second time in a row Goins beat Clay."[74]

Disagreeing, McCarthy of the *Post-Dispatch* offered a different opinion as to why blacks were angry. On March 25, 1977, he wrote: "Their campaign for write-in votes strikes a chord in the black community which many whites are trying not to hear. The chord is anger and frustration. And it could ring long enough in the muted field of race relations to break into a marching song again someday."[75]

The media refused to acknowledge that the write-in campaign was about pride, respect, and dignity on behalf of 200,000 black citizens. Our people had been effectively left voiceless by the defeat of the highest-ranking, outspoken black city official. Our people felt betrayed, ignored, and insulted by the denial of a place in the highest seat of government.

Year after year, black officials had asked their constituents to vote for white candidates. But in Bass's campaign, we were told it was unreasonable to expect white South Side voters to support a black candidate. Bass and I chose to put our political life on the line. Through ministers, teachers, and rank-and-file workers, our message was brought home to the community.

Goins Seeks Percich's Former Office

When Percich was elected comptroller, he had to vacate the sheriff's office. Under Missouri law, the filling of the vacancy was by special election. The Democratic and Republican Central Committees each selected a candidate. Democrats named Goins, and Republicans named Charles Laber, a little known South Side businessman. All other candidates had to run as independents.

Execution of the plan to exchange positions came close to suffering a major setback when Goins was almost beaten by his Republican opponent. The foregone conclusion of pollsters and party insiders was that Goins would win by 20,000 votes, based on the fact that no Republican had won a citywide patronage office in more than forty years, that Goins had been elected citywide on three previous occasions, and that his opponent had very little name recognition.

Goins himself was confident that white voters embraced his style of leadership, and that black voters had no alternative but to cast their votes on his behalf. He was incorrect on both scores. Laber ran a surprisingly strong race in the white area, winning eight of the nine white wards. The voter turnout was low, and the election outcome was in question for several weeks. Several thousand absentee ballots were disputed; Laber cited a building in the Nineteenth Ward where 150 absentee ballots had been cast. Committeeman Banks of the ward pointed out that the building was sixteen stories high and housed 315 families.

Goins's supporters sweated until the final returns showed that Goins had received 22,667 votes to 21,122 for Laber. Goins lost the nine all-white wards 16,000 to 7,000 and won the mixed wards by only 2,000. The results were telling. White voters conditioned to vote against qualified black candidates have no trepidation about applying their animosity against unqualified black candidates.

The 1,575 vote difference sent shock waves throughout the Goins camp and the Democratic leadership. His defeat would have been a great upset. Goins placed the blame for his poor showing on me. He was quoted in the *Globe-Democrat* as saying, "We heard about two weeks ago that Clay was telling people on the North Side not to vote. This is not just speculation, this is fact."[76] If I were that influential, why would he contemplate running against me for Congress? His criticism gave me power I never recognized.

Agitation for Goins-Clay Contest

Several black elected officials enthusiastically promoted the misconception that their prowess at the polls enabled Conway to defeat Cervantes in the 1977 mayor's race. They argued that it was now possible for a black person to successfully challenge me for my seat in Congress. Goins was the most prominent black mentioned to make the race. In an article written by James Floyd, the *Globe-Democrat* reported, "Clout with Conway and the city's Democratic power structure could put Goins in the North Side political driver's seat firmly enough to challenge Clay for Congress. 'This is a fight between Clay and Goins for the First Congressional District seat,' Berra said. 'It's purely a power play in North St. Louis.'"[77]

Those involved in the scheme were mistakenly and mischievously credited with carrying the black vote for Conway over Cervantes. The media conveyed the impression that they were the "new leaders" of the black community. However, official election returns revealed a different result: Conway lost in the black community.

Cervantes won the black vote in the ten North Side wards, receiving 16,118 votes to Conway's 11,914. Cervantes carried seven of the ten black wards (First, Third, Fifth, Eighteenth, Twentieth, Twenty-second, and Twenty-sixth). Conway won the election in white South St. Louis. Berra, Joseph Roddy, Francis Slay, and Albert Villa—all key supporters of Cervantes—were defeated by Conway. Conway trounced Cervantes in the eleven South Side white wards by 37,812 votes. The outcome of the election in North St. Louis, contrary to news coverage, did not indicate that I had anything to fear from Howard, Banks, and Goins. The obvious conclusion was that they posed no serious threat to my ability for re-election.

Despite the results of Goins's poor showing in his race for sheriff, Banks accused me of being a "self-serving" politician and declared his intention to "draft Goins" to run against me for Congress.[78] It was a strange declaration, to which I responded, "I don't fear his candidacy. I think it's strange that I received twice as many votes as a write-in candidate [for mayor] than he received as a machine candidate in a general election. If he's going to run for Congress, he ought to stop jawboning and file for office."[79]

Several months passed before Goins filed. For several years, he and his cohorts had floated trial balloons about a tête-à-tête contest for Congress between us. My response was always, "It only requires a one-hundred-mile auto trip to the state capital and fifty dollars to file." Goins's retort was always laced with the cautious words, "I haven't made up my mind." In my opinion, he had not been assured by the media and his financial backers that the time was ripe.

The media and white politicians insisted on portraying the differences between Goins and me as a conflict of personalities. The simple truth is personality had nothing to do with it. I viewed it as a conflict in goals, agendas, and self-determination of our people. It was a clash in political, social, and economic philosophy. My disagreement stemmed from the fact that Goins did not consider race an impairment or impediment to success when overwhelming evidence proved it was both. I was convinced he knew how destructive his role of appeasement was to the advancement of our cause. He was neither knave nor fool. His politics of accommodation were just naïve and foolish.

Goins never perceived the historical import of the civil rights campaign. His temporary political escalation was tied to tenuous footing: his ability to inflate the egos of important whites in exchange for minor achievements and his effort to convince blacks that by expanding his influence with the white power structure major benefits would accrue to the black community.

Almost twenty years of sparring, jostling, and feigning came to a grand finale in 1978. The two most touted, most successful blacks in St. Louis politics, Goins and myself, found ourselves preparing for a long-awaited showdown: my defeat for re-election to Congress.

The anticipated contest was billed as the "Super Bowl" of St. Louis politics. Elected officials, ministers, and community leaders were

Clay and Benjamin Goins, ca. 1970. Photograph by Irving Williamson, ca. 1970, MHS Photographs and Prints Collection.

taking sides. One political observer described the encounter in the following manner: "It's going to be Congressman Clay's toughest campaign (since he was first elected to Congress in 1968), and it may be decided on money and muscle. I wouldn't want to be in the middle of it."[80]

This kind of verbosity was par for the course from unnamed sources who routinely predicted that the next election would be the toughest of my career. The same public statements were printed in 1968 when Calloway was an opponent, in 1972 when a prominent Republican challenged me, and in 1974 when a former police commissioner entered the race. The big, serious, and tough campaigns always failed to materialize.

In 1975 Goins sought endorsements from city elected officials, indicating that support from county Democrats and financial help from the business community were available. McCarthy, in a *Post-Dispatch* column, reported, "One report making the North Side rounds says that [the *Globe-Democrat*] is privately urging Goins to oppose Clay. The last man to try it, Clifton Gates, was their dark-haired boy, too, but he didn't get very far."[81]

In 1978, safely insulated from the necessity of surrendering his elected position as sheriff, Goins filed for Congress. He was convinced that he had sufficient financial and political backing in the venture. His friend Jack Flach at the *Globe-Democrat* wrote, "The feeling here is that much of the downtown money—Democrat and Republican business leaders who oppose Clay—will go to Goins and serve as encouragement to him to try and knock off Clay." In the same article, Flach said, "Clay has charged previously that Goins is a pawn of the city's white downtown power structure."[82]

My opening barrage was indicative of the fierceness the campaign would take. Determined that Goins would not be defined by the white media as a highly qualified candidate capable of adequately representing 500,000 citizens in Congress, I challenged his alleged qualifications, including his inclination to protect the interests of black Americans. I also questioned his ability to articulate a defense for preserving the environment, deflect assaults on the rights of workers, and protect Social Security benefits. Such issues would be the focus of my campaign. A front-page story appearing in the *St. Louis Post-Dispatch* the day after Goins's entry revealed the extent of my rancor. I predicted that the voters of the First Congressional District would never elect a "functional illiterate" to represent them in so important an office. Goins read at a sixth-grade level and had difficulty multiplying, but he had a special talent for dividing. He had no comprehension of the monumental struggle facing deprived and denied Americans.

Goins was quoted in a featured *Globe-Democrat* story shortly after filing, saying, "I've been called an Uncle Tom and 'a functional illiterate,' and I may be called that again—and worse—before this is over. But, so be it. I'm running. Yes—I'm definitely running for Congress."[83]

Several of my close friends and advisers were surprised at the harshness of my criticism. Others encouraged even greater revelation of his inadequacies. I decided that continued silence on the question of this barnacle clinging to the black people's ship of destiny was not the most prudent option for me. Those involved in politics already knew of Goins's limitations, and most agreed it would be a tragic mistake to elect him to the U.S. Congress. My conclusion was that he constituted an ever-present danger to our thrust for a new progressive and productive politics. I believed he posed an imminent peril during our community's struggle to educate and sensitize whites to accept us as equals. Political wisdom left me no alternative but to speak out forcefully and truthfully; not once in his highly publicized career did Goins raise his voice in meaningful protest to abusive treatment heaped upon our people by the police, absentee landlords, or cynical elected officials.

What African Americans wanted least was a person in the U.S. Congress who would bring shame and ridicule to our cause. Black Americans needed articulate, combative, abrasive leaders, who, if necessary, would become disruptive but dignified in order to protect and defend the civil rights of our people. Despite objections from friends and allies appalled at my unrestrained references to my opponent, I decided the real Goins would be paraded before the community for judgment. The time had come for black people to decide the kind of leadership they wanted. I was tired of hearing the refrain that the two of us should get together. At this point, it did not matter; patience has a limit. Goins's activities had exceeded the boundaries of my tolerance and forgiveness. I was not prepared to appease those who wanted me to overlook leadership shortcomings. I gambled that the majority wanted and benefited from my type of leadership and would accept nothing less.

Yellow Power v. Black Power

Career politicians, elected officials, and candidates have always provided enough comedy to keep motion picture and television scriptwriters fully employed. Will Rogers made a fortune entertaining the public with funny political stories. Politics is not exclusively tears and wailing or incessant wheeling and dealing; incidents are often peppered with comical dimension. Many are hilarious, some just plain amusing. One such occasion happened in the 1978 campaign for Congress in the First District of Missouri.

The racially diverse list of candidates attending one congressional debate resembled a menagerie of political aspirants that would have rendered the Rainbow Coalition proud. Besides Goins and me, there was a Filipino, an Irish woman, a Negro female, and a Korean male. The Korean, Takuri Tei, had run for Congress on two previous occasions. He came to the United States in 1952, spoke five languages fluently, and had earned degrees from seminaries—Eden in England and Concordia in Missouri—but worked as a tax accountant.

Five hundred black people were in attendance at a function sponsored by the St. Louis Urban League. Each candidate was permitted to speak for five minutes. The audience was allowed to ask questions of each.

Tei, a dapper dresser, was brilliant in his scholarly presentation. In addition to his education for the ministry, he also had a Ph.D. in social work and labored with community groups in the anti-poverty program. He expressed intentions to pass legislation addressing the major problems of society and the need for new representation with ideas for leading the country in a new direction. His English was slightly broken with a staccato beat but clearly understandable.

He spoke nonchalantly of his first run for Congress against me, admitting he received only three thousand votes, or 4 percent of the total. Then he enunciated his improvements in his totals in the second race, although he only received five thousand votes, or 6 percent. He assured the all-black audience that Asians are noted for their eternal patience and proudly uttered, "I won't beat Bill Clay this time either. I will get maybe seven thousand votes this election. The next time, I will raise that to nine thousand. By the year 2000, I will get more votes than Clay. That's yellow power kicking the hell out of black power." Laughter filled the room, so much so that tears filled many eyes before the program resumed.

Congressional Super Bowl Rained Out

Fortunately or unfortunately, the community was spared the aggravating trauma of choosing between two black leaders. In the midst of the campaign, Goins was indicted on charges of racketeering, testifying falsely before a grand jury, obstructing justice, and evading income taxes. He was convicted on June 24, 1978, in the federal courts, sentenced to seven years in prison, fined eight thousand dollars, and ordered to serve five years probation after completion of his term. Although he remained in the race while on appeal, his campaign virtually came to a halt. His friend and political adviser Mayor Conway was one of the first to call for Goins's resignation.

Under the cloud of conviction, Goins only received 1,985 votes. Five other candidates received 12,000 votes, and I received 28,202. I stated that the conviction and the nullification of the long-awaited contest were both unfortunate. With abiding faith in my people, I predicted that the outcome would have been the same as in the elections with Calloway and Gates. I believe my victory would have been overwhelming. It was the same scenario described in the *Post* after a previous election: "Goins [would have] discovered what some other black politicians have learned—that white support is no big help north of Delmar Boulevard any more. Clay's place is different. No matter the outcome of the white campaign against him, he will then be at best a hero and at worst a martyr."[84]

After serving his prison term, Goins reassessed his relationship with the black community. In December 1985, he expressed remorse at a breakfast I sponsored to solidify support for a slate of black incumbents (Freeman Bosley Jr., Billie Boykins, Bass, Troupe, and Lacy Clay) running in the next Democratic primary. I invited present and former black elected officials. Goins, in an impassioned, emotional speech, stated, "I spent many nights in my cell at the federal penitentiary thinking how different my life and career might have been had I not attempted to destroy Bill Clay. I now know that those white people claiming to be my friends were only interested in keeping black people back."[85] His admission in the presence of eighty black leaders was a major change in style and substance for Benjamin L. Goins.

CHAPTER

15

VINCENT SCHOEMEHL: HOPE FOR INCLUSION

My first encounter with Vincent Schoemehl was a remarkable experience. Glib and intelligent, swift and elusive—these adjectives paint the picture I most remember of him on that fateful day. He was the white knight in shining armor who convinced Larry Williams and me that with his support our people would find our Holy Grail.

Schoemehl was a silver-tongued, gold-throat orator who said all the right things and even used the right tonal inflections when comparing his own history of hardship to the plight of many of our race. His approach was not new, but his enthusiasm and self-assurance in confronting inequities were different and persuasive. Larry and I believed he had the potential to become a permanent fixture in Missouri politics, and we reasoned that with our support he could win, despite minimum support among white voters. We further speculated that it would be several years before the political establishment co-opted his independence. Naturally, until then we expected him to dance with those who brought him to the ball.

Schoemehl was ten years younger than Cervantes or Hearnes when he decided to seek higher office. What he lacked in terms of Cervantes' charisma and Hearnes's smooth demeanor was adequately compensated for by a down-to-earth rapport with the common people and a commitment to political realism.

Two reasons prompted my personal endorsement of Schoemehl for mayor in 1981. Both were related to Homer G. Phillips Hospital. First, my judgment to support him was somewhat colored by the fact that our community was seeking a "pound of flesh" from Conway, the mayor who had made the callous political decision to close our hospital. Those who flagrantly trample on their constituents' right to adequate health care had to be taught a political lesson. Second, Schoemehl promised to reopen the facility and had to be given that chance. We realized that in a properly promoted campaign most voters on the North Side would not be pro-Schoemehl, but rather anti-Conway.

My support of Schoemehl was not based on idealistic daydreams or the reckless, wishful assumption that he would be the alpha and the omega for reforming a manipulative political system that had hindered the progress of African Americans. The decision was practical—realistically taking into account the constriction of a racially polarized city and the lack of resources available to elect a black mayor. White voters who were in the majority would have united against any serious black candidate. Further, it was evident that the black elected officials who campaigned for Conway even after he had announced his intention to close HGP Hospital had lost credibility among black voters.

A black candidate for mayor was not a reasonable option. It was impossible to mobilize the black community sufficiently to turn out the necessary votes for victory. Neither ample campaign funds nor a viable candidate was available for such a venture. Our only feasible option was to support a rising white political star who was committed to an agenda acceptable to a large number of our people.

Schoemehl Overcomes the Odds with Major Black Support

To say that Schoemehl overcame the odds to become mayor of St. Louis understates how he eventually became the victor. At a meeting in my suite at the Mayfair Hotel with Larry Williams, committeeman of the Eighteenth Ward, Schoemehl admitted to having little chance of success without our help. The three of us agreed that he had no political base, white politicians thought he followed no fixed political course, and most black people could not even pronounce his name ("Sham-mole").

Larry and I were very familiar with the long history of white candidates deceiving blacks in their bids for public office. We had become anesthetized to the deceptive dialogue of their insincere promises. But in poetic terms (not derogatorily), we envisioned this candidate to be so desperate for support that lightning had finally struck us.

Doris Moore, campaign manager for Clay, City Treasurer Larry Williams, Clay, and supporter Barbara Noble, undated.

We eagerly provided the political muscle for transforming him into a viable contender. Without leaving the hotel room, in a period of five hours, the campaign machinery was put in place through a series of telephone calls and conversations with visitors to the suite. Larry and I endorsed Schoemehl and were able to secure the backing of other important individuals. We lined up support from union leaders and attained substantial commitments from financial backers. Six black ward leaders associated with our faction agreed to support his candidacy. Several union leaders who had been hesitant in supporting Schoemehl responded to our plea and showered him with personal endorsements and the promise of financial assistance. They did not want Conway but doubted that Schoemehl could defeat him. We convinced them otherwise. After spending hours consuming beer and hamburgers and listening to other politicians who had joined us in the suite, we saw that Schoemehl's future had become very bright.

The next day, Larry and I visited the home of Fred Weathers, the dean emeritus of black politics. In meticulous detail, we outlined the basis of our agreement for supporting Schoemehl, who had only two ward endorsements at the time he walked into my hotel room. In exchange for our support, Schoemehl pledged to name two blacks of our choice to his cabinet; give us veto power over appointments to several major boards and commissions; and allow us to name blacks to manage the St. Louis Agency for Training and Employment (SLATE), the Community Development Agency (CDA), and the Housing Authority as long as he had no serious objection to the individuals.

Weathers accused Larry and me of being naïve. He said that once in office, Schoemehl would renege on his commitments. Especially, he said, no white politician would ever appoint a black who was financially and politically independent of his regime to head the CDA, which annually disbursed $35 million to neighborhood groups for federal housing.

Despite Weathers's admonition, we waged a vigorous campaign on Schoemehl's behalf. He in turn aggressively challenged Conway's laissez-faire attitude toward the concerns of our constituents. Schoemehl defeated Conway in all but one of the twenty-eight wards. Despite endorsements from sixteen regular ward organizations, the mass media, and established political and civic leaders, Conway went down in defeat.

Conway attributed his defeat to two emotional issues—the allegation that he wanted to reduce the police force by five hundred officers and Schoemehl's "promise to reopen Homer G. Phillips Hospital."[86] An important reason for Conway's lack of support on the North Side had been his refusal to establish a partnership with legitimate spokespersons in the black community. Choosing to create his own brand of ghetto leadership, he totally isolated respected black leaders from the planning and decision-making process. Without their support, he was unable to get his campaign off dead center in the black wards. Even with the endorsements of five black committeemen (Banks, Goins, Howard, Payne, and Tyus) from so-called "delivery wards," Conway's campaign sputtered, staggered, and eventually petered out.

The unpardonable sin of closing HGP figured heavily in his defeat. After the election, he admitted to being "slaughtered" because of the hospital issue. Schoemehl received 70,507 votes to the incumbent's 32,683. In the ten black wards, Schoemehl received 27,000 votes to his opponent's 3,300. In the six racially mixed wards, Schoemehl beat Conway 10,000 votes to 5,900. His total margin of victory was 37,824 votes.

Homer G. Phillips Hospital:
A Milestone in the History of St. Louis Negroes

Homer G. Phillips (HGP) Hospital came into being as the result of a twenty-three-year struggle that began in 1914 to build a medical facility staffed by black doctors, black nurses, black technicians, and black administrators. The opening of the hospital created hundreds of jobs for orderlies, aides, janitors, and ambulance drivers. At its peak, nearly one thousand black skilled and semi-skilled health-care personnel were employed in the complex. It was a first-rate institution serving the health needs of the Negro community while training blacks from across the country and around the world in the medical profession. Howard University and Meharry Medical College, unable to place graduates as interns and residents in white hospitals because of racial discrimination, were able to place graduate students at this magnificent facility.

The hospital was the cornerstone of medical, professional, economic, and employment stability for the black community. It was the glue that held the minority community together. For more than thirty years, it was the primary source of medical care for indigent Negroes. The hospital complex was the only agency of city government where blacks held significant jobs in professional positions.

From the time HGP was dedicated in 1937 until it closed in 1979, the black community was preoccupied with the struggle to keep the doors of the hospital open. Efforts to close the facility were led by numerous politicians, the two local medical schools, the publishers and editors of daily newspapers, and downtown financial leaders. These forces constituted a serious and continually agitating catalyst for closure.

Black people had no effective means of retaliating against the medical schools, newspapers, and business leaders, but they used their bloc-voting power to chastise elected officials. The judicious use of the ballot in some cases—wantonly in others—rewarded whites who were seeking elective office and supported the hospital while punishing those who did not. At least three former mayors who attempted to close the hospital were defeated for re-election because of black voter opposition.

John Poelker, who narrowly unseated Cervantes, was on the right side of all issues relating to the black community. He created suspicions, however, when he authorized studies to determine if HGP served any legitimate purpose. Aldermen Wayman F. Smith and Vincent Schoemehl circulated a petition supporting the retention of HGP as a general service facility.

Nursing students in classroom, Homer G. Phillips School of Nursing. Photograph, ca. 1960. MHS Photographs and Prints Collection.

Meanwhile, the estimates board authorized an outside group to study the hospital system to determine which of the two city-operated facilities would maintain its general services. Poelker ordered the transfer of vital medical services to the white-run city institution and refused to commit to keeping HGP open. These positions caused consternation in our community, and the mayor's job rating registered almost nil in the polls. Based primarily on that factor, Poelker decided not to seek a second term because black voters threatened his defeat over the issue.

With the assistance of several Negro politicians, Conway, who succeeded Poelker, finally accomplished what others had failed. He moved aggressively to consolidate the two hospitals into one by closing HGP and transferring all its patients to the other. The closure left a community of more than 200,000 blacks living in North Saint Louis without adequate, centrally located medical care. Blacks were forced to travel to outlying sectors of the city and county to get the medical attention they needed.

Despite the hue and cry of some ghetto politicians about whites closing the hospital, the simple truth is that most of those casting aspersions had participated in abandoning the institution. Willingly and knowingly, they aided and abetted the enemy in this nefarious plot to deny their black constituents an irreplaceable medical resource. Empowering the mayor to act unilaterally set the stage for the closure of the hospital. The decision to transfer authority evolved over a period of three years and included active participation of black leaders. They provided the political muscle for Conway to perform the egregious act.

To properly assess Conway's successful venture, it is necessary to review the circumstances surrounding his victory over Cervantes and the defeat of Bass as comptroller. Both incidents played a major role. While Bass was comptroller, the mayor was powerless to act on this issue. It required two votes on the three-member Board of Estimates to defend the facility. Bass was the swing vote on most measures. This placed him in an ideal negotiating position. The aldermanic president sided with Bass on the hospital issue. Thus, Bass served as a safety valve for continued medical services at the hospital.

Black committeemen aligned with Conway's campaign for mayor refused to make the hospital a major election issue. Conway and Percich steadfastly refused to state their intentions on the issue. Conway's black supporters placed themselves as a buffer between him and the basic interests of black people. Whatever Conway promised black leaders must have been much more important than the hospital. If he made a commitment to keep the hospital open, they did not reveal it when the move was made to close it.

Conway's official announcement of the closure caused his chief black supporters to go into hiding for two days. When they reappeared, they did not decry the action. Instead, their strategy was to identify me as the culprit and criticize me for being on a congressional trip in Southeast Asia when Conway closed the facility. Reducing the argument from a question of who closed the hospital to a question of who should have prevented its closing was a clever ploy.

Chicanery Defeats Bond Issue

Mayor Schoemehl attempted to honor his promise to reopen HGP but was defeated in his effort by black leaders associated with the former mayor. When Schoemehl made his commitment to reopen the hospital, it was not known that Conway had surrendered the hospital's license to the state and to the federal government. Now, reopening it was no longer a matter of an executive order by the new mayor. HGP had been operating under a grandfather clause that exempted hospitals in existence before 1955 from the requirement of conforming to new rules and regulations. Schoemehl was forced to apply for a new license, which required compliance with all recently imposed legal regulations, rules, and laws. Multiple-patient wards had to be converted into semiprivate rooms for two patients. Wider corridors, exit doors wider than forty-four inches, a new ventilation system, and extensive electrical rewiring were required to pass the codes.

Schoemehl recommended a bond issue for the estimated $64 million needed to qualify for the license. Five black committeemen and three black aldermen attacked supporters of the bond issue as "Uncle Toms and sellout artists." They contended that Schoemehl had not mentioned a bond issue while seeking support in his campaign. The fallacious argument influenced a small but sufficient percentage of blacks to cast votes against the proposition. When their votes were added to the strong opposition in the all-white South Side wards, the 60 percent vote needed for passage failed by a few percentage points.

The sweetness of election-night victory soon faded into bittersweet memories as Weathers's predictions unfolded. Schoemehl approached serious problems in the black community in a cavalier manner. Those who had contributed the most to his success began to hear the old familiar tune of "I had already promised that position to someone else" or "I didn't make that commitment." He denied making the deal for the CDA, failed to appoint a black to head SLATE or as an executive director of the convention center, and reneged on his promise to appoint a director of parks and recreation.

Schoemehl did, however, make several significant appointments later on in his tenure. He appointed a number of our allies, personal friends, and relatives to key positions. Among them were Gwen Giles as city assessor, Larry Williams as city treasurer, my brother Irving Clay as director of welfare, and Madeline Franklin as city judge. Other blacks appointed were Benjamin M. Phillips as city marshal and Diane Williams as director of the Civil Rights Enforcement Agency.

Election of the First Black Woman Citywide

Winter 1982 was the best of times and the worst of times. Summer soldiers and sunshine patriots were predicting my defeat in the coming election. The state lost one of its seats in Congress as the result of a population decrease recorded in the latest census. The federal court drew new congressional districts for the state because the legislature failed to reach agreement.

Adding 200,000 new residents, mostly white, to my district changed the racial composition from a black majority to half white. I was facing stiff opposition from a well-heeled veteran state senator whose district had been abolished by the legislature. In addition, the office of license collector was vacant because of the retirement of Lawrence "Jaybird" Woodson, who had been the collector for eight years. His announced retirement left a void in our ticket, which presented a potential problem for maximizing black voter turnout. But it also afforded the option of filing a candidate who could generate interest and increased voter turnout from North St. Louis.

When Freeman Bosley Jr. approached me for support for his run for circuit clerk, I informed him that I had given my word to Joseph Roddy, the incumbent, in exchange for his commitment to support our slate. I urged Bosley to file for license collector, which was an open race without an incumbent.

Roddy had held the position of clerk for fourteen years. He was the committeeman of a large delivery ward that sat in the middle of my newly formed congressional district and was the pivotal ward in Bass's senatorial district. We viewed his support as critical to our bids for re-election. Without it, we surmised that our opponents would establish a foothold that could spell disaster. Bass was confronted with the same dilemma. His district was about 50 percent white.

State Representative Billie Boykins informed me that she would not seek re-election. She said that traveling back and forth to Jefferson City and the time away from her two children had imposed a stressful hardship on her. I was looking for a candidate for the office of license collector after Bosley had rejected my request to seek the position. For Boykins, the office would substantially increase her earnings and allow her to be in close proximity to her family on a daily basis. At first she was skeptical about her chances for victory. In a meeting with Pearlie Evans, Gwen Giles, and Margaret Bush Wilson, she became convinced that she was a logical candidate who could prevent a proliferation of filings in the black area.

Our most important chore was to move swiftly in solidifying endorsements on our own turf. When that was completed, we then moved to line up support on the South Side. That was time-consuming and difficult. In fact, we were only able to secure a few key white ward endorsements and announced support from several individual politicians. Most were residents of the central corridor area and had sizable numbers of blacks in their constituencies. But, in the long run, they proved decisive in defeating Boykins's major opponent.

Boykins, Bass, and I easily turned back our opponents. One reason that Bass and Boykins were able to win handily was the endorsement of Roddy and the vote delivered in his ward. His endorsement was costly, as reported in a *Globe-Democrat* editorial printed three weeks prior to election. It stated, "Many former supporters of Roddy are upset over his alliance with U.S. Rep. William Clay, the unrepresentative

Mayor Vincent Schoemehl in 1981. © 1981, Martin Schweig Studio, transferred 1999, MHS Photographs and Prints Collections.

First District Congressman. These voters feel that Roddy should disassociate himself from Clay, rather than embrace him in an exchange of endorsements."[87]

John Bass received a total of 13,775 votes compared to the combined total of the two white candidates' 10,977 votes (Edward Sweeney and Eileen McCann). Although he amassed a sufficient number to outpoll their combined totals, had the Seventeenth Ward been in one of the other candidate's columns it would have been a different kind of election. There is no evidence that Bass would have lost, but the 1,450 votes he received from the Seventeenth Ward and the committeeman's endorsement left us free to expend our energies and money on other aspects of the campaign.

Boykins also won. Voters in Roddy's ward played a significant roll in the margin of victory for both candidates. When the final vote was tabulated in the race for circuit clerk, Roddy lost to Bosley by nine hundred votes (Bosley, 31,121; Roddy, 30,175; Thomas Connelly, 23,227; Clara Jo Roddy, 2,345).

Schoemehl Moves to Weaken Clay's Influence

During the primary election of 1986 Schoemehl and his advisers chose to challenge the entire slate of black incumbents seeking re-election. It was a strange twist of events. The mayor knew that in our history of supporting scores of candidates and campaigning for elected office, our organization had seldom lost a major race, and the slate endorsed by us usually won handily.

The squabble over candidates started at the conclusion of a meeting in the mayor's office between Schoemehl, Larry Williams, and myself. The fourth party, Kim Tucci, Schoemehl's chief political adviser, did not arrive until the business was over and we were chatting about unimportant incidents. When the secretary read back the agreement that included the mayor's support for all incumbents in the Democratic primary, all hell broke loose. Tucci declared that there was no way they would support Freeman Bosley Jr. because his father's campaign for mayor against Schoemehl had cost them $1 million. I countered that the son cannot be held accountable for the indiscretions of the father and whimsically asked, "Who is the mayor, anyhow?" Tucci's answer was, "You will see." Subsequently, we saw. Although Schoemehl admitted that he had spent over $1 million to "head off the possibility of a challenge by a Webbe-backed candidate," Tucci's argument prevailed.[88] Schoemehl attacked Bosley in a widely distributed letter, stating, "Bosley was elected four years ago through unscrupulous and deceptive political trickery. . . . He has demonstrated an arrogance toward the courts and the taxpayers. . . . His administration has been characterized by political firings, lawsuits, and mismanagement."[89] The mayor launched a campaign not merely opposing Bosley's re-election but one equivalent to a plenary attack on the city's Democratic officeholders. His plan was sweeping. It necessitated that party leaders from north and south forge an unusual coalition to stop the power grab.

The ambitious mayor, encouraged by naïve advisers and political hangers-on, declared war on my closest allies. Assured by his friends that they could raise enough money, the mayor went for the proverbial jugular vein. He filed candidates in opposition to seven incumbent Democrats: three were my personal friends, State Senator John Bass, License Collector Billie Boykins, and Clerk of the Court Freeman Bosley Jr.; and three were my close political allies, Recorder of Deeds Sharon Carpenter, Revenue Collector Ronald Leggett, and Representative Charles Troupe. Under normal circumstances, such a coming together would have been impossible. But Carpenter and Leggett were forced to join forces with Bosley and Boykins to protect their own positions. The mayor's shenanigans became very personal when he filed a candidate against my son, Representative Bill (Lacy) Clay Jr.

South side leaders Representative Tony Ribaudo and City Comptroller Paul Berra supported the all-incumbent slate. Ribaudo was chairman of the City Democratic Central Committee and house majority leader. Berra was a longtime advocate of coalition politics. When Schoemehl announced his intentions to wrest control of North St. Louis politics from our group, it took us by surprise. Yet our forces were confident that the mayor's move would be fruitless.

The media portrayed the confrontation as a struggle between two political titans, Schoemehl and Clay, but its importance was not about either. Our people perceived it as a struggle to determine who would pick our leaders. Pearlie Evans described the mayor's preemptive strike as "an attempt to disenfranchise black voters by defeating our city-wide elected officials. A black electorate without effective black spokespersons is a voiceless electorate."[90]

Schoemehl, financed primarily by construction contractors and vendors doing business with the city, waged a media-oriented campaign against the seven incumbents. His campaign expenditures for Lou Hamilton and Judy Raker, candidates for clerk of the court and state senator, respectively, exceeded $800,000. A few blacks endorsed the mayor's effort. The most prominent, Doctors Jerome Williams and Parker Word, posed no real threat to splitting our votes. Our slate of candidates raised and spent approximately $500,000. In an unprecedented show of unity, hundreds of citizens volunteered to canvass their neighborhoods, telephone their friends, and hang signs in their windows.

The black clergy joined the campaign in a well-coordinated fashion to ensure a large black voter turnout. More than two hundred ministers met and endorsed Bosley, Boykins, Clay Jr., and Bass. They registered their protests against Schoemehl's bold attempt to dictate who would speak for the black community. The issues framed in the election would pretty much determine who would speak for the Democratic Party for at least the next ten years. Rev. C. Garnett Henning, pastor of St. Paul AME Church and a spokesman for the group, however, had a different time frame: "The implications of this election reach well into the next century for black St. Louis. It is a test of the integrity of the North Side community. [Schoemehl] is the mayor today because of support from the black community. But he is like other politicians who owe their political life to blacks. Once elected, they align themselves with forces who can keep them in office, leaving blacks out."[91]

The Bosley-Boykins-Bass-Clay Jr. Campaign Committee organized a meeting to mobilize the black community for a get-out-the-vote drive. A wide range of leaders was in attendance, including Reverends James DeClue, president of the NAACP, Haymond Fortenberry, chairman of the Ministerial Alliance, and Earl Nance, a member of the school board. Most black elected officials attended. Each candidate spoke. Bass said, "If we lose these seats, politics will be over for the next generation, and we'll have to start over."[92] People in the black community, incensed and intense, were determined that blacks would decide their own leaders. Bosley put it very well in a letter to supporters: "There is presently a terrible and ugly attack being launched against your elected officials by persons who want to rule over and control our community as if they were kings. . . . Together we must put those would be political genies back into the bottle and show them that our community is going forward with progress and not backwards into the dark ages."[93] An article appearing in the *St. Louis Sentinel* described the contest in the following manner: "It appears that Mayor Vincent Schoemehl is out to capture the black vote and keep it as long as he can. Mayor Schoemehl is out to control the city, pick his own candidates, and, if anyone is in his path, 'Let the victims beware.'"[94]

The Mayor Is Humiliated

Schoemehl's dream of "controlling black politics" was not destined to occur. On election night, when all the returns were counted, he was humiliated. The seven candidates he opposed were returned to office by large margins. The difference in style and substance of the two campaigns was revealing. Our side effectively negated the mayor's grab for power. Senator Bass beat Judy Raker 11,592 to 8,433; Billie Boykins defeated Frank Killcullen 32,107 to 19,945; Freeman Bosley Jr. trounced Louis Hamilton 36,312 to 17,283; Sharon Carpenter wiped out her opponent Vel Marie King 38,921 to 4,345. For collector of revenue, the mayor's handpicked candidate, Alphonso Jackson, lost 14,683 to 33,573. Charles Troupe defeated his opponent for state representative by a three to one margin.

The crowning glory for me was the returns in the race for my son's legislative seat. The mayor personally campaigned door-to-door and spent a scandalous amount of money in his futile effort to elect Chester Hines, Lacy's opponent. According to campaign disclosure reports, Hines spent $58,000 and received 1,862 votes. His $31 per vote in a losing cause set a campaign record for expenditures in a race for the Missouri House of Representatives. My son raised $12,000 and spent $11,000. The official returns showed Clay Jr. with 3,126 votes—1,264 more votes than the mayor's candidate had.

As Les Pearson, political writer for the *Globe-Democrat*, wrote in his column "People 'n' Politics" two days after the primary: "It would be hard to characterize the beating the mayor took Tuesday at the hands of Rep. William L. Clay, Missouri's most powerful black politician, as Byzantine. It was a straight-out, old-fashioned horse-whipping of the kind that can cloud all of the mayor's political future."[95] Bill McClellan, a columnist for the *St. Louis Post-Dispatch*, summed up the election returns in the following way:

I traditionally spend election nights visiting the various campaign headquarters. . . . Tuesday night I visited several parties but was particularly struck by the differences between Lou Hamilton's party—he was backed by the mayor—and the party at the headquarters shared by State Senator John Bass and State Rep. Bill Clay Jr.

Hamilton's party was . . . kind of high-class. The people were nice and also well-dressed. They looked like the kind of civic-minded people who donate money to political causes and candidates.

The party at the Bass-Clay headquarters was a lot different. The people were very nice, but many of them were dressed casually. They looked like the kind of civic-minded people who donate time and energy to political causes and candidates.

But it was the food that really tipped me off that the Clay forces were going to beat the Schoemehl forces. At the Hamilton party, the food seemed to be coming from the restaurant's kitchen—restaurant food.

At the Bass-Clay party, the food was on a long table. It looked homemade, as if a lot of different people each brought a dish. I even saw a large bowl of Jell-O.

Right then I knew. If a candidate has people willing to make big vats of Jell-O, that candidate has committed supporters. If you have Jell-O makers, you have envelope stuffers and bell ringers. You have a political organization that's really clicking. . . . You have a machine, in the best sense of the word . . . which is exactly what Clay has. Schoemehl doesn't.[96]

I said that the election results showed that people were convinced we didn't need racial polarization in our politics. The slate of candidates that we offered was balanced and experienced. We had "two whites, two blacks, two women, and two men; two from the South Side and two from the North Side. What better choice could you give the voters?"[97]

Plan to Merge City with County

The next year (1987) Schoemehl joined Republican County Executive Gene McNary in a plan to reorganize the eighty-nine municipalities in St. Louis County. Schoemehl described the move as a potential "first step for a general reorganization of governments in the St. Louis region, such as a city-county merger."[98] To accomplish the merger, the Missouri constitution required that the city and the county each provide nine members for a board of freeholders and that the governor appoint the nineteenth person. Schoemehl and McNary recommended that Wayne Milsap, a Republican lawyer and the antagonistic prosecutor in the Jefferson Bank trial, be named chairman.

That incident alone was insulting to many in our community. In addition, the merger of the city and county threatened to diminish the influence of black voters who constituted almost half of the city population to a point of insignificance. Merging with the county would reduce their numbers to less than 25 percent.

Needless to say, the planned merger between the city and county never materialized.

"Job Swap" and the Third Term

In November 1988, to make peace, Schoemehl consummated a deal to enhance the political power of black St. Louisans. He agreed to appoint Virvus Jones city comptroller, a position of significant influence in city

State Senator William Lacy Clay Jr., Mayor Freeman Bosley Jr., Comptroller Virvus Jones, Clay, former senator John Bass, and Frederick Weathers (seated), dean of black politics in the 1960s, 1970s and 1980s.

financial affairs. The appointment involved a complex series of events in which two city officials resigned and then exchanged positions. The incident was sarcastically tagged the "job swap" by the media and those opposing Schoemehl's bid for re-election to a third term. However, the clever maneuver played a major role in garnering substantial support for the mayor in the black community.

The famous job swap—or infamous, as described by critics—was complicated, yet simple. It involved the incumbent, Comptroller Paul M. Berra, resigning his position early on the morning of November 23, 1988. He was later appointed by Schoemehl as city assessor after Virvus Jones, the present assessor, had resigned. Jones was later appointed by the mayor to fill the vacancy left by the Berra resignation.

Schoemehl was a big winner in the swap. But the black community was a bigger winner. Once again, a black person was represented on the important Board of Estimates. The three-member board was the most powerful agency of government—the city's chief fiscal body. The comptroller was the anchor. His control of finances and bonding for the city's capital improvement put the position on equal status with the mayor.

Major participants in making the deal were City Treasurer Williams, Labor Council Chairman Robert Kelley, Tyus, and myself. The final version of the arrangement called for maximum support for Jones from white Democratic committeemen in the next municipal elections. Labor leaders agreed to raise substantial money for Jones's election. A majority of black elected officials pledged support for the job swap. It worked. Schoemehl and Jones won in the March and April 1989 primary and general election.

In too many elections, we witnessed community efforts to elect qualified persons to citywide offices go down the drain because of a failure to reach consensus on candidates, low voter turnout, and the negative attitudes of disgruntled leaders. The job swap gave the black community an opportunity to get in the door of citywide politics without the bruising battle of a Democratic primary. Virvus Jones, the city assessor for the past three years, was a highly qualified candidate who marshaled the backing of black political leaders, solid support from ministerial alliances, and encouragement from many neighborhood groups. A majority of the labor unions endorsed his candidacy. Jones garnered this massive array of support because of his ability to perform a public service and conform to the high standards of conduct that the position demanded.

This election was quite different from the one two years prior. Enemies of Schoemehl in 1986 became his friends in 1988. His decision to appoint Virvus Jones as comptroller was definitely in the best and long-term interests of the black community. The community's endorsement of Jones's and Schoemehl's candidacies showed the maturity and sophistication in understanding that a compromise benefited both sides.

But the swap did not turn out the way the mayor imagined. I believe Schoemehl was of the opinion that Jones would be a puppet in his administration and that I was obligated to support Schoemehl indefinitely. Neither assumption was true. In less than two years, the deal had gone belly-up. Jones and Schoemehl squabbled over major and minor issues. It was apparent that the mayor was not going to dictate the policies of the comptroller's office. In one outburst, Schoemehl summed up the job swap, stating, "With the best of intentions, I made the worst of mistakes." He called Jones an "embarrassment" and a "joke." In reply, Jones accused the mayor of "acting like a child, throwing tantrums."[99]

Mayor Wants to Keep *Globe-Democrat* in Business

In February 1984, the *Globe-Democrat* was sold to Jeffrey M. Gluck, a young magazine publisher. Within two years, however, he was forced to file for bankruptcy, declaring that the paper was losing $120,000 a week—an annual loss of $6 million. In an effort of desperation, the new owners solicited a bailout from government agencies. They asked the city of St. Louis and the Missouri Industrial Development Board to issue $15 million in revenue bonds to forestall their financial collapse.

The *Globe-Democrat* also made inquiries to the U.S. Department of Commerce about the possibility of financial assistance to a failing business. I objected to such a stretching of the intents of Congress and pointed out that the newspaper had spent a lifetime objecting to government assistance for other businesses in financial trouble.

The trouble started in November 1983, when the owners of the *Globe-Democrat*, the Newhouse News Service, entered into an agreement with the owners of the *Post-Dispatch* to buy out the Newhouse firm and close down the *Globe*'s operations. The two papers had been operating under an arrangement to share presses and advertising profits.

The *Globe-Democrat* had a well-deserved reputation for being anti-black, anti-poor, and anti-humane. It carried editorials and news stories that inflamed racial tensions in the St. Louis community. Its last two publishers, Richard Amberg and G. Duncan Bauman, were described in a campaign newspaper, the *Point of View*, as "gutter-type, fire-eating, racist degenerates. They had no respect for the basic rights of black citizens or working people. Editorials such as 'NAACP Walks Hand in Hand with the Communists' and 'As Bad as the Congo' are just examples of its editorial bias. It often characterized black leaders as 'vicious reverse racists' and 'black Bilboes.'"[100]

The day of reckoning came when the *Globe-Democrat* faced bankruptcy. Schoemehl tried to save the newspaper with $1.5 million in taxpayers' money. The scheme called for the state to issue $15 million in revenue bonds to build the newspaper a printing plant. Schoemehl agreed to arrange another $4 million through a tax-free bond issue and $2 million through a federal grant.

Representative Lacy Clay Jr. engaged an attorney to challenge the bailout. His suit charged that subsidizing the private concern was a violation of the state constitution. Lacy's lawsuit was to be filed in the St. Louis Circuit Court and would take months, if not years, to reconcile. Because the newspaper needed financial relief immediately, the *Globe*'s owners concocted a cute ploy to obfuscate Lacy's suit. The scheme was recommended by the attorney general as a procedure to bypass the lower courts.

The suit, filed by Jesse Horstman, a longtime political operative and friend of Schoemehl, asked the Missouri Supreme Court to decide the issue. His suit requested the same opinions of the supreme court on issues to which Bill Clay Jr.'s suit was seeking resolution: 1) Does the Missouri Industrial Development Board have the authority to issue tax credits? 2) Is it unconstitutional to lend public credit to a private corporation? 3) Can the legislature delegate tax credits to the board because it creates a state liability by reducing revenues that would otherwise be collected by the state? 4) Does reducing taxes to support a privately owned newspaper fulfill the "public purpose" requirement in the law? 5) Does allowing bonds to be sold with tax credits amount to a special law to the extent that other bonds sold by the state and other political subdivisions are not accompanied by tax credits? 6) Are the U.S. and state constitutional guarantees to freedom of speech impaired by the law because "the present case creates the untenable potential for the state as primary creditor of the newspaper to direct or influence its editorial and news reporting functions"?

The Missouri Supreme Court, seeing that it was a ruse to expedite resolution of the matter, voted 4–1 to let the case go through the normal channels for judicial disposition. Time ran out on the *Globe-Democrat*, and it was forced to close its doors.

Clay Jr., in effect, hastened the death of the publication. Commenting, I said, "I have the same feeling about the demise of the *Globe-Democrat* as most people experienced with the death of Adolf Hitler. The paper was a diabolical force in our society which spread the flames of racial hatred and economic exploitation of the poor."[101]

In 1987 Schoemehl pushed a three-eighths-of-a-cent sales tax and a $5-a-month head tax to subsidize businesses that hired low-income workers at even lower pay. I opposed the gimmick, and the mayor attacked me for living in the suburbs of Washington, D.C. He said I "would not have to worry about cuts in trash collection or police and fire protection" if the tax failed.[102] He was suggesting I had no right to speak against wasteful expenditures, and I responded that that was "ludicrous—since I paid the city of St. Louis last year four times more in earnings taxes than Mayor Schoemehl, my claim to address the issue [was] four times more valid than his."[103]

CHAPTER

16

PAYBACK TIME: REVENGE OR RETRIBUTION

A cardinal principle of politics is "don't get angry, get even." In a business where no formal contracts exist, verbal ones are signed and sealed with a handshake. Enforcement of the terms cannot be pursued in a court of law. The honorable way to punish those who default is through future retaliatory action exacted at a most opportune time. Sometimes it takes years to avenge an impoliteness. When it occurs, our colleagues view it as a sign of occupational acumen. Those who renege on oral commitments must be disciplined. It's called payback.

During my career, I witnessed a number of political casualties resulting from reneging or allegedly reneging on campaign pledges. The real issue is not revenge but retribution.

Banks's State Representative Defeated

Senator J. B. Banks was a persistent critic of my positions who constantly encouraged others to challenge me for re-election. However, he never suggested that he might be an appropriate candidate. When Gates filed against me in 1974, Banks had a difficult time deciding whom to support. Again in 1978, when Goins announced his candidacy for Congress, Banks was undecided.

His hesitancy to declare his preference caused me to privately issue an ultimatum. Banks implored a South Side leader whom both of us respected to heal the breach. At the meeting he accused me of supporting the incumbent Nineteenth Ward committeewoman's choice for state representative over his candidate. I denied it but gave him time to prove the unsubstantiated charge. After the time elapsed for him to make a decision, I joined forces with Elbert Walton, who was running against incumbent representative Robert Walker from Banks's organization.

Walton, a vigorous campaigner, defeated Walker with adequate financial assistance by eleven votes (1,401 to 1,390). It was payback time.

Losing a State Senate Seat: Ray Howard's Mistake

Raymond Howard, a very popular young solon, lost his bid for re-election to the Missouri Senate because it was payback time. Every win is not a victory, and not every loss is a defeat. Oftentimes a battle is won and the war is lost. Senator Howard, much to his surprise, soon discovered the veracity of that adage.

It is difficult for an incumbent to lose a seat in the Missouri Senate. It is almost impossible to lose one designated a "safe seat." But seldom has an intelligent, energetic, suave incumbent launched such a campaign to self-destruct as Howard did. He was young, charismatic, articulate, and charmingly likable—his political career should have been unchallenged for decades. His credentials as an aggressive leader were impeccable. He had superb academic qualifications, wide legal experience, and a record of activism in the civil rights movement.

He suffered one humiliating defeat early in his career. In 1960, impetuous and impatient, Howard challenged the most respected black politician in the city, Jordan Chambers. Filing against him for committeeman and for state representative against Chambers's friend Joseph Ames proved disastrous. Chambers received 3,261 votes to Howard's 955. Ames received 25,999 votes to Howard's 767. Normally, this kind of trouncing would have been fatal. But in 1964, Frederick Weathers resurrected Howard's career. He supported him against incumbent state representative Hugh White. Howard's defeat of White should have cemented a lasting bond of respect between him and Weathers.

As time passed, Howard left Weathers's group to run for the state senate against another political legend, Michael Kinney. Kinney was the longest-serving elected official in Missouri history. Howard won because Kinney had been in office for more than fifty years, had lost touch with his constituents, and had outlived most of his avid, committed supporters. After defeating Kinney, Howard was elected committeeman in the First Ward.

Although tough, streetwise, and popular, he set in motion a classic scenario for losing an election. Involved in grassroots community activity and dedicated and committed to civil rights, somehow his politics became intertwined with the political nomads who had no appreciation of the civil rights movement. Knowingly or not, he became part of a stratagem to divide the black community.

White candidates were able to effectively neutralize the black vote by pitting black ward leaders against one other. The rift lasted ten years and crippled our efforts to capitalize on the energy of a community eager to shed its second-class citizenship. The divider equation reared its ugly head many times and took its toll in many ways. It was responsible for Weathers's defeat by one vote for clerk of the court of criminal causes in the Democratic City Central Committee. It nullified our ability to negotiate the office of public administrator for a black. It caused a re-election defeat for Bass. It necessitated the filing of two lawsuits in federal court to preserve a black-majority congressional district.

In a fight between Goins and Tyus for chairman of the First Congressional District, Howard sided with Goins. At the district organizing meeting, Weathers was proposed as a compromise candidate because he was not aligned with either faction of North Side politicians. He stayed out of the fray, viewing his role as counsel, arbitrator, and conciliator.

Howard proceeded to criticize Weathers in harsh terms. The verbal attack portraying the "dean" of black politics as old and his ideas outmoded came back to haunt Howard. In 1976, Banks filed against him for state senate. The senatorial district was composed of precincts from twelve different wards. Tyus, Payne, and Weathers held the key to election; my ward was not within the district boundaries.

Weathers once again found himself in the eye of the storm and prepared to extract political retribution from an offending colleague. He persuaded Payne and Tyus to support Banks. The final vote was close: Banks beat Howard by 417 votes, receiving 1,088 votes in the Eighteenth, Twentieth, and Fourth Wards, which provided the margin of defeat for Howard.

The Making of a Female Senator

The election of the first black female state senator in the history of Missouri was filled with suspense and intrigue. It required patience, compromise, and tact. The politician thought mostly likely to succeed to the vacant senatorial seat was denied the position because it was payback time.

It was November 1977. Cold wind whipped through the air, snowflakes slowly fell, and the temperature hovered near zero. Bass and I rang the bell at Weathers's home. He held the key vote for replacement of Fourth District state senator, whose seat was vacated when Franklin Payne, recommended by Senator Thomas Eagleton, accepted an appointment from President Carter as U.S. marshal for the Eastern District of Missouri.

If we thought the chill outside was below freezing, it became more unbearable inside once we broached the subject of our visit. Weathers was in no mood to accept our candidate, Tyus. He was persona non grata on Weathers's list of worthy politicians. Several years earlier Tyus had committed an unforgivable offense, in Weathers's estimation. It was now "get even" time. Weathers was savoring his ability to apply the ferris wheel principle: what goes around must come around.

Bass and I were pursuing a mission impossible in attempting to get the two votes that Weathers controlled (including his committeewoman). The resignation of Payne, who was also a committeeman, had left nineteen people eligible to vote on his replacement. The successful candidate needed ten votes. Rep. Fred Williams had ten votes committed, including the two from Weathers. Tyus had garnered nine votes. If Weathers remained unshakable, the nomination would go to Williams, who I thought would be disastrous for our community. During his eighteen years in the state legislature, he was most known for introducing two bills that were not enacted: one that would have outlawed noseblowing in restaurants, and another that would have made it a crime to rob people in church.

But politics is politics, and Weathers played the role of kingmaker for all its worth. He was the balance of power. He knew it. Bass and I knew it. One hour after our arrival, it was apparent that our plea was falling on deaf ears. Weathers, more closely aligned politically and ideologically with us, admitted that Williams would make a bad senator but steadfastly refused to endorse Tyus.

Finally, I posed the $64,000 question: Why is Tyus so objectionable? Slowly, meticulously, and pensively relishing each word, he launched into a long discourse about the type of representative needed for the office. His attack was not directly aimed at Tyus, but on at least three occasions he mentioned that Tyus had been in the state legislature in the 1940s and 1950s and had failed to compile a distinguished record. He spoke eloquently of racial commitment and implied it was a quality lacking in our choice for the position.

It was now payback time. Weathers, a cagey, crafty politician, had waited five years to extract an ounce of flesh. He harbored ill feelings toward Tyus for his alleged role in the Democratic City Central Committee's failure to name Weathers clerk of the court of criminal causes; he lost to George Solomon by one vote (26–25). Tyus, incidentally, voted for Weathers on a public roll call vote. But certain other factors led Weathers to conclude that Tyus had orchestrated his defeat.

Ann Voss, Pearlie Evans, and Gwen Giles, undated.

On the morning of the vote, John Conley, a black committee-man, made a speech against Weathers's candidacy. Two other blacks, Third Ward Committeepeople Mel Halston and Geneva Rhone, arrived after the vote was taken. Halston stated that his car had a flat tire. The closeness of the vote and the closeness of Tyus to Webbe, who was supporting a fellow Lebanese, caused Weathers to suspect foul play.

In private, he accused Tyus of delivering Conley and Halston to Solomon. True or not, the two votes Weathers controlled were never going to be cast for Tyus.

Immediately, I changed tactics. I inquired if a compromise candidate was in order. I began to suggest people who would possibly be acceptable. The first mentioned was Gwen Giles, former executive director of the St. Louis Civil Rights Enforcement Agency, commissioner of human relations on the St. Louis Council of Human Relations, and former director of community affairs with KMOX-TV. Without hesitation, the answer was affirmative. In fact, Weathers stated that Giles was an excellent choice whom he would support. Then he cautioned that our problem would be to convince Tyus to release his supporters for the compromise candidate.

Bass and I knew Tyus could not refuse to support Giles. She had consistently been in the forefront of progressive change in our community. Intentionally irritating those who held power, she had a knack for stimulating public debate around controversial issues. Giles was a permanent political fixture, a born and bred fighter for the rights of the underprivileged. During her fifteen years of public service, she had been active in many critical community issues, including fair employment opportunity, housing, education, community development, and youth and senior citizens programs.

Tyus respected her talent and abilities. Giles was a civil rights giant who never feared raising her voice for the rights of others. Her greatest asset was bringing people together without concern for artificial division along racial, geographical, or economic lines. She also was my campaign manager the first time I ran for Congress.

The rest is history. After a lengthy dissection of Weathers's self-proclaimed role of leadership, Tyus withdrew in favor of Giles, and the first black female state senator was elected, defeating Williams, who ran as an independent.

Schoemehl Gets Payback

In the 1986 contest for citywide elections, Mayor Schoemehl attempted to defeat the major supporters of my power base. He challenged the re-election bids of Bosley, Boykins, Bass, Clay Jr., and Troupe. Schoemehl's candidates lost every contest.

Most knowledgeable political analysts concluded that Schoemehl's arms were "too short to box with Bill Clay." The mayor's bid for support from friendly black elected officials was nipped in the bud by a series of meetings convened with ministers, businessmen, precinct captains, and community leaders. Fred Williams was the only

1992 CCC fund-raiser. From left: Committeeman Marvin Madeson, State Senator Lacy Clay Jr., Committeeman Fred Weathers, Lieutenant Governor Mel Carnahan, Clay.

black elected official who adhered to the Schoemehl party line. He spent in excess of $25,000 in his campaign. Our group opposed his re-election and supported his opponent, Paula Carter. She won handily. Her margin of victory was two to one (2,905 to 1,470). Williams was deposed because the voters believed it was payback time.

Voters endured Schoemehl at the helm of city government until the opportune time arrived. When he sought the Democratic nomination for governor in 1992, African American voters knew our time had come. He was running against Lieutenant Governor Mel Carnahan, who had a good relationship with black leaders across the state, and we were in a position to show our resentment of Schoemehl's twelve years of scorn and neglect for our community. The issues compelling black constituents to campaign against him were plentiful. The obligation to unify the black community against his candidacy and to turn out a big vote became a reality. It was of paramount importance that Schoemehl not succeed in dividing the black community.

I endorsed Carnahan early in the campaign to derail any possibility of Schoemehl suggesting that he had the solid backing of the African American community in the city. It was also to blunt the impact of his cross-state caravan to announce his filing. The *Post-Dispatch* reported, "Clay's endorsement of Lt. Gov. Mel Carnahan is still big-time news in Missouri politics . . . [it] gives Carnahan a psychological win to take with him to Hannibal for the statewide Missouri Democrat Day's gathering."[104]

Except for his support from the minority contractors of the Mo-Kan organization, a black contractors' association, Schoemehl was completely shut out of endorsements by black groups. Mo-Kan was financed by funds from the CDA, which was under the mayor's control. Their support had been predictable. It did not have great impact in the minority voting community because their arguments could not overcome the scores of instances in which Schoemehl had worked to frustrate and diminish the vital interests of the black community.

Mo-Kan entered into an arrangement with the Associated General Contractors (AGC) to lower the standards for determining what constituted a minority-owned firm qualified to participate in the city's contracting program. The mayor, Mo-Kan, and the AGC proposed that bidders for city contracts "make good-faith efforts to subcontract 25 percent of contract value to companies owned by racial minorities and another 5 percent to companies owned by women." Comptroller Jones and most civil rights activists opposed the plan and accused Schoemehl of plotting to undermine the minority set-aside program. Jones blasted the proposal as "a sellout by the minority contractors in collusion with the mayor. They have been bought and sold."[105]

The Board of Aldermen rejected the mayor's proposal by a vote of 17–11. It was a victory for Comptroller Jones, who led the fight for a more ambitious proposal. He supported a bill introduced by Alderman Terry Kennedy proposing goals of 40 percent for black-owned businesses and 10 percent for women. In managing the bill, Kennedy said, "There has to be a shared power between the mayor and the board, and [Schoemehl] just can't expect us to rush things through helter-skelter."[106]

I knew that my opposition, in spite of organized labor's vigorous support, would stymie Schoemehl's ability to create a bandwagon affect. The first task before us was to discredit the so-called "elite" labor leaders who, in overwhelming numbers, had endorsed Schoemehl for governor. Labor unions who contributed financially to Schoemehl's campaign were the International Longshoremen's Association, the International Union of Operating Engineers, the Association of Fire Fighters, the Iron Workers, the Laborers' International Union, the Brotherhood of Marine Engineers, the International Union of Painters and Allied Trades, the Operative Plasterers' and Cement Masons' International Association, the Seafarers' International Union, and the International Alliance of Theatrical Stage Employees. The state AFL-CIO and the St. Louis Labor Council were Schoemehl's strongest backers.

In an exclusive release to the *St. Louis Labor Tribune* newspaper, Robert Kelley and Richard Mantia, the executive secretary-treasurer of the Building and Construction Trades Council, angrily rebutted my charges. They accused me of having a "personal fight" with the mayor and charged that the race should not be "decided on the basis of a grudge." The two labor leaders stated, "While we respect the congressman's right to disagree with organized labor, because of the urgency of this election we expected [that] if [he] had a disagreement with the mayor . . . he would have stayed neutral in this race."[107]

State Representative Patrick J. Hickey, a labor leader, took issue with Kelley and Mantia. In a letter to Kelley, dated March 16, 1992, Hickey stated, "I find it appalling that you would chastise one of labor's major supporters in the United States Congress for exercising his right to endorse a candidate."[108] But Kelley and Mantia spoke for a divided House of Labor. Some of its leaders and many of its members were not happy with the endorsement. The St. Louis Police Officers' Association opposed its own labor council by endorsing Carnahan. Schoemehl had been successful in persuading Republican Governor John Ashcroft to veto a bill to increase pensions for police officers.

When our group began to reveal the anti-union record of Schoemehl, doubt was cast among the rank-and-file workers, and labor leaders were put on the defensive. Schoemehl's policy of contracting out thousands of city jobs to nonunion contractors was a hurdle labor leaders played down in their attempt to palm off the erstwhile mayor as a defender of working people. But we would not let it happen.

We reminded rank-and-file laborers that when the city hospital was closed, Schoemehl laid off 1,200 health care workers and hired a private management firm to run the regional hospital with lower-paid workers. Hundreds of the displaced city workers were members of AFSCME. The jobs were performed at the regional hospital by nonunion employees, earning minimum wage with decreased fringe benefits. This was a typical example of contracting out union jobs to satisfy the interests of private sector entrepreneurs. Charles Oldham, the lawyer for the AFSCME Local in St. Louis, said, "The mayor contracted out the Truman Restorative Center, a city-owned nursing home. All of the city workers were laid off. A percentage took their old jobs—but at much lower pay—with the private contractor."[109]

I then wrote to Gerald McEntee, international president of AFSCME, protesting the fifty-thousand-dollar contribution the union had made to Schoemehl's campaign. The letter stated:

> I note with some trepidation that Missouri AFSCME has formally endorsed the candidacy of Mayor Schoemehl. I perceive [the endorsement] to be an apparent conflict between what your leadership of AFSCME stands for and the record reflected by the candidate.
>
> Schoemehl is quoted as saying he would "downsize state government." The bashing of public employees and union members was typical of Schoemehl's attitude toward workers.
>
> As mayor, Schoemehl's record demonstrates that reduction in force by contracting out jobs to nonunion private sector firms is no idle threat.[110]

Kelley and Mantia took issue with my assertions to President McEntee. But the truth often hurts more than the lies. When Schoemehl became mayor in 1981, there were approximately 12,000 city employees. In large measure because of his policy of contracting out city jobs, only 4,600 existed the day he filed for governor. In 1981 there were 2,200 policemen. The day he filed for governor—with crime at its highest level and climbing—there were only 1,500 policemen. Schoemehl managed to drastically reduce personnel and city services while dramatically increasing the budget. The increase in cost to taxpayers was the result of private businessmen—usually political cronies or financial contributors to the mayor—making considerable profits from these arrangements. Leaders of organized labor were hard-pressed to explain this phenomenon to their membership.

Another anti-union issue was the role the mayor played in reopening the *Admiral* boat to the public as a stationary entertainment center. One local newspaper described the event in a headline reading "The Magic Has Returned." The magic, however, did not last long, as first-nighters were greeted by picketers from the Stagehands' Union and the local Federation of Musicians who were protesting the hiring of nonunion help at "substandard wages."

The mayor's office reportedly told union officials that they were engaged in efforts to reach a settlement of the issues involved. But the musicians' union maintained that entertainers and musicians working on the *Admiral* were entitled to the same wage as that paid at the Fox

Theatre and other major entertainment establishments. The mayor sided with the owner, who was adamant in his anti-union position. He refused to discuss the issue with union negotiators.

Schoemehl, who assisted the Admiral Corporation in securing a $7.5 million loan in tax money from an Urban Development Assistance Grant (UDAG) and the CDA, did not attempt to intervene. Instead, Schoemehl let the city-financed entertainment project proceed with nonunion musicians until it eventually filed bankruptcy and left the city with an unpaid obligation of millions of dollars.

It was a long time coming, but political reparation for Schoemehl's offenses against the community finally reached fruition. His day of reckoning came on August 4, 1992, in the Democratic primary for governor. A vigorous six-month campaign culminated the week before the primary with Virvus Jones and me distributing an "Open Letter to the Community." We attacked Schoemehl for past political sins and advised our voters to retaliate. We recalled that he closed the city's only public hospital, moving indigent patients in the middle of the night to another facility and promising better care and reduced obligations to the taxpayer. Neither happened. Voters were reminded that the federal government sent $20 million a year into St. Louis for housing block grants and that the mayor had spent the vast majority of the funds in wealthy neighborhoods, refusing to spend a fair amount on low- and moderate-income housing. In so doing, we said that "failure of the collective black leadership to oppose Schoemehl at this juncture would be an act of political ignorance and social complacency unworthy of the trust the voters have placed in us . . . we must remain free to choose representatives who speak for our community, not rubber-stamp political junkies who sell out to the highest bidder."

Mel Carnahan defeated Schoemehl for governor in the Democratic primary by a vote of 385,501 to 234,875. The black communities in St. Louis, St. Louis County, and Kansas City played key roles in the race. Schoemehl lost every black ward in the city of St. Louis by huge majorities. In the eleven all-black wards, Carnahan received over 70 percent of the vote. The same percentage of blacks voted against

Schoemehl in St. Louis County and in Kansas City. In St. Louis City, Schoemehl lost twenty-seven of the twenty-eight wards. It was judgment day for a wayward political traveler.

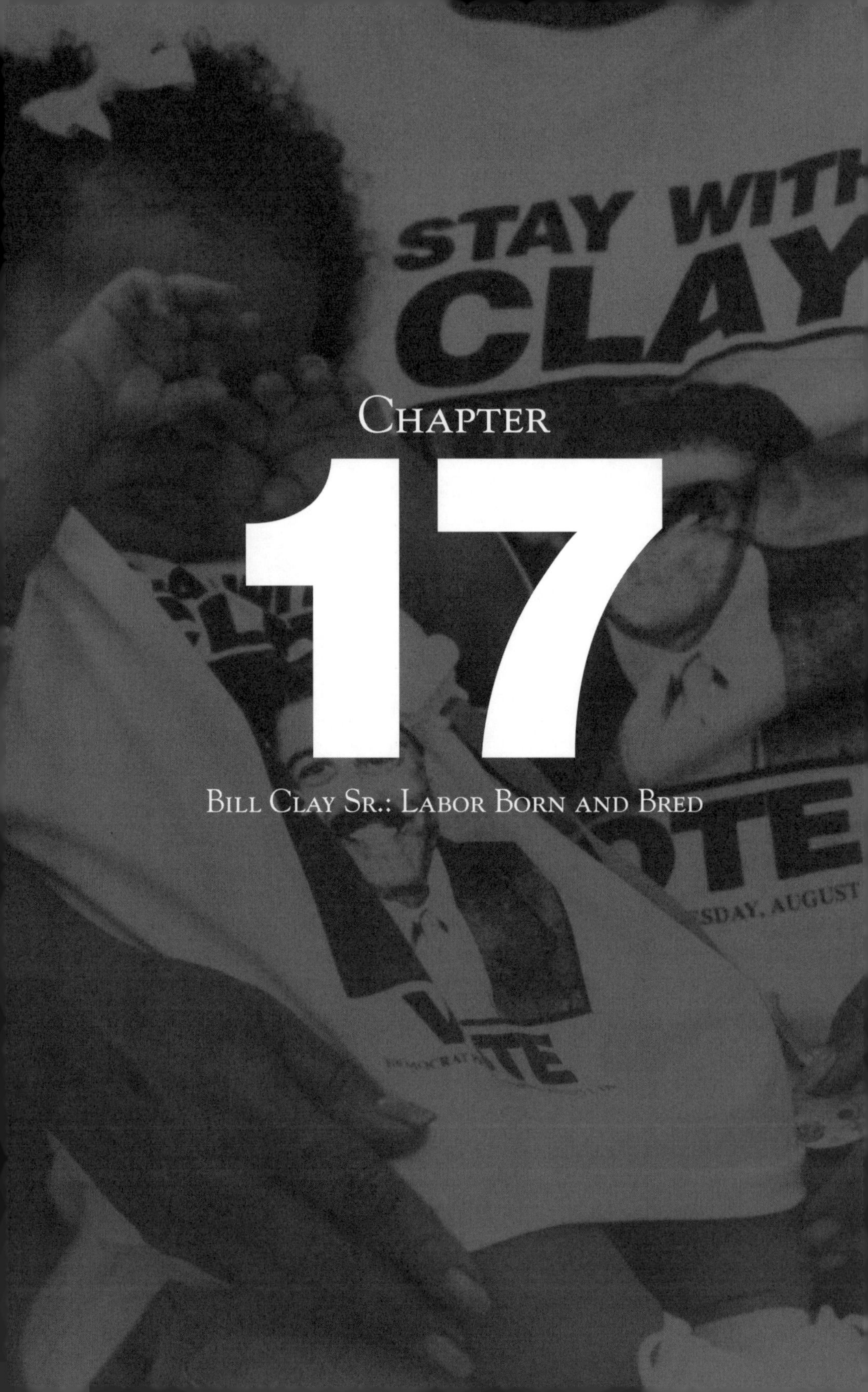

Chapter 17

Bill Clay Sr.: Labor Born and Bred

Throughout my career, I was an uncompromising advocate for the full rights of working people. Labor leaders were able to turn to me as a friend and supporter on issues addressing the interests of American workers. Amazingly, my legislative prowess in the area of protecting the rights of workers was not based on any obligation or debt that I owed labor unions for my political career. My legislative actions were motivated by a deep desire to share the benefits of our nation's great economic prosperity with the men and women who make our economy function. The first time I ran for Congress in 1968, I received the endorsements of only three unions: the Pipefitters' Union, the Seafarers' International Union, and the Leather and Luggage Workers' Union. The Teamsters supported Calloway. More than twenty unions endorsed my opponent, Milton Carpenter.

Labor leaders, union members, business tycoons, the media, Democrats, and Republicans unanimously agreed that I was the most consistent and the most effective defender of workers' rights during my sixteen terms in the Congress. There were a few others, like Bill Ford of Michigan or Augustus Hawkins and George Miller of California, with records equal to mine, but none exceeded it. I did not merely vote the right way, but, on the most critical labor issues, I organized the support and spearheaded the fight. I sponsored or managed on the House floor more pro-labor bills that became law than any other member of Congress during my term of office.

I was chairman of the two most important subcommittees in Congress that dealt with major legislation affecting organized labor. As chairman of the Subcommittee on Labor-Management Relations and the pension task force, I had jurisdiction over 65 percent of all labor legislation. In that capacity, I was responsible for or played a major role in the passage of several landmark laws: the Family and Medical Leave Act (FMLA), granting time off to tend to a sick spouse, parent, or child; the Older Workers Benefit Protection Act, which outlawed discrimination in benefit plans against older workers; the reduction from ten years to five years for pension vesting; Hatch Act reform permitting federal employees to participate in politics; the Employee Retirement Income Security Act (ERISA) Partnerships Investment Amendment, requiring employers' securities to include interests in traded partnerships; asset reversions; prohibiting raids of overfunded pension plans by employers; the Employee Polygraph Protection Act; the Economic Dislocation and Worker Adjustment Assistance Act; the Plant Closing Act, mandating sixty days' advance notice before moving or closing a facility; and other laws too numerous to mention. I also chaired the House Post Office and Civil Service Committee, protecting and advancing the interests of postal and federal employees.

My favorable lifetime rating on measures affecting issues relevant to organized labor was 98 percent. I guess for some it was not enough to warrant support for my son, who had a record identical to mine while serving seventeen years in the Missouri legislature.

My Exit from Elective Politics and Son Lacy's Campaign

Eighteen months before my thirty-second year in Congress, I announced that I would not seek re-election. Sufficient time was given to allow candidates to prepare a campaign. It also avoided the accusation that I delayed announcing to give advantage to my son, Bill Lacy Clay Jr., to run for my seat. The media speculated that several well-known figures might possibly file for the position. But the list of viable candidates eventually boiled down to three: Eric Vickers, Charlie Dooley, and Lacy Clay.

Each had name recognition, a political base, and community followers. Vickers, an attorney, was involved in many confrontational civil rights demonstrations and had filed novel lawsuits seeking equal justice for African Americans. He participated in the shutdown of U.S. Highway 70 to protest the lack of highway contracts awarded to minorities. He was involved in the high-profile investigation of fatal police shootings of black suspects. His militant stances in the courtroom and in street demonstrations, fighting for economic parity, had built a considerable support base among the grass roots. Vickers had also run unsuccessfully against me for Congress in a previous election. Initially, he was given a remote chance of upsetting the two front-runners, Dooley and Clay Jr. But as the campaign progressed, and Vickers's license to practice law was suspended for client neglect, it became apparent that he would not be a major factor in the final vote count.

Dooley had retired after thirty years as a micrographic specialist for Boeing Aircraft. He had a long career in public office: five years as alderman and twelve years as mayor of a small municipality in the district. He was at the time a member of the St. Louis County Council.

Media talking heads, academic analysts, and knowledgeable politicians—citing that Dooley's council seat was entirely situated in two thirds of the congressional district—asserted that he should easily defeat young Clay for Congress. Lacy had never faced voters in any part of the county, and most of the county's powerful elected officials— County Executive George "Buzz" Westfall and County Prosecutor Robert McCulloch—put their financial and political resources behind Dooley's candidacy. Ex-congressman Bob Young and his son, County Councilman Bob Young IV, endorsed Dooley. Thirty-three mayors in small communities announced their support for Dooley. Forty black ministers were listed by Dooley as joining his campaign. In addition, Dooley raised $750,000—$300,000 more than Lacy.

Acknowledging these assets, the more experienced media, academics, and political observers cautioned not to count chickens before they hatched. They advised against underestimating the value of the eighty-five combined years of elective and public service to the community shared by Lacy, his uncle Irving, and myself. They also mentioned that Lacy had spent most of his life training for this campaign.

In the opinion of many, Lacy had the leadership qualities to be an effective representative. He had a wealth of knowledge and experience that prepared him for the job. He had a degree in political science

Clay, Earl Wilson, Lacy Clay Jr., his daughter Carol, and Alderman Irving Clay in 1997.

and government from the University of Maryland and had served seventeen years in the Missouri legislature. But more important than formal education, he had something that only a few aspiring for public office possess: he grew up around government and politics.

He lived in a household where government and public service were frequent dinner table topics. Living and breathing the anxieties of elections, the slings and arrows of personal attacks, the thrill of campaign victories, and the deflation of legislative defeat—what could be better training for confronting the real world of congressional combat? These intangibles influenced some political analysts to predict that Dooley's county residency would not be the determining factor in the race for Congress.

The most serious charge against Dooley in the black community was his opposition to the creation of majority African American legislative districts. Other black leaders explained his stance as "attempting to curry favor" with white elected officials. They attacked him for opposing the creation of black-majority districts proposed for the county council, the state senate, and the House of Representatives. Although no black from the county had ever been elected to the St. Louis County or Missouri legislature, Dooley opposed drawing districts to make it possible.

Lottie Williams and Earl Bush, mayors of small black municipalities, accused Dooley of opposing the creation of the council district that he was elected to represent. Williams was the author of the plan that the court adopted.

According to a May 4, 2000, guest column in the *St. Louis American*, Attorney Elbert Walton, committeeman of Halls Ferry Township and former state representative, wrote:

First, Charlie Dooley appeared before the Missouri Senate Reapportionment Commission and the Missouri Court of Appeals panel to testify that we [the black population of St. Louis] did not need the majority-black Thirteenth District in St. Louis County. We got it anyway.

Second, he appeared before the Missouri House Reapportionment Commission, as well as the U.S. District Court, to testify that we did not need the seven majority-black State Representative districts that we currently had in the city [or] the four in the county. We ended up losing two black legislative districts in the city but did get the four in the county.

Third, he appeared before the U.S. District Court and testified that we did not need a majority-black county council district. Once the court ordered the district, he was selected by county white Democrats as their standard bearer and had been given over $70,000 to run for the office.

Fourth, after Dooley became the first black elected to the county council, a proposal to increase the St. Louis County townships from twenty to twenty-four was initiated. The plan presented by the Black Elected County Officials (BECO) was supported by the three Republican members of the council. The plan would have increased the number of majority black townships from one to four. . . . Of the four new townships, three of them would be majority black. The three white Democrats on the council opted for a plan to create four new majority white townships. Charlie Dooley, casting the deciding vote, voted with them and denied his black constituents three new county townships.[111]

Dooley's opposition to the right of blacks to be represented in elective government was a telling indictment of his noncommitment to political justice for his people. It adversely impacted his ability to corral African American votes.

Rewarding Dooley or Punishing Clay

The opening shot in the battle to defeat my son's campaign for Congress was fired by the St. Louis Labor Council. The executive board voted not to endorse any candidate in the First Congressional District. The action was spearheaded by Bob Kelley, the executive secretary, Terry Nelson of the Carpenters' Union, and Virgil Belfi of the International Union of Operating Engineers. Eleven of the twenty-three board members voted to leave the race open. A two-thirds vote was necessary for endorsement. Withholding endorsement was tantamount to denying union funds to Lacy. Without approval, the national AFL-CIO was prohibited from contributing to Lacy's campaign. Individual unions would then be eligible to contribute to any candidate.

In an incredible stretch of the truth, eleven members opposing Lacy proclaimed that both candidates were great supporters of organized labor. At the meeting, a joint letter from St. Louis County Executive Buzz Westfall and County Prosecutor Robert McCulloch was distributed. They announced support of Charlie Dooley and asked the labor council to endorse him because of his strong labor background.

Kelley lobbied the executive board to endorse Dooley. When it became apparent that that was not possible, he switched tactics and untiringly worked to leave the race open. He argued that "their records are exemplary. It's like choosing between your two children."[112] If Kelley was nothing else, he was consistent in recycling reasons for supporting his choices of candidates. He used the same phraseology in endorsing Schoemehl over Carnahan: "Carnahan is sincere, but he doesn't have the same exciting vitality that you see in Schoemehl. It's like asking me to pick between my kids."[113]

The question of why eleven executive board members opposed Lacy is not nearly as puzzling as the answers given by them. The advanced rationale varied from inane to ingenious. A black newspaper columnist reported that the "reasons given by the gang of eleven Labor Council members varied from 'Clay did not reach out,' to 'His opponent out-worked him,' and, according to one elected official, Clay Jr. supported a Black Trade Union candidate who had a running feud with a white AFL-CIO local union leader."[114]

Dooley's organization widely publicized the AFL-CIO's with-holding of the endorsement as a victory for their candidate. Pro-Clay labor leaders and media personalities interpreted it as a slap in the face for Lacy and me. The African American press viewed it as "a slap in the face to black voters" and proclaimed that "black elected offi-cials have taken a lot of heat from black people for their often unequivocal support of AFL-CIO unions, especially the building trades."[115]

Kelley carried his plan to block the endorsement of Lacy to the Missouri AFL-CIO. Joined by James Brown of the International Association of Machinists and Brian Fletcher of the Communications Workers of America, he successfully argued that the state was obligated to honor the decision of the local affiliate.

Rejecting the sterling record of both Clays was a reflection of the Labor Council's pettiness and an ominous signal to other legislators who traditionally supported worker issues. It was obvious to rank-and-file union members and average voters alike that something other than the qualifications of Lacy's opponent influenced the Labor Council's decision. Most surmised it was payback time for my years of defying the dictatorial attitude of insolent labor leaders.

Stalwart labor leaders were stunned by the action of the coun-cil. A majority on the Labor Council board favored an endorsement for Lacy. They fought the "no endorsement" scheme because they knew Kelley's reasoning was nebulous. An analysis of the labor record of both candidates readily exposed Kelley's contention as a gross fabrication. A cursory review of the record quickly dispelled the myth that Dooley had been a "good friend" of organized labor and had extensive legislative experience qualifying him for Congress.

Dooley had never been in a position to sponsor or support any major legislation that accrued significant benefits to the labor movement or to working people. The council that Dooley served on governed only the unincorporated areas. More than two thirds of the county is incorporated. These areas have their own city councils, fire departments, police departments, and other governmental services. Dooley served in a body that legislated only on tax assessment, public health, arterial roads, planning and zoning, code enforcement, and other mundane matters.

It would be a gross understatement if I pretended not to be disappointed by the labor leaders who opposed Lacy's candidacy. I was disheartened but not disillusioned. When Bob Kelley announced that the Labor Council would remain neutral, I realized the fight between the Clays and the leadership of organized labor had been enjoined. I also knew—and presumably Kelley's forces knew—that the Clays and our supporters never backed down from a confrontation with any adversary, no matter how powerful. I assumed Kelley and his allies were prepared for the battle that was in store. The road to my success was littered with the mangled bodies of political giants. Kelley was aligned with many of the victims our group had defeated: Mayors Tucker and Conway for re-election, Schoemehl for governor, and Jay Nixon for the U.S. Senate. The lengthy list awaited the addition of Dooley and Kelley.

An article appearing in the *St. Louis American* on April 27, 2000, hinted that Kelley played a role in the effort "to payback [Clay Sr.] for some of the feuds over the years about candidates." It further stated, "Kelley attempted to chastise Clay Sr. for his opposition to the gubernatorial aspiration of Mayor Vince Schoemehl."[116] Kelley and his allies were determined to punish me by defeating my son for Congress. I embarrassed them in several elections when we opposed candidates whom they had endorsed without consulting black leaders or manifesting concern for the basic interests of our people.

One contentious issue between Kelley, labor leaders, and me was the race for the U.S. Senate between Republican incumbent Christopher "Kit" Bond and State Attorney General Jeremiah "Jay" Nixon. The St. Louis Labor Council and the Missouri AFL-CIO endorsed Nixon while he and civil rights leaders were having a shootout over the phasing out of court-ordered desegregation in Missouri's public schools. The plan was imposed in 1980 as a remedy for the school district's historical denial of equal education to Negroes. Black leaders were not opposed to the phase-out but insisted that the settlement provide adequate protection against the resegregation of area schools and neighborhoods. Nixon's plan provided no funds to bus students to schools of their choice or to reimburse the receiving schools. If accepted, the Nixon plan would have forced 12,000 black students attending integrated suburban schools back into city schools that had an overwhelming African American majority.

The flap over Nixon's candidacy was only the latest in a series of disagreements between Missouri labor leaders and the African American community. The basic problem was the failure of local union leaders to collaborate with black elected officials in the selection of Democratic candidates. The Kelley group also refused to prioritize legislative agendas addressing the concerns of our people. Labor unions have a right to unilaterally endorse any candidate they believe will best support the agenda of organized labor and advance the rights of workers. If they choose to make selections without input from black leaders, that is also their right. But it is juvenile to expect black people's support of candidates who oppose black causes.

Despite Nixon's denials, he was playing the same negative politics as too many other Missouri politicians. Rural voters opposed the court-supervised voluntary desegregation plan. Nixon's acceleration to end the plan did not provide adequate resources to protect the interests of the children. His action was an appeal for votes in the countryside. As usual, politicians sided with white voters who could give them 40 percent of their vote over black voters who normally gave them 90 percent of their vote. But African Americans were firmly resolved that Nixon would not reap the benefit of white rural voters at the expense of black inner-city children.

Nixon filed numerous motions challenging the settlement that the Eighth Circuit Court of Appeals ruled should be negotiated. He was willing to cut off money for magnet schools after three years and eliminate extra money for upgrading all-black schools. He sought a precipitous ending of the desegregation case in order to claim he "stopped wasteful use of tax dollars on desegregation" in St. Louis and Kansas City.[117]

Kelley criticized me for asking President Clinton to cancel a campaign fund-raising appearance for Nixon, claiming that Nixon was "getting an unfair drubbing" from me.[118] I did ask Clinton not to attend a $1,000-per-plate dinner fund-raiser "unless and until [Nixon] abandons his opposition to desegregation and other equal opportunity measures for St. Louis school children."[119]

Kelley asked national labor leaders who oversaw donations to congressional candidates to take notice: "Here's the senior member of the Democratic delegation seemingly more interested in attacking Democrats than Republicans." He went one step further than the threat of unions possibly withholding campaign funds—he even gave me a bit of unsolicited career advice, saying, "If [Clay] really feels that strongly, maybe he should give up his twenty-five years of seniority and run for the U.S. Senate."[120]

With Kelley's signature, the St. Louis Labor Council sent a letter warning that officeholders who failed to support Nixon would get no labor contributions. Only two black elected officials had considered supporting Nixon's Republican opponent. But Kelley mailed his letter to all black elected officials and thirty-six white legislators, giving the impression that the threat was nonracial. But white leaders had no problem with Nixon. Mailing it to white leaders who had dodged the desegregation issue indicated a surreptitious motive. The source of contention was with labor's most consistent ally, black Democrats.

Kelley denied the obvious intent of the letter. But I countered that he and organized labor were attempting to "force Nixon's candidacy down the throats of black politicians and black voters." The threat by Kelley placed an additional strain on the already tenuous relations between organized labor and the African American community. Unfortunately, the AFL-CIO decided to draw a line in the sand with Nixon.

I also made it clear that my disagreement with Nixon was not an endorsement for Bond. The threat of withholding campaign contributions was hilarious since labor PACS only donated small amounts to black elected officials, and labor leaders were no threat to defeating any of them for re-election.

At the time of the Labor Council's refusal to endorse Lacy, Kelley and others were still sizzling about the role I played in the defeat of their candidate for governor, Vincent Schoemehl. They were embarrassed by the magnitude of his loss. He was overwhelmed by his opponent in areas most believed to be union strongholds. It revealed how impotent they were in delivering votes without forming coalitions with black leaders. I understood their desire to retaliate. That's politics—it's called payback time.

My disagreements with Bob Kelley did not extend as far back as the ones with Goins and G. Duncan Bauman of the *Globe-Democrat*, but they were just as terse. Early in my congressional career, I invited a number of labor leaders to a luncheon at a popular restaurant on Oakland to discuss my upcoming election. As I was outlining the seriousness of my challenger and suggesting what I needed from them, Kelley blurted out, "You assume we are all endorsing your candidacy. Some of us have not decided who we will support. I personally don't like your position on abortion." For a moment, there was silence at the table. Then, I said, "That is your wife's agenda, not high on the list of workers' priorities. Do we have to let George Meany settle this dispute?" There was laughter and then unanimous agreement that I was organized labor's favorite son.

Another incident took place in Bill Stodghill's office involving Virvus Jones. I had asked Stodghill to call a meeting to solidify labor's support for Jones's re-election as comptroller. Representing labor was Duke McVey, head of the state AFL-CIO, Leonard Robinson of the United Auto Workers, and Kelley. Also present was Donald Suggs, publisher of the *St. Louis American*. While trying to wrangle an endorsement out of Kelley, Dr. Suggs implied that the labor movement owed our community this type of political support. Kelley, apparently reluctant to support Jones, deliberately provoked an argument with Suggs and abruptly left the meeting. McVey remained and assured us that he would persuade Kelley to change his mind.

Kelley's bark was loud but his bite feeble. Diatribes and trumpeting retaliation against black leaders were becoming a common occurrence for Kelley. He threatened to punish me if I supported Jesse Jackson over Richard Gephardt in the Democratic presidential primary. In a telephone conversation, he screamed that "labor would defeat me for re-election" if I did not appear on the platform when Gephardt made his formal announcement for the presidency. I need not acknowledge my rebuttal, but I can assure you that it would be considered pornographic by any standard of decency.

As it turned out, I was not on the platform when Gephardt announced, and Jackson won our district by an overwhelming margin. Organized labor had to seek our support to get several of their candidates named as delegates at the state convention.

Richard Gephardt and Clay, undated.

Kelley and his minions always had difficulty understanding that sledgehammer diplomacy was counterproductive and constituted the sort of action that jeopardized the long-standing relationship of coalition politics between organized labor and the black community.

The continued rift between labor and the African American community unveiled basic weaknesses in the labor movement. The St. Louis Labor Council, without realizing the decline in its political power, continued to possess an exaggerated opinion of its ability to deliver votes. It failed to give sufficient credit and maximum support to black voters who constituted the basis of labor's political power. It was necessary to come to grips with political reality. Disagreeing over candidates was a nonviolent way that we hoped would jolt them from their dreamlike state. When African Americans and St. Louis labor disagree on candidates and issues, organized labor becomes a paper tiger. A sizable number of white union members are more interested in nonunion—sometimes anti-union—issues than in the "bread and butter" union priorities of job security and decent working conditions. Unfortunately, they are more concerned about the right to own guns, to stop abortions, to authorize prayer in public schools, and to lower capital gains taxes. Basic rights of workers are secondary to those union-negotiated contracts that allow them to live in upper-income neighborhoods and send their children to private schools.

I have spoken at some St. Louis local union meetings where the members' demeanor indicated that legislation to prevent companies from hiring replacements for striking workers, preserving the prevailing wages in the area for construction workers, pension protection, and increased minimum wages were not high on their list of priorities.

The political pundits, university political scientists, and city hall gossipmongers were baffled by the labor leaders' spirited drive to defeat a state legislator who had provided them with seventeen years of gallant support. Additionally, Lacy was the son of labor's greatest supporter in Congress. Initially, it looked as if Kelley would succeed in his effort to drive a wedge between labor and the Clay family. He was able to secure for Dooley the maximum legal contributions from international unions such as the Communications Workers of America, Carpenters' International, and the Operating Engineers. James Brown, president of the Association of Machinists and Aerospace Workers, even forced Aerospace Workers' Local 837 to demand that Lacy return a measly $250 contribution.

With the help of the county supervisor, Dooley enticed Jim O'Mara, the business manager of the once politically powerful Pipefitters' Local 562, to withdraw his endorsement of Lacy. O'Mara was an original sponsor of Clay Jr. for Congress. His endorsement was strong and unambiguous, stating, "We have reviewed the records of all announced candidates and find that Lacy Clay has served the state and our members extremely well. Clay has protected the vital interests of the labor movement and effectively represented working people on all paycheck issues." Three months later, O'Mara did an about-face. It was obvious that what finally motivated him to dump Lacy had nothing to do with labor credentials or legislative ability. O'Mara, a fellow colleague of Dooley on the county council, needed Dooley's vote to change the mechanical code and transfer most construction jobs to the Pipefitters at the expense of other AFL-CIO construction union members.

The manner in which O'Mara withdrew his support for Lacy irritated many rank-and-file members of his own union. He accused Lacy of labeling Democratic members of the county council as racists for denying Ethiopian cab drivers with green cards the taxicab permits needed in order to pick up passengers at the airport. A front-page article in the *Labor Tribune* quoted him as incensed because Lacy showed no concern for generating jobs or revenue for the county.

After the election, O'Mara fired Representative Pat O'Connor, who worked for the union, because he introduced Lacy at the victory celebration and appeared with him on all major media outlets in St. Louis that night. Subsequently, O'Mara rehired him.

An organized, united labor effort might have posed a serious threat to the chances of my son winning. But under the circumstances, the majority of labor leaders and their membership did not forsake the mission of the labor movement for the personal vendetta of a few disgruntled union bosses. The giants of the labor movement stepped forward and put "union-made short pants" on Kelley and his disoriented cohorts. Premier union leaders took center stage and rallied behind Lacy. He picked up the support of the Teamsters, the United Auto Workers, Laborers' International Union, the AFL-CIO Teachers' Union, gas workers, transit workers, postal letter carriers, postal clerks, Service Employees' International, the Coalition of Black Trade Unionists, United Food and Commercial Workers, iron workers, Painters' International, airline pilots, firefighters, hotel and restaurant workers, the Boiler Makers' Union, Seafarers Local 5, the Fraternal Order of Police, and others.

Embarrassed by the failure of the council and the state AFL-CIO to endorse Lacy, they waged the maximum effort on his behalf, independent of the city and state labor bodies. They raised funds to offset the thousands of dollars contributed to Dooley by friends of Westfall, the business community, and the eleven unions that voted against Lacy's endorsement. Grant Williams of the Service Employees' International Union said, "Lacy is the best candidate in the race. . . . He's been a leader on every issue that has made a positive impact on the lives of [workers]."[121] A leader of the Coalition of Black Trade Unionists stated, "For labor to abandon young Clay is odd and borders on insanity."[122] Joseph A. Galli Sr., local Teamsters president, said, "Eleven members of the Labor Council made a mistake when they voted not to endorse Lacy Clay. He has a consistent record of supporting Missouri's families during his seventeen years in the Missouri House and Senate."[123]

Lacy spent years in the Missouri legislature waging a battle against those who would exploit the labor of working men and women. His favorable rating among organized labor groups was in the high nineties. While serving as chairman of the House and Senate Labor Committees, he led the fight for key labor issues such as collective bargaining for state employees, increased retirement benefits, legislation to enhance workers' compensation, increases in the minimum wage, creation of safer workplaces, and a ban on the use of strikebreakers. He never wavered on the question of workers' rights. He sponsored more than fifty key labor bills that won him praise and loyalty among working people. He sponsored legislation to allow local law enforcement personnel to form unions. Lacy pushed two prominent bills that authorized up to twelve weeks of paid compensation to new parents following the birth or adoption of a child and one bill, the landmark Hate Crimes Law, which outlawed intimidation based on race, religion, ethnicity, or sexual orientation.

These labor leaders rallied to Lacy's support because his record was factual—not theoretical or intangible, but there to see and touch. For more than seventeen years, he had been a champion for working families, senior citizens, women, public education, health care, and diversity.

Lacy Clay Jr. and mother Carol on election night 2000 after Lacy won the Democratic primary for Congress.

Black Community Behind Lacy

There was no doubt in Lacy's camp about the outcome of the election. Weeks before election day, they felt confident that their highly organized campaign structure was vastly superior to the one promoting Dooley. Newcomers and strategic consultants Michele Clay and Darryl Piggee professionally laid out the campaign battle plan. Veteran campaign manager Pearlie Evans, assisted by headquarters manager Gwen Reed, efficiently directed the program. The engines of the campaign were rolling smoothly as Committeewoman Virginia Cook, Representative Betty Thompson, and Mayor Errol Bush oversaw the St. Louis County section of the district.

The black clergy was instrumental in uniting the community on behalf of Lacy's candidacy. Reverends Willie J. Ellis and B. T. Rice were co-chairs of the committee comprising more than one hundred ministers. Every ward in the city endorsed Lacy. Most were part of his state senate district. Additionally, he had the strong backing of Larry Williams, the city treasurer, former mayor Clarence Harmon, and former mayor Freeman Bosley Jr. Lacy's colleagues in the state senate and house from North County, including Senator John Schneider, endorsed him.

Lacy Clay Jr. won because he surrounded himself with the most experienced political operatives in the area. In addition to Evans, Cook, and Reed, he selected Committeewoman Colleen Roche and consultant Mark Odom as field coordinators and Representative Pat O'Connor, former state senator John Bass, and unionist Lew Moye as campaign advisers. The campaign staff was adept at developing issues and cultivating volunteer support. They were veteran politicians and political activists who assured that the daily operation was promoted effectively and efficiently.

The end of the campaign was not to the liking of Kelley and his dissident labor cohorts. Lacy easily trounced Dooley in every sector of the district. He ran extremely well and beat Dooley in the areas where the pipefitters, communications workers, machinists, and carpenters were supposed to be the strongest. He won every precinct in their stronghold by large margins. The final count was Clay Jr. with 34,393 votes to Dooley's 15,612.

The election of Lacy Clay Jr. was justified because he was the most qualified candidate seeking the office. His background, association, and identification with pertinent public issues plus his nearly eighteen years in the state legislature prepared him for a greater career in a higher office. One of my fondest memories in politics was the night the results came in showing that Lacy had won the Democratic primary for Congress.

The general election between Lacy and his Republican opponent, Z. Dwight Billingsly, was really a nonelection. The reactionary Republican was underfinanced, outmanned, and overshadowed by Lacy's record—as he had been on two previous occasions when he ran against Clay Sr.

CHAPTER

18

A SUMMARY OF THE BLACK STRUGGLE

I n 1968 Missouri Democrats had an ironclad grip on state politics. Both U.S. senators, nine of the ten members of the U.S. House of Representatives, the governor, the lieutenant governor, the state treasurer, the attorney general, the state auditor, and the secretary of state were Democrats. Democrats controlled both houses of the state legislature. In every city, township, and hamlet, "happy days were here again" for Missouri Democrats.

The lopsided majorities for Democratic candidates produced in black precincts enabled the party to dominate politics. Casting 90 percent of their ballots, Negroes constituted the margin of victory for Democrats in election after election. Most Democrats left South St. Louis trailing Republicans by 10,000 to 20,000 votes, but the figures were quickly reversed as North Side black wards were tallied.

Yet the Negroes' party loyalty for more than thirty years was never fully appreciated or returned. Except for the courageous and unwavering fight for civil rights at the national level waged by a continuous, unbroken string of U.S. senators and representatives—Harry S. Truman, Tom Hennings, Stuart Symington, Edward Long, Thomas Eagleton, Leonor Sullivan, and Richard Bolling—the political investment of black voters was hardly recognized. In most instances, Democrats at the state and local levels operated similarly to other officials in southern states. The hierarchy of the party's decision-makers refused to share power with African American leaders or to address the problems of their constituents.

Negroes were considered excess baggage—ripe for political exploitation. In the 1950s and 1960s, Democratic mayors and a Democrat-controlled Board of Aldermen promoted schemes to deny blacks decent housing, fair employment, and access to public accommodations. They uprooted 50,000 blacks in the three-hundred-acre Mill Creek area and flung them across the city without sympathetic concern for their relocation or fear of political retaliation. Under the guise of "imminent domain," a Democratic administration allowed developers to seize their property at prices insufficient to purchase new homes.

In the 1970s and 1980s, Democrats engaged in another breach of faith with black citizens. They closed the city hospital that provided medical care for most black indigent patients and employed most of the city's black doctors, dentists, x-ray technicians, nurses, and other professional staff. The other city hospital, preferred by white patients, both university medical schools, and business tycoons—although much older, less cost-efficient, and less central to the indigent population—remained open.

Black Political Disenchantment

An increasingly lower voter turnout in African American precincts began to send a signal that was obvious: In ignoring the dynamics of race and politics, the chickens will come home to roost. General disgust with the lack of fairness reached a high point in the late 1980s and early 1990s. From the beginnings of Negro assertiveness manifested in 1960, many white Democrats fought to stem the tide of black influence in party politics. The failure of Democratic officeholders to yield patronage to newly elected black ward leaders was a mistake that impaired the ability of ward organizations to deliver large volumes of votes for party candidates. Refusal to hire blacks left precinct captains disillusioned and ward leaders embittered. Hundreds of whites who moved to St. Louis County continued to hold high-paying political jobs. Their talents were no longer available or required to energize the electorate and get voters to the polls.

Most Negroes held the view that campaign promises of both parties were meaningless; voting Republican was no viable alternative. Republicans offered pie-in-the-sky fantasies to address real minority concerns and expected blacks to migrate to the party of Abraham Lincoln because he had signed the Emancipation Proclamation. Promoting trashy, condescending slogans such as "Blacks should be in both parties" or "Under our wide tent, we welcome Afro-Americans" while simultaneously championing states' rights, opposing affirmative action, and supporting reactionary white candidates is demeaning and insulting. Democrats, on the other hand, operate as if they have a manifest destiny to keep blacks economically subservient and politically paralyzed. Unconditionally wedded to the philosophy that catering to the needs of blacks alienates white support, they suppress any meaningful agenda for minorities. Neglecting the needs of their black supporters is believed to be the safest and most expedient option. Democrats rationalize that blacks are in a catch-22 predicament, with no place to go. Blind to political reality, unperceptive white Democrats march on, losing election after election.

The policy of benign neglect has played an important role in the reversal of the Democratic Party's fortunes. A significant number of blacks no longer places a premium on electing indifferent Democratic candidates, and they shudder at the thought of casting votes for ideologically attuned Republican zealots. Refusing to choose between the insincere and the insensitive, they have found they do have a positive place and a relevant role in politics. The place is home. The role is boycotting elections. Withholding their votes also presents a catch-22 for Democrats.

Black St. Louisans do not vote Republican because Republicans are part of the conspiracy to keep our race politically impotent. Republicans in the city have voluntarily abolished their GOP Party identification by switching to the Democratic Party in order to prevent black voters from becoming the balance of power in choosing Democratic candidates. Abdicating party principle and abandoning personal responsibility, lifelong Republicans have determined that deterring the progress of the black race is more important than advancing the interests of their own party.

In the highest-income areas where the very rich contribute substantial sums to GOP candidates for the U.S. Senate and president, Republicans do not file viable candidates. Instead, they cross party lines to campaign for Democrats in the primary, contending that a vigorous two-party system would dilute the white vote and allow African Americans to determine who is nominated and subsequently elected.

In recent elections, every white elected Republican committeeman and committeewoman has publicly endorsed and openly campaigned for the Democratic candidate. Ironically, a media that without hesitation alleges voting irregularities in black wards ignores these violations of state law, or at least the spirit of it. The two major political parties, established by state statute, have the exclusive right to elect two committeepersons from each party in each of the twenty-eight wards. They are legally authorized to name polling clerks and judges to assure honest elections. When all Democratic and Republican committeepeople in the same ward endorse the same candidate, who protects the integrity of the voting booth and who prevents improper or illegal behavior? The arrangement has been good for individual Democratic candidates, but the fallout has been disastrous for the party. Discontent among African Americans is the major reason Democrats no longer dictate or control politics in Missouri. In 2004 the pendulum swung 180 degrees; Republicans gained both U.S. Senate positions and six of the nine seats in the U.S. House of Representatives and controlled both houses of the state legislature.

Democratic pollsters wonder why black leaders in St. Louis and Kansas City are cantankerous and their constituents rebellious. The answer is not difficult or profound. Their apathy is a reflection of their disgust with Democrats who sound like, act like, and vote like their Republican counterparts.

Winds of Change

In the mid-1950s, the winds of change were blowing in every municipality where black Americans lived. The desire for economic justice and social equity was the dynamic force driving the pursuit of a new political agenda among blacks. Negro masses, emboldened by the 1954 Supreme Court decision declaring separate but equal to be inherently unequal, divorced themselves from the debilitating clutches of fear and hopelessness that had stifled their assertiveness for more than a century. Experiencing a sweeping readjustment in attitude and a sea change in realistic expectation, Negroes pursued their rights with reckless abandon. They flexed their muscles through sit-ins, economic boycotts, and political action.

While liberals and their conventional black allies were congratulating each other for the limited, gradual racial improvement achieved in the 1940s, a new generation of impatient, angry blacks emerged, demanding freedom immediately. Young visionaries, freshly off the picket lines and out of southern jails, were projecting far more innovative strategies for opposing Jim Crow conditions. They exhibited a passionate determination never before manifested by black Americans. Skills learned in organizing marches, sit-ins, and boycotts were readily converted into organizing registration drives, establishing political clubs, and conducting get-out-the-vote campaigns.

Following the advice of new leaders, blacks who had usually skirted around the perimeter of the political game plunged into the heart and soul of it. They began to recognize common concerns, common interests, and, more important, common enemies. They became aware that latent power, if activated, could overthrow entrenched political

Congressman Louis Stokes, his wife Jay, and Clay, undated.

bosses. Self-determination became the password driving blacks to organize and take control of elected positions in predominantly black districts. Racial togetherness represented a pregnant milestone in devising effective campaigns to oust insensitive officials, most of whom did not live in the run-down, dilapidated, rat-infested districts they pretended to represent.

Blacks, nationally as well as in St. Louis, were caught up in the euphoric atmosphere created by the exciting rhetoric of Stokely Carmichael, the bravado of H. Rap Brown, the stubborn endurance of John Lewis, the militancy of Malcolm X, and the radical confrontation of Huey Newton. Abetted by the awe-inspiring leadership of Dr. Martin Luther King Jr., young blacks across the country were undoubtedly inspired to challenge the invidious system of racial discrimination and exploitation.

The years between 1960 and 1993 can accurately be described as the "golden years" of African American politics in Missouri. During this period, despite stringent resistance from recalcitrant white Democrats and objections from reactionary black leaders, African Americans reached the pinnacle of success. The dramatic increase in elective officeholders and appointments to government boards and commissions resulted when old-guard and new insurgent leaders entered into a pact for the common good. Positions of power escalated for blacks and even blossomed—some negotiated, others won at the polls. The achievements were unprecedented in any other southern state: Two of the state's ten representatives in the U.S. House were African Americans. Two blacks from St. Louis and one from Kansas City were elected to the state senate. The election of T. D. McNeal to the state senate in 1960 was a historic occasion. He joined the distinguished list of four other black state senators in the nation. Blacks maintained control of the Fourth State Senatorial District in subsequent elections: Franklin Payne, Gwen Giles, John Bass, and Lacy Clay succeeded McNeal in office. In 1972 Raymond Howard won the second senate seat in St. Louis. He was followed in the district by J. B. Banks and Paula Carter. Phillip B. Curls Sr. of Kansas City was elected to the state senate in 1983. Freeman Bosley

Jr. was elected mayor in 1993. Three blacks held the city comptroller's office at separate times: John Bass, Virvus Jones, and Darlene Green. Citywide patronage offices were held by Benjamin Goins, license collector and sheriff; Larry Williams, city treasurer; Freeman Bosley Jr., clerk of the circuit court and mayor; Mavis Thompson, clerk of the circuit court; and License Collectors Lawrence Woodson and Billie Boykins. The first black elected to the school board was Reverend John J. Hicks in 1959. Afterward, James Hurt, Adella Smiley, Anita Bond, Reverend Earl Nance Sr., and numerous others were elected to the Board of Education.

The appointment of blacks to decision-making positions—unimagined in the 1950s—was attained during these golden years: T. D. McNeal, as chairman of police commissioners; several African American St. Louis metropolitan chiefs of police; Theodore McMillian, federal appellate court judge; three federal district court judges; twelve state court judges; cabinet members in each of seven mayoral administrations; appointees to the Metropolitan Sewer District Board and the Board of Elections; commissioners of higher education, the Bi-State Development Agency, and the St. Louis Housing Authority; city counselor; acting president of the Board of Aldermen; and others too numerous to cite.

Indeed, it was the golden age of progressive politics for African Americans. The impressive record of accomplishment can be traced to three crucial developments: effective coalescing with a small but influential group of white politicians; the melding of older, more experienced black leaders with younger, more energetic leaders into a united front; and the grooming of a family spirit among important, diverse centers of influence in the black community.

Effective Coalition Politics

A minority community, no matter how dynamic or forceful its leaders or how profound its proposals, can only succeed by uniting with other power interests in a common cause. Such a coalition was formed from elements of organized labor, blacks working for the white media, and educators at the university level. The unity pact enabled blacks to gain power sufficient to protect themselves from predatory forces. However, reaching agreement with people who were considered the wearers of "black hats" was the most beneficial step in attaining political clout. Alliances with leaders who had been castigated by the political, economic, and social barons strengthened the position of black leaders and enabled us to parlay our voting potential into concrete results. Without the support of Cervantes, Webbe, Callanan, and Lawler—the designated wearers of the "black hats"—it is doubtful that I or any other black would have been elected to the U.S. Congress or to a citywide office, or appointed to an important board.

Support for the advancement of racial and political causes from reformers commonly referred to as blue-ribbon citizens never materialized. In my opinion, assistance from them would not have come under any circumstance. The good guys in "white hats" were too busy consolidating their own positions to bother with such mundane issues. When opportunities surfaced that would have advanced the causes of black people, the establishment forces invariably drafted cleverly worded statements justifying their opposition.

The good guys were often in direct contradiction to their overly publicized declarations of efforts to improve minority conditions. The reason the business community and the Democratic power structure would support policies to keep blacks subservient was not readily apparent. The position of liberals was discernible and understandable because it was based on practical, self-interested politics. Their influence, in many instances, was inexplicably tied to support provided to them by the Negro community. Except for pervasive, ingrained racism, blacks would have been a critical political mass in their own right. However, it was necessary to sanction white liberals as spokespeople to make our concerns heard. The arrangement created for liberals a power base worthy of recognition by other power entities. As Negroes began to chart their own destiny, to execute their own programs, to assert their independence, and to speak for themselves, the influence of white liberals was greatly reduced.

In a very real sense, the progress of blacks undermined the stability of the liberal bloc and raised questions of its legitimacy.

The second major factor in the development of a successful campaign for inclusion in the greater society was the coming together of old-line politicians such as Weathers, Grant, Goldston, Broussard, and others with the new element headed by Larry Williams, Giles, Evans, Clay, Tyus, Payne, Bass, and others.

The merging of the forces made a vast difference in enabling a once badly splintered community to move ahead in reaping major political benefits. Weathers and Payne took the lead in negotiating agreement on many contentious issues. Although there was constant sniping by the nihilists, their defiance never completely stalled the drive for racial progress.

The third significant reason for the advancement of blacks in the political sphere was the coming together of leaders commonly referred to as the Family. It was an informal gathering of numerous black leaders, many without title or portfolio, who gathered to discuss issues and devise strategies. It replaced the loose-knit network that formerly met at Tate Sisters' and the Deluxe Restaurants. There were no membership lists, dues, bylaws, officers, or regularly called meetings. It was not a syndicate led by a "boss of bosses" or a highly structured cartel of elected officials. It existed merely as a clearinghouse for ideas and as an instrument for assembling supporters for direct political action projects.

The original participants in the Family were elected officials, civic leaders, and community activists. Among the more active were Larry Williams, Pearlie Evans, Doris Moore, Gwen Reed, Weathers, Payne, Tyus, Nat Rivers, Leonard Robinson, Giles, Bass, Margaret Wilson, Bill Stodghill, Virvus Jones, Leroy Wilson, Ted Daniels, Billie Boykins, Louis Ford, Hank Thompson, Wayman Smith, and Elliot Davis. In later days, Bosley Jr., Mike McMillan, Lacy Clay Jr., Harold Crumpton, Paula Carter, and Claude Brown became important participants. Landmark breakthroughs came about because strong, independent individuals devoted their efforts to eradicate racial inequities. They believed political pressure was the most effective means of eliminating it.

Despite the negative attitudes and contradictory activities of some black leaders, the submerging of personal ambition for the benefit of the whole prevailed. The Family succeeded in overcoming the disruptive, obscene behavior of the nihilists. The Family usually met in my suites at the Bel Air West Motel or the Mayfair Hotel whenever I was in town. The committeemen and the heads of civil rights organizations usually met at the home of Weathers, the dean of black politics. Doctors, lawyers, and other professionals gathered at two Negro-owned private clubs—the Vagabonds and the Lambs. They were informed of issues and briefed on strategies by Weathers, Tyus, Bass, and others.

Development of a black agenda and execution of its provisions were key to the Family's success. They were the basis of its quest, its objectives, and its hope for the future. Proposals always included a demand that blacks actively participate in planning the expansion and vitality of the city. Underpinning all plans was the insistence that minorities get a fair share of jobs and contracts on government-financed projects and that they be appointed to important boards and commissions.

In most instances, educators, lawyers, doctors, neighborhood organizers, civil rights leaders, newspaper editors, and reporters were included in ratifying the final plan. Involving them was crucial in preventing outside forces from compromising and dividing North Side voters. No matter how often the establishment tried to create legitimacy for their handpicked leaders or in how many different ways they attempted to portray them as community voices, the schemes failed.

The Family maintained its integrity because its agenda was influenced by those who pursued politics as a career, a vocation, and a profession. Diverse personalities were independent enough to resist monetary temptation and skillful enough to put down pernicious internal defection. Respect in the community enabled Family members to control the machinery and direction of North Side politics. The strength of black politicians resonated from the ability of the Family to relate to the black church, the black media, black professionals, and black activists who supported the concept of togetherness and were dedicated to the principle of self-determination. In essence, the Family gave voice to

Mayor Freeman Bosley Jr. and Clay, 1997.

black pride and, through the forceful exercise of political power, made its impact upon the way St. Louis related to its minority citizens.

Black politics, black self-determination, and black pride reached their apex in the mayoral race of 1993. Freeman Bosley Jr., the clerk of the court, was elected in a bitterly fought, intense campaign. Four candidates, two whites and two blacks—each with considerable name recognition, political savvy, and experience as elected officials—vied for the office. The two whites, Tom Villa and Anthony Ribaudo, were state representatives. Steve Roberts, the other black candidate, was a former member of the Board of Aldermen. All four waged viable campaigns. Bosley, in victory, received 49,955 votes; Villa received 33,055; Ribaudo, 11,389, and Roberts, 6,870.

In the same primary, incumbent comptroller Virvus Jones was renominated over challenger James Shrewsbury, president of the Board of Aldermen, by 44,941 votes to 42,962. A minor candidate, Penny Alcott, received 3,280 votes. Jones went on to win the general election, giving blacks a majority on the powerful Board of Estimates for the first time.

Diminution of Political Power

Four years later, St. Louisans witnessed the beginning of the end of a strong, effective black political presence. The power that had begun to wane several years earlier was dealt a devastating blow in Bosley's 1997 re-election defeat. A media harshly critical of his administration and opposition among black leaders took its toll on his governance. Two blacks, incumbent Freeman Bosley Jr. and challenger Clarence Harmon, the chief of police, crystallized the festering, bitter discontent between black leaders and permitted the white power structure to become the swing and decisive vote in the election.

White Democrats, aided by the downtown business community and the media, surmised it would be too difficult for a white to defeat the charismatic Bosley. Following the example of other cities similarly situated, they united behind a black candidate who presumably would be easier to defeat in a future election. Thus, Harmon unwittingly became the unanimous candidate of those who were more opposed to Bosley than personally committed to Harmon. The plot thickened when Harmon admitted that four months after Bosley had first been elected mayor, downtown business leaders invited him to lunch and asked him to run against Bosley for mayor in the next election.[124]

Harmon was endorsed by every white elected official residing in the city, Democrat and Republican, with the exception of Senator Thomas Eagleton, Francis Slay Sr., and Francis Slay Jr., who endorsed Bosley. In the Twenty-third Ward, where the senior Slay had been committeeman for more than twenty years, Harmon received 5,646 votes to Bosley's 227 votes. The ward organization endorsed Bosley but obviously did not campaign for him. It was part of a commitment designed to get Bosley's support for Slay's son, who ran for president of the Board of Aldermen.

Organized labor was divided. The carpenters, police, firefighters, and painters supported Harmon. The electricians, service employees, and teachers were for Bosley. The St. Louis Labor Council was undecided. Sylvester Brown Jr., writer and publisher of a monthly news chronicle, described Bosley's opposition in blunt terms in a special column to the *St. Louis American*. He wrote, "Harmon's candidacy is a carefully orchestrated plot by the 'powers-that-be' to derail the progress of black economic and political gains. What better way to defeat an 'undesirable' black politician than with another black man who has been accused of ignoring black concerns for the purpose of white advancement?"[125]

Republican elected officials openly joined white Democrats in support of Harmon's candidacy. In the predominantly Republican Twelfth and Sixteenth Wards, Harmon beat Bosley 5,936 to 114 and 6,678 to 199, respectively. Evidence of Republican defection is manifested in the vote count. Three candidates in the Republican primary only received a total of 1,368 votes citywide. In the Sixteenth Ward, Democratic Committeeman James Wahl confirmed the Democratic-Republican conspiracy when he heaped praise on Republican activists and thanked Republicans Jerry Wamser and Steve Doss "for helping set up and staff an organization that included telephone banks and teams of people who visited anyone who had not voted [for Harmon] by midafternoon."[126]

The race was decided by the distinct preference between white and black voters. In his victorious campaign, Harmon won every white ward by large margins (86 percent); outran Bosley in the central corridor, the base of white liberal voters, by 65 percent; and lost every black ward (receiving only 15 percent). Harmon received 56,894 votes (56 percent) to Bosley's 43,150 votes (43 percent).

Four years later, Mayor Harmon was defeated for re-election by Francis Slay Jr., president of the Board of Aldermen. Harmon did not have a scandal during his term of office. His administration was so top-heavy with white South Siders appointed by him that the black aldermen who had supported his candidacy over Bosley's publicly complained. Amazingly, Harmon, endorsed by 99 percent of white elected officials in 1997, received the endorsement of less than 1 percent of white elected officials in 2001.

The Passing of the Torch

In reviewing the resiliency of blacks throughout the history of politics in St. Louis, it is evident that leaders who pioneered a new frontier in black politics did not fail. But many of their contemporary associates, too enamored with mentalities that equated positive representation with the ability of white leaders to dispense personal welfare, were responsible for the failure.

But that must not deter the drive to bring black Americans to full and equal citizenship. The transition of power, leadership, and commitment has to pass to a younger people. When quizzed about the transfer of power from the older generation to the new, John Bass said, "We need to ask ourselves—who are we going to turn the gauntlet over to? Who will stand on the shoulders of those who have gone before? Young people need to understand about coalition politics, about working together with other groups. They need to develop a council of elders to advise them."[127]

Bass is correct. Young politicians should reflect on the past before leaping into the future. Knowledge gives strength, vitality, and, above all, insight for long-range planning. The struggle must continue, and the torch must pass to new warriors. They must be strong advocates of racial and economic justice. Turning the tide for change is still the critical challenge facing minority constituents.

Recently, African Americans in St. Louis have lost most of the hard-earned gains of the golden years. In 2003 blacks were no longer holding office as mayor, clerk of the courts, sheriff, or license collector. Only the offices of city treasurer and comptroller were held by blacks. In addition, blacks lost one of their two state senators. The loss of four citywide offices and one state senate seat has crippled the ability of African Americans to exert maximum political influence.

Unless the politics of suicide, which results in massive black dis-unity, is abated and reversed, the gallant struggle of black warriors of the past will be nullified. If blacks in St. Louis are to re-establish themselves as a viable political force, the cannibalism among their leaders must end.

After a brief pause and a long sigh, I assertively suggest that the kind of unselfish leadership manifested by the Family of yesteryear is needed more today than anything else. Black politicians must forgo their ego-tripping and devote their energies to eliminating the existing barri-ers still prohibiting equal justice and equal opportunity for African Americans. They must focus attention on the immense disparity of the races: pervasive black unemployment, excessive numbers of black women heading households, deplorable black-on-black crime, phenomenal rates of high school dropouts and drug addiction, and all the other tragic and sordid conditions that form a panorama of the black experience.

The mind-set that separates the progress of minorities from the advancement of the whole society must be obliterated. In the twenti-eth century, the myth that a democratic nation could live peacefully in safety and comfort while tolerating racial injustice was exposed. In the twenty-first century, through effective community organization and judi-cious use of the ballot, that myth must be destroyed.

Notes

1. William L. Clay, *Just Permanent Interests* (New York: Amistad Press, 1992), 55.

2. Nathan B. Young, ed., *Your St. Louis and Mine* (St. Louis: N. B. Young, 1938), 39.

3. Ibid.

4. John Hope Franklin, *From Slavery to Freedom: A History of Negro Americans*, 3rd ed. (New York: Vintage Books, 1969), 486.

5. Ibid., 68.

6. Tillman was appointed a Missouri circuit judge on November 12, 1970, by Governor Warren E. Hearnes.

7. *St. Louis Globe-Democrat*, September 22, 1960, p. 10.

8. *St. Louis Argus*, November 11, 1961, p. 1.

9. *St. Louis Globe-Democrat*, September 5, 1972, p. 4A.

10. *St. Louis Post-Dispatch*, October 14, 1963, p. 4.

11. *St. Louis Globe-Democrat*, October 25, 1963, p. 1.

12. Ibid.

13. "Law and Order Upheld," *St. Louis Globe-Democrat*, October 25, 1963, p. 8A.

14. "Police State Tactics," St. Louis CORE report, February 15, 1964, p. 1.

15. Norman R. Seay, letter commemorating the twenty-fifth anniversary of Jefferson Bank Demonstrations, November 12, 1988.

16. *St. Louis Globe-Democrat*, February 23, 1965, p. 26.

17. *St. Louis Defender*, March 18, 1965, p. 2.

18. "Either Clay or Negro Jobs," *St. Louis Globe-Democrat*, September 3, 1965.

19. "Bill Clay Our Choice," *St. Louis Argus*, July 19, 1968.

20. *St. Louis Mirror*, July 3, 1968, p. 6.

21. "In the First District," *St. Louis Post-Dispatch*, July 24, 1968, p. 2E.

22. *People's Guide* (St. Louis publication), February 7, 1968.

23. *St. Louis Post-Dispatch*, May 22, 1968, p. 9D.

24. John Angelides and James Floyd, "Doc Lawler: A Behind-the-Scenes Political Kingmaker," *St. Louis Globe-Democrat*, September 5, 1972, p. 4A.

25. Ralph G. Martin, *The Bosses* (New York: G.P. Putnam's Sons, 1964), 264.

26. Official Manual of the State of Missouri, 1966, p. 1155.

27. Ibid., p. 1122.

28. *St. Louis Globe-Democrat*, January 14, 1972, p. 4A.

29. Robert Christman, *St. Louis Post-Dispatch*, n.d.

30. Ibid.

31. Samuel Slade, *St. Louis Sentinel*, May 1971.

32. Ibid.

33. *St. Louis Post-Dispatch* editorial, May 6, 1971.

34. Press release, Margaret Bush Wilson, chairperson of Committee of 100 for the First Congressional District, April 1, 1981.

35. "Call for Unity-Clay-Goins," *St. Louis Argus*, September 14 , 1972, p. 1.

36. Ibid.

37. "Clay and Goins Say They've Made Peace," *St. Louis Globe-Democrat*, September 11, 1972, p. 1.

38. *St. Louis Sentinel*, October 3, 1972, p. 1.

39. Ibid.

40. *St. Louis Post-Dispatch*, May 17, 1974, p. 3A.

41. *People's Guide*, April 10, 1974, p. 1.

42. *St. Louis American*, August 1, 1974, p. 1.

43. Gerald M. Boyd, "CORE Accuses Clay of Losing Identity with Blacks," *St. Louis Post-Dispatch*, August 1, 1974, p. 1.

44. Ibid.

45. George Judge Johnson, vice chairman, ACTION news release, St. Louis, Missouri, August 4, 1974.

46. *St. Louis Post-Dispatch*, May 17, 1974.

47. "Rep. Clay Calls for Investigation of Sverdrup's Donation to Gates," *St. Louis Post-Dispatch*, July 18, 1974, p. 1.

48. "Clay-Gates Fight Escalates," *St. Louis Post-Dispatch*, August 4, 1974, p. 18A.

49. Ibid.

50. Attorney Frankie M. Freeman, letter to T. D. McNeal, president of St. Louis Board of Police Commissioners, July 29, 1974.

51. George E. Curry, "North Side Poll Security Called Discriminatory," *St. Louis Post-Dispatch*, July 31, 1974, p. 12A.

52. "Hoodlum Support for Clay," *St. Louis Globe-Democrat*, August 6, 1974, p. 1.

53. *St. Louis Globe-Democrat*, August 7, 1974, editorial page.

54. In 1998 all sixteen black members serving on the dialogue committees became disgusted with the arrangement and resigned en masse. James Buford, president of the Urban League and one of the leaders withdrawing from the dialogue committee, said, "If we are going to be a Renaissance city—a world-class city—we are going to have to start dealing with race straight on. Civic Progress is very concerned that its African American members of the dialogue committee have left. It is not as concerned with prioritizing the issues we feel are important." It

was a great loss to the city that the dialogue concept failed. Business leaders were presented with a wonderful opportunity to interface with blacks, and, through honest discussion, perhaps some of the distorted notions about African Americans might have been dispelled. Alvin A. Reid, "Civic Progress Dialogue Group Resigns En Masse: Sixteen Black Civic Leaders End Talks," *St. Louis American*, September 3, 1998, p. 1A.

55. Jake McCarthy, "Campaign against Bill Clay," *St. Louis Post-Dispatch*, May 9, 1975, p. 3.

56. *St. Louis Post-Dispatch*, April 8, 1976.

57. "Clay's Campaign for Mayor," *St. Louis Post-Dispatch*, March 10, 1977, p. 1.

58. Ibid.

59. "Deeply Disturbed," *St. Louis American*, March 17, 1977, letter to the editor.

60. Partial statement by Congressman Bill Clay, from transcript of March 9, 1977, meeting with ministers, pp. 2–3.

61. Rev. James Cummings, ibid., p. 4.

62. Rev. J. H. Oxley, ibid., p. 4.

63. Farley Wilson, "Three-Ring Political Circus Has Race for Mayor in a Turmoil," *St. Louis American*, March 17, 1977, editorial page.

64. Ibid.

65. "Our Choices," *St. Louis Argus*, March 31, 1977, editorial page.

66. Wilson, "Three-Ring Political Circus."

67. Jack Flach, "Banks Accuses Clay of Being Self-Serving," *St. Louis Globe-Democrat*, March 25, 1977, p. 1.

68. "A Reply to Mr. Ernest Calloway," *St. Louis Sentinel*, April 7, 1977, p. 5.

69. "An Open Letter," *St. Louis Argus*, March 24, 1977, editorial page.

70. "Clay's Campaign for Mayor May Split City Democrats," *St. Louis Post-Dispatch*, March 10, 1977, p. 1.

71. *St. Louis Globe-Democrat*, April 7, 1977, p. 12A.

72. "An Interesting Election," *St. Louis Argus*, April 7, 1977, editorial page.

73. "An Open Letter," *St. Louis Argus*, March 24, 1977, editorial page.

74. James Floyd and William Poe, "Write-in Move Called a Clay-Goins Power Struggle," *St. Louis Globe-Democrat*, March 12, 1977, p. 1.

75. Jake McCarthy, *St. Louis Post-Dispatch*, March 25, 1977.

76. *St. Louis Globe-Democrat*, February 18, 1978, p. 3F.

77. Floyd and Poe, "Write-in Move," p. 1.

78. *St. Louis Post-Dispatch*, May 18, 1977, p. 14.

79. J. Pulitzer and David Fink, "Goins Sheriff in a Squeak," ibid., p. 1.

80. *Globe-Democrat*, February 2, 1978, p. 1.

81. McCarthy, "Campaign Against Bill Clay," p. 3.

82. Jack Flach, "Political Power Tussle Looms in 1st District," *St. Louis Globe-Democrat*, May 21, 1977, editorial page.

83. *St. Louis Globe-Democrat*, February 2, 1978, p. 1.

84. McCarthy, "Campaign against Bill Clay," p. 3.

85. Benjamin Goins, speech in St. Louis, Missouri, restaurant on West Florissant, December 1985.

86. Jo Mannies, "10 Years with Vince Schoemehl," *St. Louis Post-Dispatch*, April 21, 1991, p. 1B. Conway was correct in both instances.

87. "Bosley for Circuit Clerk," *St. Louis Globe-Democrat*, July 10, 1982, editorial page.

88. Robert L. Koenig, Louis J. Rose, and Michael D. Sorkin, "Schoemehl Rewards Donors," *St. Louis Post-Dispatch*, May 4, 1986, p. 1.

89. Mayor Vincent C. Schoemehl Jr., letter to the voters, August 1, 1986, on official stationery with the mayor's seal.

90. Pearlie Evans, *Point of View* (campaign newspaper), June 1986, p. 5.

91. Frank Elam, *St. Louis American*, May 29, 1986, p. 1B.

92. Frank Elam, *St. Louis American*, May 22, 1986, p. 2B.

93. Bosley, letter to constituents, dated May 12, 1986.

94. *St. Louis Sentinel*, April 10, 1986, p. 1.

95. Les Pearson, "Schoemehl—Nowhere to Go but Up," *St. Louis Globe-Democrat*, August 8, 1986.

96. Bill McClellan, *St. Louis Post-Dispatch*, August 8, 1986, p. 3F.

97. Pearson, "Schoemehl."

98. Margaret Gillerman, "Schoemehl Praises Reorganization Plan," *St. Louis Post-Dispatch*, May 31, 1987, p. 1D.

99. Tim O'Neil, "'Never-Ending Story': Vince-Virvus Shenanigans Strain City's Politics," *St. Louis Post-Dispatch*, February 17, 1992, p. 1B.

100. "Mayor Wanted to Keep Globe Democrat in Business," *Point of View* (campaign newspaper), August 1992, p. 6.

101. "Efforts to Save, Sink Newspaper Made as Globe Fought for Life," *St. Louis Post-Dispatch*, October 31, 1986, p. 15A.

102. *St. Louis Post-Dispatch*, March 13, 1987, p. 3A.

103. Karen Koman and Mark Schlinkmann, "Clay Seeks Mayor's Apology," *St. Louis Post-Dispatch*, March 13, 1987, p. 3A.

104. Mark Schlinkmann, "Clay's Backing Is Feather in Carnahan's Cap, Blow to Schoemehl," *St. Louis Post-Dispatch*, March 7, 1992, p. 3.

105. Tim O'Neil, "Schoemehl, Jones Groups Squabble over Contracts," *St. Louis Post-Dispatch*, February 27, 1992, p. 3A.

106. *St. Louis Post-Dispatch*, April 1, 1992, p. 3A.

107. "Kelley and Mantia Rap Clay for Carnahan Endorsement," *St. Louis Labor Tribune*, March 12, 1992, p. 1.

108. Representative Patrick J. Hickey, letter, March 16, 1992.

109. Jo Mannies, "Mayor's Clout," *St. Louis Post-Dispatch*, March 29, 1987, p. B1.

110. Letter from Clay to Gerald McEntee, president of AFSCME, February 25, 1992.

111. Elbert Walton, *St. Louis American*, May 4, 2000.

112. Alvin Reid, "Clay Boasts Labor Clout; Dooley Cries Foul," *St. Louis American*, May 3, 2000, p. A3.

113. Fred W. Lindecke, "Labor Council Urges Support for Schoemehl," *St. Louis Post-Dispatch*, February 13, 1991, p. 1.

114. "Not a Labor of Love," *St. Louis American*, May 4, 2000, p. A12.

115. Ibid.

116. *St. Louis American*, April 27, 2000, p. 8A.

117. "Labor Leader Raps Clay over Nixon Censure," *St. Louis Post-Dispatch*, October 8, 1997, p. 4A.

118. Ibid.

119. "Democrats Divided over Nixon," *St. Louis Post-Dispatch*, October 8, 1997, p. 6B.

120. "Labor Leader Raps Clay," p. 4A.

121. Reid, "Clay Boasts Clout," p. A3.

122. Samuel Slade, "What You Don't Know Can Indeed Hurt You," *St. Louis Sentinel*, June 1, 2000, p. 5A.

123. Letter to the editor, *St. Louis Post-Dispatch,* April 27, 2000, p. 1B.

124. *St. Louis Post-Dispatch*, February 27, 1997, p. 5A.

125. Sylvester Brown Jr., "Clarence Harmon: The Man Who Wore the Gold Badge," *St. Louis American*, February 27, 1997, p. 5A.

126. Tim O'Neil and Jo Mannies, "South Side Turned Out in Force for Harmon," *St. Louis Post-Dispatch*, March 6, 1997, p. 1.

127. Doris A. Wesley, *Lift Every Voice and Sing* (Columbia: University of Missouri Press, 1999), 39.

Index

Aboussie, Martie, 232
AFL-CIO, 288–300
Akins, Virgil, 12
Albert, Lawrence, 193–194
Ames, Joe, 131
Anderson, Richard, 121

Banks, J. B. "Jet," 213–214, 230, 269, 271, 308
Bass, John, 88, 100, *186*, *197*, *211*, *227*, 251, *262*, 299, 308, 309, 316; re-election campaigns, 223–232, 255, 257–259; runs for comptroller, 196–199
Bauman, G. Duncan, 213, 264, 293
Bell, James, 178
Berra, Louis "Midge," 69, 94, 235
Berra, Paul M., 262
Billingsly, Z. Dwight, 300
blacks: discrimination in hiring, 116, 148–150, 218–219; "golden years" in Missouri, 308; Jefferson Bank protests, 108–129; low voter turnout, 304; Mau-Mau mentality, 8; political parasites, 189–206; stratification of leadership, 191–195; support of white politicians, 7; underrepresentation in public office, 1–8, 23–25
Bledsoe, Frank, 4, *55*, 88
Bolling, Richard, 303
Bond, Anita, 185, 309
Bond, Christopher "Kit," 290–292
Bosley, Freeman, Jr., 94, *262*, 299, 308–309, *313*; loses re-election as mayor, 314–316; race for circuit clerk, 254–256; re-election as circuit clerk, 256–259
Bosley, Freeman, Sr., 194, 256
Boykins, Billie, 185, 220, 309; race for license collector, 254–256; re-election as license collector, 257–259
Brady, Bill, 34, 45
Brewster, Mary, 228
Broussard, C. B., 90, *163*, 225
Brown, Claude, 311

Brown, Sylvester, Jr., 315
Buckowitz, Georgia, 48–49, 135
Buckowitz, Louis, 49, 144, 148, 150
Bush, Errol, 299
Bush, James, *203*
Butler, Jacqueline, 121

Cahill, Clyde, 111
Callanan, Larry, *101*, 134, 143, 168; background, 88–89; Clay's Congress run, 156–157, 163–165; involvement in politics, 98–100; integration of Pipefitters, 101–104
Calloway, DeVerne, 73, 177–178
Calloway, Ernest, 18, 48, 72, 74, 230; head of NAACP Youth Council, 75–79; runs for Congress against Clay, 157–165
Calloway, Olivia, 15, 177
Calvin, Michael, 194
Carnahan, Mel, *275*, 276, 280
Carpenter, Milton, 156–165, 283
Carpenter, Sharon, 257, 259
Carter, Paula, 308, 311
Catholic Laymen's Organization, 92
Cervantes, Alphonse J., 56, 143–153, *146*, *151*; loses re-election, 235–236
Chambers, Jordan, 4, 15, *41*, 69, 80–81, 84, 89, 93, 131, 270; first meeting with Clay, 40–43; impact on St. Louis politics, 94–95
Citizens Liberty League, 1–8
civil rights protests, 17, 58–61, 108–129
Clark, Crittenden, 1
Clay, Bill: alliance with Pipefitters, 100; army life, 16; arrested at Jefferson Bank, 113; campaigns for Goins, 212; conflicts with Goins, 236–240; conflicts with Hearnes, 133–140; conflicts with Schoemehl, 253–266, 275–281; demands jobs for blacks, 55–58, 218; early life, 11–19; enacts public accommodations law, 58–61; family, 173–175; feud with *Globe–Democrat*, 20–21, 63–65, 119, 212–217; forms

NAACP Youth Council, 17–18; home meetings, 37–40; Howard Johnson protests, 58–61; influences election of Cervantes, 147; Jefferson Bank protests, 108–129; labor unions, 283–300; loses Baptist preachers' endorsement, 34–35; makes peace with Goins, 205; opposes revision of the city charter, 18; opposition to, 20–21, 209, 212–217; protests, 17; purges arrest records, 62–66; runs for alderman, 23–29; runs for Congress, 156–171; runs for mayor, 228–232; sponsors Equal Employment Opportunities bill, 61–62; working with women, 178–182

Clay, Carol Ann Johnson, 15, 17, 67, 173–174, *174*, *298*

Clay, Irving, 12, 150–152, 285, *286*

Clay, Lacy, *67*, 257, *262*, *275*, *286*, *298*, 308; and labor unions, 297–298; campaign for Congress, 284–300; re-election, 257–261; works to close *Globe–Democrat*, 265–266

Clay, Luella, 12, 173

Clay, Michele, *67*, *174*, 175, 299

Clay, Vicki, *67*, 175

Clay, William Lacy, Jr. *See* Clay, Lacy

Club Riviera, 83–84

Conley, John, *91*, 215, 274

Conway, James: closes Homer Phillips Hospital, 225, 245, 248–249, 251–252; elected mayor, 231–232, 235–236; loses re-election attempt, 248

Cook, Blondell, 88

Cook, Virginia, 299

CORE, 58–61, 91, 213; Jefferson Bank protests, 108–129

Crawford, Curtis, 166

Crumpton, Harold, 311

Cummings, James, 225–226

Cunningham, Nettie, 228, 230

Curtis, John, 31, 88, 179

Curtis, Julia Child, 4, 46

Curtis, Robert B. (Bob), 88, 136; Jefferson Bank protests, 109–129

Daly, Richard, 109

Daniels, Ted, 311

Davis, Elliot, 311

Dearing, Myrtle, 179

Dease, Magnolia (Maggie), 32, 88, 179

DeClue, James, 259

Deeba, Charles, 194

Deluxe Restaurant, 83, 311

Democrats, 303–306, 310

dialogue groups, 218–219

discrimination in hiring, 1, 116, 148–150, 218–219

Diuguid, William, 79–80

Dooley, Charlie, 284–300

Dugas, June, 96, 121

Dwyer, John "Jack," 15, 79–80, 144

Dyer, L. C., 5

Eagleton, Thomas, 272, 303, 314

Easter, Jerri, 179

Edwards, William D., 225

Elbert, Harold I., 49–50, 57, 60, *61*, 61–62

Ellis, Willie J., 225, 299

Equal Employment Opportunities bill, 61–62

Evans, Pearlie, 88, 156, *181*, *185*, *197*, 228, 258, *273*, 299; campaign manager, 186; Clay's district director, 180–182

"Family," the, 311–313

Faulkner, Reverend Curtis, 35

Ford, Louis H., 113–129, 184, 220

Fortenberry, Haymond, 259

Freeman, Frankie, 84, 216–217

Galli, Joseph A., Sr., 297

Gates, Charles, 46

Gates, Clifford W., 209–211

Gephardt, Richard, 294

Gibbons, Harold, 164

Giles, Gwen, 88, 156, 183, *229*, *273*, 308; assessor, 185; campaign manager for Congress run, 160, 185, 186; state senator, 274–275

Glenn, Ronald, 113–129

Globe–Democrat, 20, 63–65, 119, 143, 212–217, 231, 233, 238; declares bankruptcy, 264–266

Goins, Benjamin L., 133, 135, *211*, 223, *237*, 309; appointed license collector, 94, 100, 166–171; campaign manager for Austin Wright, 70–74; campaigns for Bass, 198–199,

230; campaigns with Clay, 212; chairman of the First Congressional District, 205–206; conflicts with Clay, 236–240; convicted and imprisoned, 241; elected committeeman, 96–97; Jefferson Bank protests, 113–129; makes peace with Clay, 205, 242; political sabotage, 193–195; runs for Congress, 235–242; runs for sheriff, 160–161, 234–235

Goldston, Samuel, 91

Grand, Ian, 113–129

Grant, David, 56, 62, 65, 84, 90, 120–121; defends Jefferson Bank protestors, 111

Grant, Dr. Edward, 46, 177

Green, Darlene, 309

Guillaume, Robert, 12

Haley, Johnetta, 118

Harmon, Clarence, 299; runs for mayor, 314–316

Harris, Ida L., 70–74, 163, 178, 186

Hatton, Beatrice, 135

Hawkins, Sonny, 156

Hayes, John W., 4, 46

Hayes, Walter, 109

Hearnes, Warren E., 131–140, 137, 168; and Jefferson Bank demonstrators, 135

Henning, Rev. C. Garnett, 258

Hennings, Tom, 303

Hickey, Patrick J., 278

Hicks, Rev. John J., 47–48, 90, 309

Hill, Elsa, 135, 162, 185–186

Hill, the (St. Louis), 169–170

Hogan, Edward "Jellyroll," 15, 79–80

Holly, Clarence, 95

Homer G. Phillips Hospital, 6, 249–253, 304; in Tucker's administration, 144–145; plans to close, 225, 251

Hoover–Young, Wyvetta, 111

Howard, Raymond, 59, 157, 308; insults Weathers, 206, 270–271; Jefferson Bank protests, 109–129

Howard Johnson protests, 58–61, 159

Hudson, Zelda, 179

Hurt, James, 309

integration of public facilities, 17

Irish control of St. Louis politics, 88–90

Jefferson Bank protests, 108–129, 135

"job swap," 261–264

Johnson, Zenobia Shoulders, 46

Jones, Billy, 111

Jones, Charlene, 203

Jones, Ethel, 179

Jones, Taylor, 113–129

Jones, Virvus, 262, 277, 293, 309; becomes comptroller, 261–264

Kavenner, Dick, 205

Kelley, Bob. See Kelley, Robert

Kelley, Robert, 263; backs Schoemehl, 277–279; opposes Lacy Clay, 288–300

Kennedy, Arthur, 80, 83, 144, 181

Kinney, Michael, 270

Lawler, John "Doc," 148, 165; integrates Pipefitters, 101–104; involvement in politics, 98–100; supports Cervantes, 143–144; supports Goins, 168, 170–171

Lee, Kenneth, 113–129

Leggett, Ronald, 257

Liston, Sonny, 12

Littlefield, Joyce, 143

Lloyd, Aaron W., 1

Lloyd, Lee, 179

Long, Edward, 303

Lowe, Walter, 1

Lynch, Alphonse J., 111

lynching, bill against, 6

Mack, Willie, 72, 79, 88

Madeson, Marvin, 275

Mayberry, T. H., 23, 34, 57, 60, 66, 79–80, 84

McDaniel, Ralph, 225

McDonald, Joseph P., 60

McDuffie, Joseph, 111

McLemore, Joseph L., 4

McMillan, Mike, 311

McMillian, Theodore, 309

McNeal, Theodore D., 55, 158, 308, 309; state senate campaign, 81–83

McTague, Mickey, 143

McVey, Duke, 293

merger of the city and county, 261

Mill Creek redevelopment, 36, 84, 96, 144, 303–304

Miller, Herdy, 88
Millsap, Wayne, 109
Mitchell, Frank, Sr., 33, 156
Mitchell, J. E., 1
Mo–Kan, 276–277
Moore, Doris, 186, 209, *247*
Morrell, Leo, 90–94
Moye, Lew, 299

NAACP Youth Council: destroyed,
    75–76; formed, 16–17
Nance, Earl, 259, 309
Nicholson, Dr. Lawrence, *203*
Nicholson, Father Joseph, 46
nihilists, 192–193, 204–205
Nixon, Jeremiah "Jay," 290–292
Noble, Barbara, *247*

O'Connor, Pat, 299
Odom, Mark, 299
old guard, 191–192
Oldham, Charles, 55, 73, 88, 278; Equal
    Employment Opportunities bill,
    61–62; Jefferson Bank protests,
    109–129
Oldham, Marian, 73, 88, 179; Jefferson
    Bank protests, 109–129
O'Mara, Jim, 296
Oxley, J. H., 225–226

Payne, Franklin, 88, *91*, 156, 272, 308
Peake, James, 112
"Penny Brigade," 113
Percich, Raymond, 198; elected comp-
    troller, 223–225
Perkins, Reverend Charles, 109–129
Perry, Ivory, 88
Piggee, Darryl, 299
Pipefitters union, 99–104, 156
Poelker, John H., 152, 250–251
Pointer, Reverend Samuel, 35–36
Polizzi, Salvatore, 12
polling place dishonesty, 32, 44–45
Porter, Ruth, 183–185
Priest, H. Sam, 109
public accommodations, 49

Quarles, Raymond, *211*

Raiffie, Harry, 183–185
Randolph, A. Philip, 32, 81–83

Ratterman, Robert, 111
redistricting, 18, 155, 199–204
Redmond, Sidney, 46
Reed, Gwen, 185, *186*, 299; campaign
    manager, 186
Reid, Rev. Frank Madison, 80
Republicans, xi, 303–306; blacks as, 5
Rice, Addie, 31–32, 88, 179
Rice, B. T., 299
Rice, James, 31
Richards, Lucien, 109–129
Rivers, Nathaniel, 29–30, 88, 156, 162,
    163, 179
Roberts, Steve, *229*, 313
Robinson, Leonard, 311
Roche, Colleen, 299
Roddy, Joseph P., 57; named clerk of
    the courts, 168–169; re-election,
    254–256
Russell, William, 111

Sansone, Anthony, 147
Schneider, John D., 214, 299
Schoemehl, Vincent, 245–266, *255*;
    labor unions, 277–280; payback from
    Clay, 275–281; promise to reopen
    Homer Phillips Hospital, 246,
    252–253; re-election loss, 276–281
Schwerdtman, Robert, 59
Scott, Judge Michael J., 109–129
Seay, Norman R., 54, *55*, 60, 70–74, 83;
    Jefferson Bank protests, 109–129;
    opposes Morrell's election, 92–93;
    parts ways with Clay, 96
Shaw, Arthur, 60
Shenker, Morris, *101*
Slay, Francis, 94, 314, 315
Sleeping Car Porters' union, 81
Smiley, Adella, 185, 309
Smith, Wayman, II, 15, 23, 45, 84,
    229, 250, 311
St. Louis Globe–Democrat. See
    Globe–Democrat
St. Louis Labor Council, 277, 288–295
Stodghill, Bill, 293, 311
Stokes, Jay, *307*
Stokes, Louis, *307*
Suggs, Donald, 293
Sullivan, Leonor K., 177, 303
Sverdrup, Lief J., 214
Symington, Stuart, 303

Tate Sisters' restaurant, 83, 311
Tei, Takuri, 240–241
Thomas, Joyce, 185
Thompson, Betty, 299
Thompson, Herman, 14–15; Jefferson
    Bank protests, 109–129
Thompson, Mavis, 309
Thornton, Oliver, 40–43
Tournour, Roberta, 113–129
Tozer, Martin L., 26–27, 32, 44, 69–79
Troupe, Charles, 257, 259
Troupe, James P., 23, 45, 157, 202, 220
Troupe, Quincy, 203
Tucci, Kim, 256–257
Tucker, Raymond, 61, 96, 144–145
Turpin, Charles Udell, 1, 3
Tyus, Leroy, 23, 55, 81, 83, 88, 91, 156,
    168, 197, 227, 229, 263; alliance
    with Pipefitters, 100–104; campaign
    for state senate, 272–274; resigns as
    chairman, 205–206

Vaughn, George L., 1
Vickers, Eric, 284–285
Ville, the, 81
Voss, Ann, 156, 273

Wallace, Al, 15
Walton, Elbert, 269–270, 287
Washington, Arthur "Chink," 95
Weathers, Frederick N., 69, 83, 84, 88,
    91, 144, 248, 262, 275; becomes
    dean of St. Louis politics, 95; dis-
    cord with Leroy Tyus, 272–274; dis-
    cord with Ray Howard, 206,
    270–271; runs for clerk of the crimi-
    nal court, 90–94; runs for
    Eighteenth Ward committeeman, 15
Webbe, Sorkis, Sr., 98, 168, 193; enlists
    Callanan's support for Clay,
    163–165; runs for public administra-
    tor, 90–94
White, Anna, 70–74, 83, 96
White, Hugh, 55, 80, 83, 84, 144, 270;
    Jefferson Bank protests, 113
Williams, Emanuel, 111
Williams, Fred, 157, 197, 203, 223,
    272, 275–276
Williams, Grant, 297
Williams, Larry, 94, 203, 247, 263, 309;
    fights redistricting, 202–204; sup-

ports Lacy Clay, 299; supports
    Schoemehl, 245–249
Williams, Willie, 96
Wilson, Earl, 286
Wilson, Leroy, 311
Wilson, Margaret Bush, 55, 80, 84,
    138, 203, 217; defends Jefferson
    Bank protestors, 111; fights redis-
    tricting, 202–204
Wilson, Robert, 111
Witherspoon, Robert, 46, 111
women in politics, 173–187
Woodson, Lawrence "Jaybird," 58, 60,
    66, 309; Jefferson Bank protests, 113
Wright, Austin, 70–74
Wright, Cecil, 60

Young, Robert, 200–204
young turks, 192
Younge, Dr. Walter, 46